Conflict of Myths

CONFLICT OF MYTHS:

The Development of American Counterinsurgency Doctrine and the Vietnam War

LARRY E. CABLE

NEW YORK UNIVERSITY PRESS
New York and London

First published in paperback in 1988.

Library of Congress Cataloging-in-Publication Data

Cable, Larry E., 1942–
  Conflict of myths.

  Bibliography: p.
  Includes index.
  1. Vietnamese Conflict, 1961–1975—United States.
  2. Counterinsurgency. 3. United States—Military
  policy. I. Title.
  DS558.C33 1986   959.704'33'73   86–2420
  ISBN 0-8147-1401-3 (alk. paper)
        0-8147-1409-9 pbk.

*New York University Press books are Smyth-sewn
and printed on permanent and durable acid-free paper.*

CONTENTS

Foreword   *vii*

Abbreviations and Acronyms   *xi*

Shadows of Substance   *1*
   1. Introduction   *3*
   2. The Greek Civil War   *9*
   3. South Korea, 1948–1954   *33*
   4. The Philippines, 1946–1954   *44*
   5. The Malayan Emergency   *71*
   6. The Banana Wars, 1915–1934   *96*

Totems and Tribal Memories   *111*
   7. Selecting and Erecting the Pole   *113*
   8. Carving Totems: At the Top and at the Bottom   *141*
   9. Tribal Memories   *158*
  10. Intrusions and Conclusions   *174*

Fetishes That Failed   *183*
  11. The COIN of Camelot   *185*
  12. Fetishes and Failures   *205*
  13. Doctrine of Predestination   *237*
  14. Auguries of Janus   *279*

Bibliography   *287*

Index   *305*

FOREWORD

According to an operational plan named 37D, the head of the American camel was supposed to enter the Vietnamese tent at eight in the morning of 8 March 1965 at a place called Red Beach 2. As had already proven to be the case so often, things did not go according to plan. The troops who went ashore that day, members of Item and Kilo Companies of the 3rd Battalion of the 9th Marines, did not consider that possibility; neither is it likely that any thought about the possibility that they constituted the advance party of an enormous American ground combat force commitment. While no one except the individuals themselves can be certain, it is likely that each simply dealt as best he could with the conflicting feelings of fear and elation which characterize the imminence of combat, while those with experience in Korea or World War II were grateful for the anesthetic which is automatically provided by the routine procedures of soldiering. The demands of details deadened the imagination, much to the good of all hands.

The landing had been complicated by a sudden and unexpected deterioration in the weather, which at 6 a.m., the landing time originally scheduled, had been merely miserable with an intermittent drizzle. Within the next two hours the waves had grown to ten feet, and the marines were forced to reload their equipment to larger and more seaworthy landing craft. Even with this unscheduled delay, the eleven amphibious tractors carrying the assault echelon of Battalion Landing Team (BLT) 3/9 lurched ashore only three minutes behind the rescheduled H-hour of 0900. A mere fifteen minutes passed before the fourth and final assault wave was ashore, and the American invasion of South Vietnam was temporarily at an end. In the meantime, the marines were putting forward a spirited and, as the photographs transmitted around the world clearly showed, a not altogether successful defense against the attacks of local university students whose female vanguard, wearing the traditional *ao-dai*, hung flowers on the combat-laden and -ready troops. The marines, equipped and briefed to expect hostile action, were instead greeted not simply by girls armed with garlands but also by schoolchildren lining the road to Danang and signs welcoming them in English, Vietnamese, and, confusingly, French. Although none of these signs read "Welcome to Vietnam where promise and reality are never the same," they perhaps should have, for such was certainly the case.

The rest of the 9th Marine Expeditionary Brigade (MEB) landed in the next twenty-four hours by both landing craft and airlift from its base at Okinawa. After many false starts and false alarms culminating in an attempt by Assistant Secretary of Defense McNaughton to replace the marines with the politically less noisy paratroops of the 173rd Airborne Brigade, the unopposed landing of American ground combat forces had been accomplished without a real hitch, although with a touch of surrealism.[1] There can be no doubt that the basic character of the war had changed and could not easily revert to its previous, more restrained complexion. A new phase of the conflict had commenced, one about which many questions can and should have been raised.

Basic questions such as what they were doing in Vietnam and how events had worked so that they were in the country did not loom large in the minds of the marines at the time. That would come later as they cowered, cringed and cursed while the incoming mortar rounds and rockets shook the ground which gave shelter; later, as they, eyes clenched against the stinging sweat and legs cramped with protest against steep slopes and heavy loads, humped themselves up one hill and down another without any sight of the Viet Cong enemy; later, as the land mine and invisible sniper took out yet another buddy without the relief of response. Then these existential questions, expressed in profane form and with heartfelt passion, would come. Neither were the questions of how and to what end raised by the policy formulators and decision makers from Saigon to Washington. They were men of action and intellectuals of decisiveness, not reflection, although reflection would come as the explanatory and exculpatory memoirs were written in a calm and cool place far removed from the paradox-ridden jungle and uncertainty-laced swamps of Vietnam. But even later, even under the impetus of frustration and the desire for self-justification, one essential question would be absent from the agenda: considering that the decision-making process and the experiences upon which it had been predicated were so riddled with basic errors of perception and understanding, is it possible that the marines and their successors should have been issued white flags, as they were doomed to defeat even before they waded ashore or walked down the aircraft ramps?

It is obvious that a question of this nature subsumes many lesser parts and is surrounded by an array of subsidiary concerns. But at the center it forces us to derive an understanding of the American theory of victory, not only in conventional and nuclear warfare generally, but in guerrilla war as well. Having done this, it becomes possible to critically evaluate the then prevalent American understanding of its capabilities to define and achieve policy goals in Southeast Asia. It also becomes possible to state whether or not the United States had any realistic chance of achieving those goals with the means at its disposal.

*   *   *   *

This book, like all works of history, represents, at bottom, a collaborative effort in which the services, support, and assistance of many have been necessary. It is impossible to express properly the gratitude felt for the contributions of so many. However, two individuals in particular occupy positions of prominence: Professor James Kirby Martin of the University of Houston, whose criticism and encouragement have contributed materially to the existence of this book, and David Humphrey, Archivist at the Lyndon Baines Johnson Library, without whose efforts and professionalism this book would have life only as a vague concept and not a reality.

NOTES

1. LBJ/NSF/CF/VN/14/M30/109, Telegram from OSD/ISA to American Embassy Saigon dated 2 March 1965, (declassified, 24 July 1980), p. 1.

ABBREVIATIONS AND ACRONYMS

AID	Agency for International Development
ARCOV	Army Combat Operations in Vietnam (U.S.)
ARVN	Army of the Republic of Vietnam
BCT	Battalion Combat Team
BLT	Battalion Landing Team
CASF	Composite Air Strike Force (U.S.)
CCF	Chinese Communist Forces
CF	Country File
CIA	Central Intelligence Agency
CIC	Army Counterintelligence Corps (U.S.)
CINCPAC	Commander in Chief, Pacific
COMUSMACV	Commander, U.S. Military Assistance Command, Vietnam
CNO	Chief of Naval Operations
DAS	see ELAS
DCI	Director, Central Intelligence (U.S.)
DMZ	Demilitarized Zone
DRV	Democratic Republic of Vietnam
DWEC	District War Executive Committee (Malay)
EAM	National Liberation Front (Greece)
EDCOR	Economic Development Corps (Philippines)
ELAS	Greek People's Liberation Army, later known as DAS
FM	Field Manual
GHQ SWPA	General Headquarters, Southwest Pacific Area
GNA	Greek National Army (Government force)
GNN	Nicaraguan National Guard

GVN	Government of (South) Vietnam
HMB	Huk guerrilla units
HQMC	Headquarters Marine Corps
IMT	International Meetings and Travel Files
ISA	International Security Affairs
JCS	Joint Chiefs of Staff
JUSMAG	Joint US Military Assistance Group (Philippines)
JUSMAPG	Joint US Military Advisory and Planning Group (Greece)
JUWTF	Joint Unconventional War Task Force (U.S.)
KKE	Greek Communist Party
KMAG	Korean Military Assistance Group
LBJ	Lyndon Baines Johnson Presidential Library
LOK	Greek National Army Commando Force
MAAG	Military Assistance Advisory Group (Vietnam)
MAB	Marine Amphibious Brigade
MAC	Military Area Commands
MACV	Military Assistance Command, Vietnam (successor to MAAG)
MAF	Marine Amphibious Force
MAROPS	Maritime Operations (U.S.)
MAU	Marine Amphibious Unit
MCP	Malayan Communist Party
MEB	Marine Expeditionary Brigade
MEU	Marine Expeditionary Unit
MPC	Military Police Command (Philippines)
MPLA	Malayan People's Liberation Army
MRLA	Malayan Races' Liberation Army
NIE	National Intelligence Estimate (U.S.)
NKPA	North Korean People's Army
NLF	National Liberation Front (Vietnam)
NSAM	National Security Action Memorandum
NSC	National Security Council
NSF	National Security Files
OPLAN	Operational Plan (U.S.)
OSD	Office of the Secretary of Defense
OSS	Office of Strategic Services

PACOM	Pacific Command (U.S.)
PAF	Philippine Armed Forces
PAVN	People's Army of Vietnam (North Vietnam)
PLA	People's Liberation Army (China)
RAF	Royal Air Force (British)
RLAF	Royal Laotian Air Force
ROAD	Reorganization Objective Army Division
ROCID	Reorganization of the Current Infantry Division
ROK	Republic of Korea (South Korea)
ROTC	Reserve Officers' Training Corps
RVN	Republic of Vietnam (South Vietnam)
RVNAF	Republic of Vietnam Armed Forces
SAS	Special Air Service (British)
SC	Special Constables (Malaya)
S.E.A.	South East Asia
SEACORD	Southeast Asian Coordinating Committee (U.S.)
SFG	Special Forces Group (U.S.)
SKLP	South Korean Labor Party
SNIE	Special National Intelligence Estimate (U.S.)
SOE	Special Operations Executive (British)
SVN	South Vietnam
SVNAF	South Vietnam Air Force
SWEC	State War Executive Committee (Malaya)
TAC	Tactical Air Command (U.S.)
UNC	United Nations Command (Korean War)
UNRRA	United Nations Relief and Rehabilitation Agency
USAF	United States Air Force
USCONARC	U.S. Continental Army Command
USGPO	United States Government Printing Office
USIA	United States Information Agency
USOM	United States Operations Mission
VC	Viet Cong

SHADOWS OF SUBSTANCE

1.
Introduction

Although ranking somewhat below the holy writ in either authority or permanence, military doctrine does constitute the conceptual skeleton upon which are mounted the sinews of materiel, the muscles of battalions and brigades and the nervous system of planning and policy decision. At the risk of slight oversimplification, it is useful to understand doctrine as being the officially sanctioned theory of victory outlining the conduct of war on all levels, from the broadest aspects of operational planning down through tactics and standard operating procedures to the most minor details of squad patrolling. Generally, doctrine is historically derived, in that it is the synthetic product of actual experience in previous conflicts. While doctrine can be altered with the advent of new weapons or new technologies of communication and transportation or according to the demands arising from a new conflict, the doctrine in effect prior to the start of a war powerfully conditions the military and civilian perceptions and decisions which lead to the onset of hostilities.

In April 1966, a year after the first U.S. ground forces landed, a thorough review of American combat operations in Vietnam was transmitted to the U.S. Army's Chief of Staff by the Commander of the U.S. Military Assistance Group, Vietnam (COMUSMACV), General William Westmoreland. An evaluation team of sixty military officers and six civilian operations research specialists, acting at the direction of the Chief of Staff, had spent three months in the field extensively examining the experience of the major U.S. Army units involved in combat in the Republic of Vietnam (RVN). The group was specifically charged with the development of recommendations as to "improvements in doctrine, organization and materiel."[1] Recognizing that maneuver battalions constituted the crucial combat element in low-intensity war, the evaluation effort paid particular attention to these formations. With respect to the doctrine applicable to maneuver battalions in a guerrilla war, the team concluded, "evaluation of the four type infantry battalions employed in Vietnam revealed that doctrine is essentially sound. . . ."[2] A similar conclusion is seen concerning the doctrine governing brigades and divisions although "expansion and emphasis are required to take advantage of the lessons learned in Vietnam. . . ."[3]

It is necessary to inquire into the nature and origin of the doctrine in effect during the period 1958–1965, so highly thought of by the ARCOV (U.S. Army Combat Operations in Vietnam) report, in order to appreciate properly the intellectual and perceptual matrix surrounding primary policy and consequent military decisions made regarding American involvement in Vietnam. My purpose is to evaluate the accuracy and suitability of the doctrine itself and to examine the experiences underlying the American view of guerrilla war and counterinsurgency. In order to do this, it is necessary to chart the course and isolate the salient characteristics of insurgencies or the guerrilla aspects of conventional conflicts, which either involved American personnel or directly affected American perceptions. From this, it will be possible to track the evolution of American counterinsurgency doctrine.

A powerful but unspoken assumption lay beneath the discussions concerning the nature and extent of the American involvement in the developing conflict within South Vietnam. This assumption, which continued to underlie the debate which followed direct American engagement in the Vietnamese War, consisted simply of the belief that the United States was a successful, experienced, warlike power whose vast military competence comprised a capability in matters of guerrilla warfare. The accuracy of this assumption, as well as its effect upon military decision making and concomitant policy planning, must be questioned.

As was evidenced by the verbal and conceptual morass surrounding the terms "guerrilla," "partisan," and "insurgent" war, in 1960 or 1965 the United States was a rank amateur in the arena of unconventional, low-intensity conflict. Indeed, in the years following the Spanish-American War, the U.S. Army had been directly involved in only three "guerrilla" campaigns: the Philippine Insurrection, the Greek Civil War of 1946–1949 and certain peripheral portions of the Korean War of 1950–1953.

The Huk Insurrection in the Philippines, 1946–1954, had only tangentially involved uniformed American personnel. The Marine Corps had been involved extensively in a long series of counterinsurgency operations in the Central American "Banana Wars" of the 1920s and 1930s, but this experience had been integrated into the doctrine of the armed forces in only a very poor and distorted fashion.

The lack of direct, recent and relevant experience with guerrilla war led in the late 1950s to a spate of literature both analytic and synthetic in nature intended to shed some light on guerrilla war and to provide models useful in countering this new threat of guerrilla conflict, particularly the war of national liberation which had been adopted by the Soviet Union as an instrument of policy. While much of the resulting material was superficial, and even more was tinged with the color of service-related special pleading, or had a focus made overly rigid by cold war considerations, or overly narrow by obeisance to the requirements of the nuclear battlefield, the chief sin was that of conceptual confusion.[4] Terms such as "guerrilla," "partisan," "insurgent," "internal," "irregular," "unconventional," and "bushfire" were attached to "war" quite interchangeably and without any indication that major differences might exist between the two major varieties of guerrilla war: partisan and insurgent, or that totally different types of military, let alone policy, responses might be appropriate to each.

Despite the confusing terminology, there are indeed only two basic types of guerrilla war: partisan and insurgent. In the first type, the guerrillas operate as an auxiliary to the regular military forces of a nation. Partisans do not exist without external support, sponsorship and control. Insurgents operate as armed political dissidents within a society seeking revolutionary social and political changes. The insurgent force has the potential and ability to operate without any external material support or sponsorship.

The American view of guerrilla war was simply that all such wars were partisan in nature; all had support from an external sponsoring power and all were backed, at least implicitly, by an over-the-border presence of a regular army. Any seemingly domestic insurgent movement was either externally sponsored or was soon captured by an external sponsor. Additionally, guerrilla war was seen as the early warning sign of an impending conventional cross-border attack from a hostile, Soviet-dominated state. These two basic principles convinced the military planners that the key to victory in guerrilla war was to be found in destroying the lines of supply and communication connecting the guerrillas with their sponsors. The severing of the lines of supply and reinforcement was to be coupled with the destruction of the guerrilla forces in the field by the vigorous application of conventional military tactics by regular military units, including tactical air forces. Contrary lessons were not seen.

This skewed view of historical experience combined with the nature of general purpose land combat and air forces designed to operate in the presumably nuclear battlefields of Europe to assure that the American view of guerrilla war would be Clausewitzian. The theory of victory appropriate to its defeat would emphasize the utility of conventional forces, the necessity of employing tactics aimed at the physical destruction of the guerrillas in the field as well as the lines of support from outside and, if these measures were not sufficient, the use of force directly against the presumed external sponsoring power to persuade it both to refrain from conventional invasion and to put its guerrillas on a leash.

The literature of the late 1950s and early 1960s discussed the two major types of guerrilla war without using the terms "insurgent" and "partisan" and without noting properly that each requires a different type of approach to defeat successfully. In short, the writers of this period failed to recognize that the partisan war required an emphasis upon the more strictly military aspects and that the insurgent model required a greater emphasis upon the nonmilitary programs of nation building and preemptive redress of social and economic grievances. Additionally it was not seen clearly that the insurgent conflict required that the military employ low-lethality weapons and tactics, give the highest priority to intelligence and police-type activities, as well as effectively use psychological operations and civil affairs programs.

An examination of the nature of partisan and insurgent war as each was experienced or perceived by the United States is necessary. Also deserving examination is the question of how each fits in with the larger view of war and the theory of victory employed by American doctrine, as well as the role force organizations and configurations developed originally for nuclear combat on the battlefields of Europe played in affecting American decisions regarding Vietnam. It should be noted that the examination not only of the experiential origins of the American doctrine but of the nature of the Indochinese conflict is predicated upon material available in the early 1960s and thus presumably at the disposal of the U.S. authorities and their advisers.

NOTES

1. BG George Mobry et al., *US Army Combat Operations in Vietnam (ARCOV)*, 9 vols., (Saigon and Washington, D.C.: U.S. Army 1966 mimeo) I: p. 2.

2. Ibid., II: p. 18.

3. Ibid., II: p. 43.

4. Examples include: Special Operations Research Office, *Case Studies in Insurgency and Revolutionary Warfare*, 2 vols., (Washington, D.C.: American University 1963); Andrew Molnar et al., *Undergrounds, Resistance and Revolutions*, (Washington, D.C.: American University [SORO] 1963); Paul Jureidini, *Case Book on Insurgency and Revolutionary Warfare*, (Washington, D.C.: American University [SORO] 1963); Otto Heilbrunn, *Partisan Warfare*, (New York: Praeger 1962); Otto Heilbrunn and C. D. Dixon, *Communist Guerrilla Warfare* (New York: Praeger 1955); Fred Barton, *Salient Operational Aspects of Paramilitary Warfare in Three Asian Areas* (Chevy Chase, Md.: Johns Hopkins University [ORO] 1963); Edgar Howell, *Soviet Partisan Movement 1941–44* (DA-Pam 10-244) (Washington, D.C.: Department of the Army 1950); A. H. Peterson et al., *Symposium on the Role of Airpower in Counterinsurgency and Unconventional Warfare* (Santa Monica, Ca.: Rand, 1963).

2.

The Greek Civil War

The protagonist in this guerrilla war, like its counterparts in other areas of the world, was born in the chaos of World War II. The Greek People's Liberation Army, generally known by its Greek initials, ELAS, together with its political arm, the National Liberation Front (EAM), were controlled by the Greek Communist Party (KKE) and comprised the most efficient guerrilla force engaged in resistance activities against the occupying German Army. The British provided arms and other support to ELAS, as they did to other resistance forces in the Balkans. As proved to be the case in other countries such as Albania and Yugoslavia, the Greek Communist forces proved to be the best organized and most militarily effective subrosa fighters in the mountains. Quite unsurprisingly, at the end of World War II the British were unable to negotiate or enforce any meaningful cease-fire between the ELAS troops and their counterparts among more rightist groups. Neither were the British able to forstall the KKE bid for power which came upon the heels of the German withdrawal in 1945 and quickly precipitated a civil war with the British troops caught in the cross-fire. The patched together internecine agreement was doomed to fail from the start and, when it did, the British were too impoverished and preoccupied with weightier matters to intervene in support of the beleaguered central government: that privilege was left to the United States.

In August 1946 the thirty-five member KKE Central Committee selected Vaphiadis Markos to be commander of the newly renamed and resurgent guerrilla forces; DAS replaced ELAS as the designation of an emerging guerrilla army with ambitions of coherent organization leading to success against the ill-trained and poorly led National Greek Army.

General Markos, as he became known, had no experience as a regular soldier, quite unlike his predecessors, but he was an experienced political commissar with a flair for intelligence activities who had gained some practical experience with the guerrillas of ELAS during World War II. He was probably the most able individual available who met the stringent tests of previous KKE and Comintern loyalty. By the end of September Markos had established twenty-two small DAS bases throughout mainland Greece with even smaller excrudescences on the islands of Crete, Chios and Lesbos. His main headquarters was at the training and logistics camp at Bulkes, Yugoslavia, but he maintained a small, mobile "GHQ in the field" which did allow his presence in Greece to be advertised with a desirable degree of legitimacy.

As 1946 progressed and DAS activities increased in scope and daring, so also did the Soviet-orchestrated diplomatic support for the KKE insurgency. During the preceding two years the Yugoslavs had demanded an independent Macedonia while the Bulgarians pressed for control of western Thrace.[1] In this there may be seen the rationale for Tito's support of DAS as well as the seeds of eventual factionalism within KKE and DAS; the demoralization resulting from this would impair the combat efficiency of the insurgents even more than the eventual closing of the Yugoslav border. The less than subtle hand of Stalin was seen more directly in the Ukrainian charge before the United Nations Security Council on 24 August 1946 that "monarcho-fascist" Greeks were provoking border incidents throughout the Balkans in an attempt to seize southern Albania.[2] It should be recalled that Albania was now firmly under the control of the hardline pro-Soviet regime of Enver Hoxa whose wartime communist resistance movement had defeated its royalist competitors. This propaganda offensive helped to inhibit the Greek National Army (GNA) attempts to strike at the DAS camps along the north-central borders which held approximately 8,000 guerrillas.[3]

Throughout the autumn of 1946 the DAS activities followed the pattern which had become stereotyped during the Second World War: small hit-and-run attacks on undefended villages for food and recruits or on isolated police installations for arms and moral effect. The desired psychological perceptions of governmental impotence and guerrilla competence were inculcated in the peasants of Macedonia and northern Greece such as to facilitate the rapid growth of DAS manpower and the sway of KKE. Athens was progressively demoralized by the appearance of a steady deterioration in the military sphere which was paralleled by a collapse in the civilian economy. Deterioration degraded into disaster when it was discovered that KKE had successfully penetrated and suborned units of the National Guard. The government's response was threefold: The court-martial of sixty officers and men of the GNA, the demand for an investigation by the United Nations of foreign aid for DAS and, finally but most importantly, the urgent request for massive economic and military aid from the U.N. Relief and Rehabilitation Agency (UNRRA), Great Britain and the United States.

That the aid was needed and that economic conditions within Greece facilitated instability there cannot be doubted. Subsequent to the German invasion, over five percent of the Greek population had hid as a direct or indirect result of the war while a further fifteen percent had become refugees. The public health system had collapsed; malaria and tuberculosis ran rampant. The country was without reserves or immediately convertible resources. Unemployment and underemployment constituted the norm. This low level of economic activity was exacerbated by the effective collapse of nonsubsistence agriculture as a result of distribution system disruption attendant upon the insurgency. Overall, nonfarm production was but one-third of the pre-1940 average and the situation in agriculture was even worse. All in all the Greek government estimated in late 1946 that an aggregate of four billion dollars' damage had been wrought upon the civilian economy by the war and its immediate aftermath.[4] Even if the Greek estimates are inflated, the need for economic and infrastructure assistance was distinct and urgent.[5]

In 1946 Greece received a total of $700,000 in aid from UNRRA, Great Britain and the United States.[6] It was not enough. In early 1947 Paul Porter, Chief of the U.S. Economic Mission, determined ". . . unless Greece received immediate assurances of large scale military and financial aid, the authority of the elected Greek government would disintegrate. . . ."[7] There were initial misgivings by Secretary of State Marshall who predicated upon a perception that neither Congress nor the American public would long tolerate "support to a Greek government which does not enjoy [the] popular support of the Greeks themselves."[8] Events outran this perception when two of the major economic underpinnings of Greece gave notice of termination. UNRRA was scheduled to cease its program in Greece at the end of March 1947 while the British advised Athens and Washington on 21 February that their assistance could not extend beyond 31 March 1947.[9] The British believed that the Greeks would need not less than 240 million dollars successfully to extend national authority over the KKE insurgents.[10] In a critical *Aide-Memoire* the British specifically referred to the estimation by their military authorities that "in order to meet the present emergency caused by the bandits the Greek armed forces should now be reorganized to enable them to make an all-out assault on the bandits in the Spring."[11] Previous British plans based on a Greek National Army of 100,000 men were now obsolete. Verification of the gravity of the situation came from the American Ambassador in Athens, Lincoln MacVeagh, and the American Chief of the UN Observation Mission which was in the country to investigate the Greek frontier incidents.[12] The nature of the military threat had been well conveyed on a continuing basis to the State Department, with a full appreciation provided by the intelligence section of the Greek General Staff via the US Military Attaché as recently as 17 February.[13] Under Secretary of State Dean Acheson prepared a memorandum on 21 February in response to the interlocked problems of economic disaster and armed uprising which he entitled quite fittingly "Crisis and the Imminent Possibility of Collapse in Greece" in which, as he later recalled, he and the Director of the Office of Near Eastern and African Affairs Loy Henderson argued to Secretary Marshall that only substantial American aid could save Greece.[14] Significantly, he urged that the U.S. reconsider its previous position and provide military aid to the Greeks as the army would otherwise simply not be able to deal with the guerrilla activities and maintain domestic order.[15] In short, Acheson concluded that the more important threat to Greek survival was presented by the guerrillas whose task was merely facilitated by the underlying economic problems and social weaknesses; the challenge was to defeat the first in order that time might be purchased to deal with the second.

Within two months the American response to the Greek problem was forthcoming.[16] President Truman's initial request for 300 million dollars in aid to Greece "to support free people who are resisting attempted subjugation by armed minorities or by outside pressure" was approved.[17] The model of the Greek Civil War as a partisan conflict with the guerrillas operating as auxiliaries supported by a regular, over-the-border, force was emerging but not yet developed. This would await the fixative bath of combat and its assessment.

The Greek National Army, motivated by the impending arrival of American aid, but laboring under the now obsolete British timetable as well as the fact that the DAS guerrillas had seized the initiative, launched its first major counter-offensive in April 1947. The plan called for a multiple division sweep through central Greece to the Yugoslav/Albanian border. Thereafter, the border was to be secured in order that future guerrilla infiltration could be interdicted. Any bypassed insurgent pockets would be reduced by police units of lower caliber. The effort lasted for several months but with diminishing energy and morale as it became obvious that the operation was a ponderous fizzle. Owing to superior DAS intelligence and mobility, the lethargic and lightly dealt GNA blows were easily evaded or, when convenient, repelled. The Americans were unhappy with the size and failure of the operation.[18] The Greeks, while not too concerned about the American disappointment, were not at all pleased at the results of the campaign as related by Field Marshall Papagos:

Despite their losses and numerous defections, the communist bands succeeded in refilling their ranks through compulsory recruiting of peasants. They also retained their fighting spirit. In June [1947] they actually attacked a significant urban center with large forces. That attack failed but it was another proof that the numerous military operations undertaken against them had neither destroyed their fighting ability nor curbed the warlike disposition of their leaders. . . The result of the 1947 operations was disheartening.[19]

This constitutes an intriguing understatement considering that the intelligence officer of the American Military Mission in Greece reported that by the end of 1947 DAS had 23,000 guerrillas within Greece while 8,000 replacements were immediately available in camps located within the three neighboring Balkan countries.[20]

With the end of the 1947 counteroffensive, the GNA withdrew to positions of static defense awaiting the arrival of the American military aid. The initial American Aid Mission to Greece was established on 15 July 1947 under the direction of the former governor of Nebraska, Dwight Griswold. According to the letter of instruction given Governor Griswold, he was to oversee some sixteen programmatic areas and was to enjoy "supreme authority in Greece over all such assistance, both civilian and military."[21] Given the magnitude of the job and the crying need for vast improvement in the command and general staff efficiency of the GNA, it is not surprising that within two years the Mission had grown to a formidable operation, having over 100 military personnel, 220 civilians in the economic mission, 100 diplomatic and intelligence officers and 80 functionaries in the Joint Administrative Services.[22] The flood of American materiel comprised 74,000 tons of military equipment between August and December of 1947.[23] The problem with the American largess was simply that it could not be effectively used by the Greek National Army.

The decision was made in December to face this problem by forming a Joint U.S. Military Advisory and Planning Group (JUSMAPG). This clumsily named entity was intended to plan and coordinate GNA operations, training and logistics following the obvious reality that the situation in Greece was deteriorating markedly and rapidly.

> The guerrillas appear to be gaining in strength and boldness while, reports of satisfactory morale on the part of the National Forces notwithstanding, the efforts of the Greek Government and its forces to control the situation seem increasingly less effective. . . .Were other things to be equal, the giving of operational advice by American officers might serve to turn the tide.[24]

Regardless of the specific intent or denials, the inevitable effect of JUSMAPG was to divert the conduct of military operations into American hands.

The seeming necessity of this action was clearly indicated at an interdepartmental meeting in late December 1947 attended by General Livesay, the senior U.S. officer in Greece who commented, "there is much inertia and a habit of fighting at long range instead of coming to grips with the guerrillas."[25] Paradoxically, considering the later insistence that the presence of external support for the DAS guerrillas made them difficult to defeat, General Livesay took the position that foreign recognition of the "Government of Free Greece" and the possible dispatch of foreign troops by the communist Balkan states to aid the DAS would operate to improve the morale and combat efficiency of the GNA by "resolving the

doubts of the Greek troops and intensifying their determination to resist."[26] Livesay believed that a massive increase in the size of the Greek
National Army and the second line National Defence Corps was absolutely
essential to counter the guerrillas and that "with the addition of American
observers they [the Greek forces] would conduct a more active campaign
against the guerrillas."[27] It might be noted that General Hap Arnold suggested at this point the introduction of two American divisions to Thrace
since this "would have an excellent effect on the general situation."[28] Far
from being rejected, this idea received approval of a cautious sort, with
high ranking State Department official George Kennan suggesting that
the idea be given careful consideration, "especially if they were to go as
part of a mixed United Nations force."[29]

Considering this militant background it is scarcely surprising that Gen.
James Van Fleet became the defacto senior tactical officer of the Greek
National Army when he assumed command of JUSMAPG in early February 1948. Neither is it surprising that JUSMAPG took a hard line with
their Greek counterparts, insisting that all its recommendations be carried
out fully and speedily. This new American policy introduced a sense of
urgency quite foreign to the Greek government, general staff and army.
JUSMAPG saw the Greek Civil War to be simply a war and, like any war,
amenable to simple direct military resolution.

This interpretation was not unique to the military and accurately reflected the basic policy of the United States as expressed in the National
Security Council paper 5/1 entitled "The Position of the United States
with Respect to Greece," which stated in paragraph 10:

> The United States should, therefore, make full use of its political,
> economic and, if necessary, military power in such manner as may
> be found most effective to prevent Greece from falling under the
> domination of the USSR either through external attack or through
> Soviet-dominated Communist movements within Greece, so long as
> the legally elected government of Greece evidences a determination
> to oppose such Communist aggression.[30]

To some, most notably Loy Henderson, this position was not quite robust
enough. It was argued that the situation in Greece was of such gravity
and its rectification of such importance to the American national interest

that U.S. forces should be committed without delay. Henderson commented on NSC 5/1 in a memorandum:

> I regret that the paper does not contain a clear and definite statement that the United States should decide now that, with the consent of the Greek Government, it will send troops to Greece if necessary to prevent Greece from falling under Soviet domination. Such a decision may be made under Paragraph 10 of the "Conclusions". However that Paragraph registers hesitation and indecision.[31]

Even before JUSMAPG had commenced effective operation, the weight of American materiel made itself felt in the key battle for Konitza. On 25 December 1947, fourteen DAS battalions comprising over 2,000 combatants under the direct personal command of General Markos invested and assaulted the sizable city of Konitza, the intended capital of "Free Greece." Meanwhile, another 1,000 guerrillas undertook diversionary and blocking efforts to the north and east of Konitza through the plains of Thessaly and Epius.

Initially the attackers dug in on the ridge line overlooking the town, following which they took the Boprazans bridge, cutting the main road over the Roos river and threatening the town's most vulnerable side. The attackers had an ample number of mortars, both medium and heavy, as well as two batteries of mountain guns and at least four 105mm howitzers. These latter pieces were emplaced in Albania and fired at extreme range, but the lighter pack howitzers, Skoda weapons of 75mm caliber, were moved well forward to positions from which they were not dislodged until 4 January 1948.

After a preliminary mortar and artillery bombardment of impressive volume but dubious accuracy, the guerrillas assaulted the town from several directions but were repulsed. Despite the failure of the assault, the DAS troops were not disheartened and settled in for an artillery siege as no GNA relief attempts were anticipated due to the difficulty of the terrain. The continuous, heavy volume of incoming fire convinced the defenders that the DAS not only had unexpectedly large munitions stockpiles in Albania but motor transport at least much of the way to the siege lines. They advised GNA headquarters of their conclusions by radio and dug a little deeper into the rocky soil to await relief.

Although heavy rain delayed the GNA response, relief columns advanced from two garrison centers and made contact with the DAS lines on 30 December 1947. In a series of disjointed meeting engagements, GNA infantry supported by tactical air and recently arrived American 105mm howitzers cleared the ridge line. The guerrillas at the bridge held out a little longer, until the new U.S-supplied automatic weapons and bazookas were brought into action. The GNA, without any encouragement, had adopted the American emphasis on firepower with gusto; they now had the means to expend copious quantities of ammunition in lieu of blood. This experience with heavy fire, including artillery and aerially delivered rockets, was a new and distinctly unpleasant one for DAS but the guerrillas gave ground slowly and, although some panic-driven withdrawals occurred on 1 January 1948, the majority of the DAS troops, including the artillerymen with their 75mm guns, fought tenaciously, not being ejected until the fourth. It was not until three days later that the GNA was able to declare Konitza secure with the DAS formations withdrawing into their defensive positions adjacent to the Albanian frontier.

The spring of 1948 constituted a period of uneasy equilibrium between the opposing forces as both regrouped and prepared for the next round. DAS, having made good its losses of 1947 with an ever more repressive system of conscription, but not yet ready to risk large unit actions, continued a program of raids and ambushes aimed primarily at further dislocating the still extremely frail Greek economy and secondarily at the diversion of GNA from active operations to those of static defense. Nominally, a DAS brigade at this time had a troop strength of 1,500 men armed with 963 rifles, 393 submachine guns, 81 light machine guns, 6 heavy machine guns, 27 light mortars and 6 medium mortars.[32] Actually, the typical DAS tactical formation was the thirty man platoon armed with an adequate but not impressive miscellany of weapons. Often a platoon of this nature would operate in subunit detachments but only rarely would it link with others for larger actions. The intelligence and logistics functions of the DAS were provided by an efficient organization of clandestine cells collectively known at this time as "Yiafka," from a term meaning a place of conspiratorial meeting. It has been estimated by an individual then engaged in intelligence evaluation functions that the Yiafka organization comprised some 15,000 active personnel and a mass support base of 750,000 passive sympathisers.[33]

Yiafka and allied organizations handled recruiting, supply procurement and intelligence functions. Direct supply of DAS field platoons was carried out by nocturnal pack trains organized as area supply units of roughly sixty men. These detachments collected, forwarded and guarded food and ammunition caches, served as information and liaison conduits and arranged for the removal and care of wounded or sick guerrillas in areas distant from friendly borders. The system was efficient and well tailored to the Greek terrain.

At the outset of 1948 the Greek national forces consisted of a bewildering hodgepodge of six different types of infantry: the field divisions and mountain divisions of the GNA, the commando groups of the GNA, the territorial static defense formations of the National Defense Corps, the paramilitary gendarmerie and the local irregulars. The major components of the GNA were the three field divisions and the four mountain divisions. The former were motorized formations of 10,500 men and the latter were animal-transported units of 8,500 troops.[34] Because of the wide disparity in mobility between these two types of division, JUSMAPG worked overtime to create and deploy a new standard division with an authorized strength of 9,300 men and organic motorized transport, artillery, engineer and reconnaissance capabilities. This task was completed with such success that by late May it was possible for the National Security Council to delete the introduction of U.S. combat troops as a contingency option.[35] Although the full fruits of this reconstruction of the GNA would not be felt until the end of the year, when a total of eight standard divisions had been fabricated, the initial results were of such a quality that Van Fleet was quite optimistic, predicting that the insurrection would be crushed by the end of the year unless the Soviets intervened directly.[36]

During the dark days of winter and early spring, as the Americans struggled to reconstruct the GNA and develop plans for an effective offensive command, it was essential that some sort of pressure be maintained on DAS. To do this it was necessary for the officers at JUSMAPG to swallow the normal American distaste for elite forces and utilize the British-developed commando groups of the GNA known by their Greek initials as LOK. This was done to the extent of expanding the LOK commandos to a total of four groups, with the result that the 2,000 troops of these special units became and remained the best offensive force at the disposal of JUSMAPG and the GNA throughout 1948. The LOK troops engaged in such intense and successful activity that they rapidly developed a high esprit de corps and offensive spirit. Subject to abusive misuse by local commanders who wished to employ a certain winner rather than the less effective, nonelite GNA units, the LOK commandos suffered rapid attrition and JUSMAPG became their protector, carefully conserving this effective combat force by defining its missions in a limited fashion to raiding, deep penetration patrolling and as an air mobile strategic reserve. Their detractors questioned the efficiency, mobility, staying power and cost-effectiveness of the LOK commandos and, by implication, all similar units as indicated by this excellent example of the typical American postwar assessment:

> It is doubtful if the functions assigned to commandos were of such a nature as to warrant the maintenance of special units, with the concentration of effort and dislocation of morale that such a course of action entails. To a degree, the effectiveness of the commando was achieved at the expense of the standard infantry units.[37]

This analysis overlooks the reality that with the best will in the world there was not enough time for JUSMAPG to have trained the regular infantry to undertake the same type of mission with the competence which the LOK units already possessed. The use of the expensive commandos was to purchase the most precious commodity in the military realm: time.

The LOK, although effective, were insufficiently strong to bother significantly DAS in its mountain stronghold. Consequently, JUSMAPG gave its concurrence to the long-planned GNA spring offensive using elements of two field and one mountain divisions. The goal of this 20,000 man force employed in Operation DAWN was the clearing of 2,000 square miles in the Roumeli mountains across the waist of the Greek peninsula. Of the estimated 7,000 guerrillas in the operational area, 641 were killed, and 1,300 captured between 15 April and 6 May 1948, with friendly losses of 145.[38]

The success of DAWN, coupled with the refurbishment of more of the GNA divisions, led JUSMAPG to authorize a second major operation, dubbed CROWN, involving 40,000 men in a three-pronged advance into the Grammos mountains where there were believed to be some 8,000 DAS guerrillas. A total of six divisions was employed with the three most mobile being used in the assault role and the less mobile formations being placed in static blocking missions. If this operation proved successful, JUSMAPG concluded, a third of the DAS effective strength would be neutralized. CROWN was intended by JUSMAPG to break the back of the insurrection.[39]

CROWN ground attacks started on 19 June 1948 following three days of extensive artillery and air bombardment of the target area, including the first use of napalm in the war. The campaign was designed to be concentric in nature so as to prevent a DAS withdrawal into Albania. The plan failed completely when the guerrillas fought with unsuspected tenacity. By 22 June the advance was bogged down in an ignominious stalemate which extended for six weeks. With only the lower half of the pocket surrounded, DAS rushed in 4,000 reinforcements while GNA responded with increased tactical air strikes and artillery barrages. At the cost of heavy casualties, GNA regained the initiative in the first week of August with the result that a key section of the Albanian frontier was seized. Morale in the DAS ranks was shaken as, in a battle of attrition, the odds were on the side of the government forces with their heavier firepower and aircraft. Markos allowed his guerrilla instincts to surface at the last possible moment and conducted a masterful fighting retreat into Albania.[40] Markos' troops, despite occasional morale and discipline problems, fought exceptionally well and in a surprisingly coordinated fashion given the sketchy nature of DAS command and communication capabilities.

GNA was left in possession of the field and could legitimately claim a victory. They had lost 801 killed, 5,000 wounded and 31 missing while inflicting an estimated 9,000 casualties upon the insurgents.[41] By some accounts the GNA had fought well while the air force had performed quite creditably, flying over 2,400 offensive sorties as well as 750 reconnaissance and 180 supply missions.[42] Nonetheless, the GNA had failed to accomplish its major goal, the destruction of the DAS force in the Grammos. The guerrillas had successfully withdrawn to Albania where, despite U.N. protests, they would be rearmed, re-equipped, reinforced, and return.[43]

After the sanguine predictions of Van Fleet and the seeming promise of DAWN, the bloody and quite inconclusive CROWN had served to lower morale in GNA, JUSMAPG and some echelons in Washington. A general perception had grown that the war in Greece would necessarily be inconclusive until some way of closing the borders was discovered. This and similar despondent attitudes were conveyed to Secretary of State Marshall when he arrived on a fact-finding trip in mid-October. He related his impression of the situation to the State Department:

> I found a rather depreciated state of morale in Athens among our Mission, particularly the Military and in the Greek Cabinet. . . . The reasons are easy to find. The Greek Army was never fully trained. Its officers are of a rather distant past in all grades, the men are very tired, particularly as they see no conclusion in sight so long as the United Nations permits the guerrillas to utilize Albania and Yugoslavia for retreat, refitting and particularly for lateral tactical moves.[44]

He approved of a proposal by Van Fleet to increase the GNA by some 15,000 which would allow the removal or retirement of some of the older and more worn-out troops while not increasing the overall size of the army.[45] While Marshall referred to this as a "minimum," it is significant that he did not give approval at this stage for Van Fleet's more grandiose conception embodied in a telegram of 16 October. Here he proposed the creation of a 12-division field force backed by a static defense force of 30,000 with the result that the armed forces would be brought to a total strength of 240,000, not including the 22,000 member gendarmerie.[46] Marshall, the organizer of American victory in World War II, in all probability saw that overly rapid increases in force strength would be expensive but ineffective and that more time was required for the impact of aid already in the country or en route to be felt.

Overestimating the recuperative powers of the GNA as well as the positive effects of the ever-increasing amounts of U.S. materiel, JUSMAPG authorized the mounting of a limited follow-up to CROWN in the Vitsi mountains adjacent to the Grammos. Markos had forseen this possibility and had redeployed DAS units through Albania to the threatened area. The GNA offensive bogged down immediately and was administered a sharp check by a surprise guerrilla counterattack. Clearly the insurgents still had sharp teeth and the will to bite.

A month later Markos tried a flank attack on the GNA defensive positions in the Vitsi; this time the DAS broke a tooth. Markos then undertook the guerrilla equivalent of a root canal procedure, reorganizing his forces so as to disband inept units and shoot inept commanders. He merged other formations, promoted his best commanders and ended with a trimmed down, firmed up and hardened force of some seventy-five main-force battalion equivalents comprising an overall strength of 23,000.[47] The majority of the guerrillas were originally unwilling conscripts molded into effective and dedicated fighters by a fascinating synergy of leadership, indoctrination and naked fear.

JUSMAPG and the U.S. government were rather disappointed that the war had not been successfully liquidated during 1948. While GNA had performed creditably during the spring and summer, and the training and reconstruction efforts of JUSMAPG were quite impressive, the fact remained that by fall the Greeks were barely hanging on despite the massive influx of American weapons, equipment and money, and despite the best efforts of the American tactical advisors-cum-commanders. The Grammos operation had been a hollow victory and the premature Vitsi follow-on had been an unmitigated failure as the numerically superior GNA, backed with ample aircraft and artillery, had been fought to a standstill and nearly driven from the mountains. Although the official line that the DAS successes in the Grammos and Vitsi campaigns had been made possible because of the tactical displacement capabilities provided by the sympathetic Balkan states and the open borders, the fact remained that the Greek Army and its U.S. operators had not been able to implement their tactical and operational plans, which took the borders into account, and would have effectively interdicted them had the troops been able to win the ground. The Greek Army was not yet well enough supplied with aggressive and competent commanders; there was a lack of professionalism, and an "absence of a strong will to fight."[48]

The overarching reason for the lack of Greek success was simply that it was nearly impossible to equip and train in American methods and doctrine an army which was simultaneously expected to perform effectively in sustained offensive combat against an able and motivated adversary. Whether the American error is seen as initiating premature offensives or, more charitably, as responding in the only way possible to the exigencies of the situation, the problem remains at heart the attempt to address two incompatible missions with the same small force. To this must be added the command misperception which saw the superficial adoption of U.S. methods and doctrine as equating with a genuine capability to employ these effectively. The American combined arms approach to combat, with its mixture of infantry, artillery and mechanized or armored formations, constitutes a challenge almost beyond belief to an army lacking completely the fundamentals for understanding this sophisticated array of communications, transportation and weapons technology. A second error was the American belief that, by controlling the decision-making echelon of the GNA and formulating the operational plans, they had sufficient leverage to force the desired amount of energy and offensive mindedness among the Greeks. This overlooked the reality that in the warfare of mountain and bush, in guerrilla war, the small unit commander is the real supreme commander. Without a constant and integrated American presence at the battalion level, it was impossible to energize the critical formations.

Although it was not apparent at the time, as the winter of 1948 rolled into the spring of 1949, the balance of the war slipped from stalemate to victory for the Greek government. The conventional explanation for this was the rift between Tito and Stalin and the consequent denial of Yugoslav bases to DAS. Although only partially true, this deceptively straightforward explanation has found great favor with American commentators for whom the existence of secure base areas has been the *sine qua non* of successful partisan warfare.

While this traditional model has a certain accuracy, it was not the sole reason for the gradual slippage of events in favor of the GNA. It deserves note that the improvement in the situation was evident to the Department of State, if not to the Athens Mission which was rather too close to events, as early as the end of October.[49] Other reasons for the perceived improvement in the Greek situation included the completion of the training and equipping phase of JUSMAPG's activities and the deployment of the augmented Greek field forces on a program of systematic sector clearance. A third contribution came as a result of severe factionalism within the KKE Central Committee over the question of Macedonian nationalism. The result of this politburo bickering can be best understood as being a case of losing the hearts and minds of the people; the government did not so much gain support as the insurgents lost adherents.

The Greek government finally responded to concerns expressed by Secretary Marshall by appointing Alexandros Papagos, a hero of the 1940 war with Italy, to the supreme command.[50] Papagos assumed command of a three service armed force numbering 169,000, of which 145,000 were troops of the GNA backed by the large National Defense Corps and the local defense irregulars.[51] Paradoxically, the first few months of Papagos' command saw the initiative resting with the DAS. Through December 1948 and January 1949, the guerrillas engaged in a series of successful forays against medium-sized towns on the verges of the Vitsi and Grammos mountains. These attacks were pressed under the cover of fierce and increasingly accurate artillery fire. However, the repeated successes proved to be a DAS undoing. Although the guerrillas made no real effort to hold the towns in the face of determined GNA counterattacks, the very size of the targets necessitated the concentration of many independent bands into ad hoc conventional formations, thus providing attractive and rewarding targets to the emerging Greek Air Force. The not-always-Greek pilots responded to these attractions with a will, inflicting severe physical and even more grevious morale casualties on the guerrillas. Affairs with the partisans reached such a sorry pass that units went to ground when a solitary reconnaissance aircraft was sighted. Additionally, the DAS fixation on taking towns and holding them as long as possible facilitated JUSMAPG in attaining its goal of enforcing concentration on the often widely dispersed GNA field force.

Not only was the DAS "town campaign" terminated with disastrous effects for the guerrillas, but late spring saw the Yiafka structure in south and central Greece obliterated in the previously mentioned series of sector by sector search and clear operations.

> The general plan, matured with American aid, was applied with strict attention to the minutest details. The combined force, aided by the local military units, successively cleared one district after another from south to north. Their job was not too difficult, for the campaign had been so thorough that all but a small number of the roving bandits had been exterminated and the local (Yiafka) organizations which maintained them had been wiped out.[52]

All that remained was the liquidation of the DAS mountain redoubt in the Grammos range.

This task was facilitated, but not made possible, by Tito's closure of the Yugoslav border which was a process and not an event; a gradually tightening constriction of the cross-border traffic resulted in a total stoppage only in July 1949, less than a month before the insurrection was finally suppressed. Arguably, Tito's action did not so much lead to the DAS defeat as recognize its inevitability. He had been keenly aware of the course of battle, having been furnished direct and timely intelligence by General Popovich, the Yugoslav military advisor on General Markos' staff. When Markos and, incidentally, Popovich were dismissed by the KKE Central Committee in the course of the Fifth Plenary Session following the bad results of the "town campaign," Tito was undoubtedly apprised of the decreasing military capability of DAS vis à vis GNA, whereupon he saw no further potential in backing a palpable loser, particularly a loser who happened to espouse the political line of his Stalinist opposition. Tito had been the most successful practitioner of partisan war in World War II and had the ability to assess the potential of DAS with the utmost precision. He did so and ordered the slow strangulation of cross-border traffic.

It is significant that the border was not closed with suddenness; it is also important to consider that the closing of the Yugoslav border did not mean that DAS was either isolated or deprived of "off stage" tactical displacement capability. The main routes of supply and maneuver for the DAS strongholds in the Vitsi and Grammos mountains ran to Albania, whose borders remained wide open throughout the DAS endgame. Had the guerrillas not already been on the ropes, the Yugoslav action would have been an inconvenience at most and if they had ever shown any ability to recover their battlefield prowess, Tito not only would have noticed, he would have responded by reversing the constriction.

Militarily the situation had deteriorated for the DAS as spring flowers bloomed in the passes of the Grammos. Markos had been replaced by a politician and self-described general, KKE Chairman Zakhariadis. He commanded a force whose morale, materiel and blood had been drained by the GNA counteroffensive and the sector clearing operations. The Greek government was gaining in confidence and coherence as a result of the victories in the field and the influx of American aid. The KKE was rife with factions over the question of Macedonia: was it to be included in postwar communist Greece or was it to be spalled off into a quasi-independent sop to the recrudescent pan-Slavism as demanded by Bulgaria and Stalin? The degree of defeatism within the command echelons of DAS and its effects upon the guerrillas may be inferred from the conciliatory peace feelers broadcast by the KKE radio in Albania on 21 April 1949.[53] This approach was followed and reinforced by the Soviet representative at the United Nations, Andrei Gromyko, who initiated a demarche with Assistant Secretary of State, Dean Rusk.[54] Despite American concern, the Greeks firmly turned aside these hints of negotiation with vigor as influential members of the Greek government smelled military victory.[55]

Even though a new 3,000 man brigade, armed and equipped by the Soviet Union, was infiltrated through Albania in May, the DAS had no immediate hope of regaining the initiative. Their indigenous intelligence and logistics arm had been amputated. They were blind to GNA intentions, preparations and movements. The deployment of LOK units into the Grammos-Vitsi, coupled with aerial reconnaissance, gave Athens the eyes and ears formerly possessed only by the guerrillas. Continuing their momentum and exploiting the intelligence generated by LOK and other information-gathering assets, GNA drew the noose tighter around the southern and eastern mountains, setting the stage for the final annihilation of DAS. Papagos was able to concentrate six of his eight field divisions against the central DAS positions in the Vitsi range and its salient, the Grammos. The terrain was formidable and the guerrilla defenses well prepared, but not so well manned. From 10 to 16 August 1949, very heavy conventional, positional combat raged. Finally, the weight of GNA air and artillery support tipped the balance and the guerrillas withdrew precipitately into Albania from which many displaced by infiltration into the Grammos where the GNA presence was lighter. Again, heavy fighting ensued, with the Americans rushing an additional fifty "Helldiver" fighter-bombers into the fray. This additional increment of flying artillery decisively assisted the GNA, with the result that government units took the two main passes serving as infiltration routes from Albania and dominated the Grammos.[56] As both Hoxa and Stalin now recognized, the Greek Civil War was over.

The Americans viewed the conflict, though called a "civil war," as having been a partisan war in which DAS operated as auxiliaries of the Soviet Army whose intervention was possible and, for a while, seen as probable. As a partisan war, the solution would have to be sought and found in the military context. Civilian programs and civic action goals, including economic and infrastructure aid, were clearly seen as adjuncts to the military effort. Success in "nation building" with failure in combat was perceived as equalling defeat. Although 473 million dollars were provided by the United States as economic aid during 1948 and 1949, compared with 345 million dollars in purely military aid, a close reading of the purposes for which this aid was employed indicates persuasively that in large measure it was intended directly and immediately to support the military program.[57]

The introduction of massive amounts of U.S. materiel required an equally massive set of U.S.-controlled training programs to insure the proper employment of the equipment furnished. In order to maximize the effectiveness of the training program, U.S. doctrine, procedures and methods were introduced not only to the troops but among the officer corps as well. Later it was seen that the equipping, indoctrinating and training of the Greek forces, particularly as coherent combined arms formations, should not have been undertaken while those forces were required to continue combat operations. The interposition of U.S. combat forces as a temporary shield behind which orderly training might occur was suggested as a desirable alternative. It might be recalled that such an action came close to being dictated by the realities of the time.

Air power was uniquely effective due to the Greek Air Force's unrestricted ability to reconnoiter and engage the DAS guerrillas, who were bereft of any air defenses.

The record of the . . . Air Force operations during the war leads to the conclusion that the return from the air effort immeasurably exceeded the return from any comparable effort on the ground . . . moreover, casualties sustained in the air were infinitesimal as compared with those sustained on the ground.[58]

The same author argued for the combination tactical air and light infantry penetration forces as the proper mix for effective counterguerrilla operations.[59]

The clearance of guerrilla formations and their mass support base elements could be most effectively obtained within interior zones by the tactic of search and clear. Although some civilian population dislocation would result and not all members of the support organizations be apprehended, the structural integrity of the guerrilla combat, intelligence and logistics systems would be severely compromised or even completely destroyed, leaving at the most a shattered and demoralized remnant well within the capabilities of local police or defense volunteers to handle. In order for systematic search and clear operations to succeed, tight command and control was necessary, as was an advanced communications capability. Further, the troops would require a high degree of mobility both on and off the road. Deficiencies in the latter category embarrassed both search and clear missions and ground attacks on guerrilla base areas, as well as government responses to partisan attacks.

Cross-border sanctuaries were seen as having been essential to the guerrillas. The belief grew that the partisans could not have existed without the privileged sanctuaries in friendly countries which were connected with operational areas by secure infiltration routes. If the cross-border sanctuaries could not be directly neutralized, then full and uninterrupted interdiction of the infiltration routes was essential. From this appreciation derived the undeserved emphasis upon the crucial importance of Tito's closure of the Yugoslav frontier to the success of the final Vitsi–Grammos offensive. Although inhibited from doing so by the potential threat of direct Soviet involvement, there is strong reason to believe that JUSMAPG and GNA considered cross-border operations by both air and ground forces against the Albanian base camps.

Partisan wars could be successfully prosecuted, it seemed, by well-trained and -equipped general purpose ground forces, if given adequate mobility and good air support. There was no apparent requirement for specific, elite antipartisan units. Without high cross-country mobility capabilities, LOK and similar commando units had no unusual utility in reaction or pursuit roles. Their only definite mission, other than morale building, was in the long-range, deep penetration role. In this, they were seen as important but not vital. Provided that the infantry had good subunit commanders, mobility and communications, it remained the "queen of battles" in partisan war.

Firepower kills in partisan as in conventional war. The infantry needed air and artillery support of a high quality and in copious quantity. In battle after battle, up to and including the final Grammos mountain offensive, the Americans saw that it was artillery and tactical air power which cracked the defensive nut and allowed the infantry to winkle out the emplaced partisans. Finally, the rapid and resolute dedication of

American support was understood as having allowed an endangered government, even though coterminous with hostile Soviet bloc states, to engage and defeat a large, well-equipped and well-led partisan force. It appeared, in fact, as though the job had been accomplished expeditiously and at a relatively low cost: two years and under a billion dollars. The perception was formed that proxy partisan was a quick and clean proposition.

On balance the lessons ultimately derived from the U.S. experience in the Greek Civil War were seen to have been highly positive. By using American doctrine and equipment to construct a reasonable simulacrum of U.S. general purpose light forces, it would be possible successfully to defeat the guerrilla. This seeming proof in the laboratory of guerrilla war served to color future American planning because the results fitted so well with the expectations. The combination of heavy firepower, close air support and good mobility, which had been the American way of war in World War II, was seen to be appropriate for fighting new forms of war. Comfortingly, doctrine and self-image coincided and the accuracy of fit for the coincidence was good; there would not need to be any rethinking of doctrine or force configurations: big battalions seemed to work in any type of conflict.

NOTES

1. Joseph Jones, *Fifteen Weeks*, (New York: Viking 1955), p. 68.

2. UNO, Security Council, *Official Reports: First Year, Series Two, Number Four*, (New York: UNO 1946), pp. 33–39.

3. J. C. Murray, "The Anti-Bandit War" in T. N. Greene (ed.), *The Guerrilla and How to Fight Him*, (New York: Praeger 1962), p. 73. Originally published under the same title in *MCG*, vol. 38 (Jan. 1954) 14–23; (Feb. 1954) 50–59; (March 1954) 40–47; (April 1954) 52–60; (May 1954) 52–58 in a somewhat longer and more detailed form.

4. Greek Ministry of Public Works, *Sacrifices of Greece in the Second World War*, (Athens: Graphic Arts, Aspiotis-Elka 1946), passim.

5. U.S. Department of State, *Foreign Relations of the United States, 1946: Africa and the Mid-East*, (Washington, D.C.: USGPO 1969), pp. 480ff, passim, while disagreeing with the Greek figures in detail, supports the gloomy picture completely and in some areas such as health is even more alarmist.

6. U.S. Department of State, *Assistance to Greece and Turkey: Second Report to Congress*, (Washington, D.C.: USGPO 1948), Chart, p. 46.

7. Jones, *Fifteen Weeks*, p. 76.

8. Telex from the Secretary of State to the American Embassy in Greece, dated 21 January 1947, in U.S. Department of State, *Foreign Relations of the United States, 1947: The Near East and Africa*, (Washington, D.C.: USGPO 1971), pp. 7–8:8.

9. *Aide-Memoire* from H.M. Embassy in Washington, D.C., transmitted informally on 21 February 1947 and formally on 24 February, reprinted in U.S. Department of State, *Foreign Relations of the United States, 1947: Mid-East and Africa*, (Washington, D.C.: USGPO 1971), pp. 32–35.

10. Jones, *Fifteen Weeks*, p. 76.

11. *Aide-Memoire* of 21 February 1947, p. 33.

12. U.S. Department of State, *The United Nations and the Problem of Greece*, (pub. 2909 Near East Series 9), (Washington, D.C.: USGPO 1947), pp. 52, 77.

13. U.S. Embassy in Athens to the Secretary of State, dated 7 February 1947 but not received until the 21st, reprinted in U.S. Department of State, *Foreign Relations, 1947*, p. 15.

14. Reprinted in *Foreign Relations of the United States, 1947*, pp. 29–31. Compare with Dean Acheson, *Present at the Creation*, (New York: Norton 1969), p. 290.

15. Ibid., p. 31. Interestingly this portion of the argument is soft-pedaled in the Acheson memoirs.

16. U.S. Department of State, *Assistance to Greece and Turkey: First Report to Congress*, (Washington, D.C.: USGPO 1947), pp. 28–29.

17. U.S. Department of State, *Aid to Greece and Turkey*, (pub 2802), (Washington, D.C.: USGPO 1947), p. 829.

18. See the dispatch of 7 May 1947 from the American Embassy in Athens to Secretary of State in *Foreign Relations, 1947*, p. 163.

19. Alexander Papagos, "Guerrilla Warfare" in Mark Osana, *Modern Guerrilla War*, (New York: Free Press 1962), p. 237.

20. Edward Wainhouse, "Guerrilla War in Greece," *Military Review*, vol. 36 (June 1957), p. 2. Compare with the Greek government figure quoted in Charilaos Lagoudakis, "Greece," in D. M. Condit et al., *Challenge and Response in Internal Conflicts*, Vol. 2 (Washington, D.C.: Center for Research in Social Systems, 1967), p. 504 of between 20,000 and 28,000 guerrillas within Greece and 10,000 to 20,000 replacements and trainees in the external base camps.

21. Letter of Instructions to Governor Griswold from the Secretary of State in *Foreign Relations, 1947*, p. 227.

22. *Assistance to Greece and Turkey: Second Report*, p. 12.

23. U.S. Department of State, *Assistance to Greece and Turkey: Eighth Report to Congress*, (Washington, D.C.: USGPO 1949), Chart on p. 10.

24. "Memorandum by the Political Section of the Embassy in Greece" dated 6 December 1947, reprinted in *Foreign Relations of the United States, 1947*, p. 441.

25. "Memorandum of Conversation" dated 26 December 1947, reprinted in *Foreign Relations of the United States, 1947*, p. 466.

26. Ibid.

27. Ibid., p. 467.

28. Ibid., p. 468.

29. Ibid.

30. U.S. Department of State, *Foreign Relations of the United States, 1948: Eastern Europe; the Soviet Union*, (Washington, D.C.: USGPO 1974), p. 40.

31. Reprinted in ibid., p. 39.

32. Murray, "Anti-Bandit War," p. 85.

33. Wainhouse, "Guerrilla War," p. 22.

34. Murray, "Anti-Bandit War," p. 82.

35. "Report to the National Security Council" dated 25 May 1948, reprinted in *Foreign Relations, 1948*, pp. 93–95. The actual NSC decision was embodied in NSC 5/4 dated 3 June 1948.

36. Letter, COMJUSMAPG to JCS dated 31 March 1948, CCS 092 BP 2 (sec. 11).

37. Ibid., p. 84.

38. Lagoudakis, *Challenge and Response*, p. 514; Kenneth W. Condit, *The History of the Joint Chiefs of Staff: The Joint Chiefs of Staff and National Policy, 1947–1949*, (Wilmington, Del.: Glazier 1979), p. 51 gives the total number of guerrillas in the Roumeli as 2,000 and does not provide casualty figures, citing JUSMAPG Operational Report, number 6.

39. JUSMAPG Operational Report to JCS, number 19 dated 24 June 1948, CCS 092 (8-22-64) BP 2.

40. JUSMAPG Operational Report to JCS, number 28 dated 27 August 1948, CCS 092 (8-22-46) BP 2.

41. W. C. Chamberlan and J. D. Iams, *Rise and Fall of the Greek Communist Party*, (Washington, D.C.: Department of State, Foreign Service Institute Mimeo, 1963), p. 369.

42. Ibid., p. 372.

43. U.S. Department of State, *Assistance to Greece and Turkey: Fifth Report*, (Washington, D.C.: USGPO 1949), p. 51.

44. "Memorandum by the Secretary of State" dated 20 October 1948, reprinted in *Foreign Relations of the United States, 1948*, pp. 162–63.

45. Ibid., p. 164.

46. "Telegram from the Ambassador in Athens to the Secretary of State" dated 16 October 1948, reprinted in *Foreign Relations of the United States, 1948*, p. 160.

47. Wainhouse, "Guerrilla War," p. 24.

48. Murray, "Anti-Bandit War," p. 94.

49. "Telegram from the Acting Secretary to the Embassy in Greece" dated 30 October 1948, reprinted in *Foreign Relations of the United States, 1948*, pp. 177–78.

50. See *Foreign Relations of the United States, 1948*, pp. 162–65, 183.

51. *Assistance to Greece and Turkey: Fifth Report to Congress, 1949*, p. 51.

52. Papagos, "Guerrilla Warfare," p. 240.

53. U.S. Department of State, *Foreign Relations of the United States, 1949: The Near East, South Asia and Africa*, (Washington, D.C.: USGPO 1977), p. 305n.

54. Ibid., pp. 303–9.

55. Ibid., pp. 315ff passim.

56. For details including maps, consult Chamberlan and Iams, *Rise and Fall*, pp. 450–60.

57. *Assistance to Greece and Turkey; Eighth Report*, pp. 10ff passim.

58. Murray, "Anti-Bandit War," p. 107.

59. Ibid., pp. 107–8.

3.
South Korea, 1948–1954

The partisan war aspects of the Korean conflict not only served to reinforce the lessons learned from the Greek Civil War, they introduced a new and compelling focus to American planners. This new wrinkle was the perception that guerrilla activities served as the first signal that a conventional cross-border attack was impending. Thus, after the Korean War, the presence of guerrillas in an area adjacent to a country under supposed communist domination was taken as the harbinger of conventional attack.

In Korea the North Korean partisans acted directly and classically as irregular, albeit sometimes uniformed, adjuncts to the North Korean People's Army (NKPA) and the Chinese Communist Forces (CCF). Even before NKPA crossed the thirty-eighth parallel, indigenous guerrillas operated as partisans, preparing the way for external conventional forces. By 1948 the Americans had created within the newly independent Republic of Korea (ROK) a 45,000 man national police force, organized in eight brigades, and a 50,000 man ROK Army, divided into five divisions of three regiments each. Although withdrawing the majority of its occupation forces, the U.S. maintained a rather small Military Advisory Group in Korea (KMAG) and provided redundant American military equipment for the ROK forces under the authority of the Surplus Property Act.[1] The forces created by the United States were organized as a constabulary and had been furnished with a miscellany of elderly Japanese and American weapons. Care had been taken to restrict the ROK forces to light weapons including mortars and machine guns.

The primary concern of the Korean constabulary forces at this time was an organization called the South Korean Labor Party (SKLP), which was sponsored by North Korea's leader, Kim Il Sung, but actually directed by the longtime Seoul resident and Marxist, Pak Hon Yong.[2] After a brief flurry of overt activity, SKLP was outlawed in 1946 by the U.S. occupation authorities and forced to go underground.

SKLP adapted to the underground milieu quite readily, developing a sizable party membership and a significant armed guerrilla force. While no verifiable numbers exist, at the time the ROK was formed in 1948 SKLP probably had something over 140,000 adherents, of whom 20,000 were hard-core communists and followers of the Kim Il Sung line.[3] Its subordinate armed force was a motley aggregate of party members, sympathizers, noncommunist opportunists and free-lance bandits numbering perhaps 5,000.[4] Virtually all the guerrillas were concentrated in three mountainous regions of the peninsula, particularly in the longitudinal Taebaek range along the east coast and, to a somewhat larger extent, the area of Chiri mountain. This 750 square mile area in the country's southwest corner had been a haven for bandits, dissidents and fugitives since the Japanese conquest. It now served as the principal SKLP base.

SKLP missions reflected the objectives of the North Korean regime. Prior to 25 June 1950, the party and its guerrillas worked to disrupt ROK governmental control and to interrupt communication and transportation arteries. The first recorded guerrilla operation occurred not on the peninsula, but on the Island of Cejudo, eighty miles south of Pusan, the major port on the southeast coast of Korea. There, on 1 October 1948, a small partisan force based in the Haela hills struck shoreline fishing villages, killing 550 islanders and burning hundreds of buildings before ROK troops arrived and restored order.[5] This escapade was followed on 10 October by an uprising in the ROK 14th Regiment at the port of Yogu, which was engineered by an SKLP cell. A mutiny of 300 enlisted men and noncommissioned officers was followed by the occupation of the twenty-mile-long peninsula upon which Yogu is located. Over 500 loyal police and troops were killed as was a somewhat larger number of civilians.[6] The rebellion was quashed but many of the rebels escaped to link up with guerrillas in the nearby Chiri mountain region. Immediately thereafter a rapid succession of smaller mutinies and "bandit" raids erupted throughout the Taebaek and Chiri regions with the twin goals of governmental destabilization and the obtaining of supplies.[7]

North Korea was unable to infiltrate supplies or weapons on a regular basis, which reinforced the necessity of continual guerrilla raids for provision purposes. However, the North was able to enhance the combat effectiveness of the partisans by infiltrating cadres specially trained in guerrilla warfare. An NKPA school at Kandong was established with both Korean and Chinese instructors to provide trained guerrilla leadership. The students were drawn in part from the North but the majority were Southerners. Before the NKPA invasion at least 1,000–2,000 partisan leaders were infiltrated.[8]

The presence of the first wave of these freshly minted specialists was felt throughout 1949, particularly after June, as the American troop strength was reduced to a few hundred military advisors and logistics personnel concentrated at the installation known as Ascom City located on the road between Seoul and the port of Inchon. The increased raiding tempo effectively denied ROK authority over the north and central Taebaek region and severely disrupted the social and economic fabric in the areas abutting on the Chiri stronghold. In psychological and physical support of these partisan activities, NKPA units carried out cross-border raids. The military rhythm received a political counterpoint harmony from SKLP's underground activities which provoked strikes and riots, threatened ROK authorities, stimulated widespread terrorism including arson and violent expropriations, as well as sabotage directed against telephone and telegram facilities.[9] SKLP agitprop activities utilizing rumor, leaflets, and street theater heaped opprobrium on the ROK government and promised a communist redress of popular grievances within a unified Korea. While these actions had the cumulative effect of reducing support for President Rhee in the May 1950 elections, they did not succeed in causing the transference of any significant amount of primary political allegiance from Seoul to Pyongyang, thus aborting Kim Il Sung's hopes for a "popular front" amalgamation between the ROK Parliament and the NK Presidium. Political subversion having failed, military conquest was attempted.

When the NKPA tanks crossed the thirty-eighth parallel, SKLP had approximately 7,000 partisans available for support operations.[10] The partisans had already made a significant contribution to the speedy NKPA success, as fully three division equivalents of ROK police and army had to be committed to antiguerrilla operations.[11] As a result only five division equivalents were available to oppose the invasion which further lengthened the odds against the South. The effect of the prewar partisan activities in interfering with the ROK army training programs was severe but quite unquantifiable. Suffice it to say that the South Korean Army had been so preoccupied with counterguerrilla operations that large-scale conventional war training had been severely curtailed and maneuvers of larger than battalion size units had not been possible.[12] In addition, the presence of the ongoing partisan threat had served to convince the KMAG as well as their political superiors in Washington that the major threat to South Korea was presented by internal unrest and guerrilla warfare, not from cross-border invasion by large, conventional armored forces.[13] This strengthened the position of those who wished to deny the ROK forces heavy weapons, such as tanks and artillery, for fear that President Rhee would attempt to implement his bellicose rhetoric.

While the partisans had little, if any, discernible role in the NKPA drive to the Pusan perimeter, the guerrilla presence assumed a greater importance once the battle lines had stabilized. Partisans infiltrated the U.N. lines with comparative ease to execute ambushes of supply roads and rail lines as well as to attack rear area facilities, collect information and induce unrest among the civilian population. The United Nations Command (UNC) was obliged to dedicate significant assets, primarily ROK, but including U.S. Army military police battalions to reduce this threat.[14]

The Inchon landing and the Pusan breakout resulted in thousands of NKPA stragglers taking to the hills and joining the previously established SKLP partisans. By November the total guerrilla strength had jumped astronomically to 40,000, of whom roughly half were armed; the largest concentrations were in the Chiri region.[15] While the UNC forces ranged north of the thirty-eighth parallel, the guerrillas existed as powerless shadows cut off from any possibility of contact with the North, short of supplies and engaged primarily in efforts directed at self-preservation. They were capable only of mounting raids on nearby farms or isolated police posts.

This situation was changed radically, as were so many others, by the explosive entrance of the Chinese Communist Forces (CCF) upon the Korean stage. The retreat of the UNC to a line south of the thirty-eighth parallel enabled the partisans to reestablish liaison with North Korean authorities. They were reorganized under the political and operational control of the NKPA's 526th Army Unit, also called the Partisan Guidance Bureau, commanded by one Bae Choi, a Soviet-trained professional, who had garnered practical experience in operations against the Germans in the southern Caucasus.[16] Through this organization the SKLP guerrillas would be harmonized with the new communist drive to the south.

Although UNC did not properly appreciate the fact at the time, the mission of the guerrillas was unchanged by the regularization of their status within the NKPA and the centralization of command and control. The partisans were to facilitate the southward movement of the NKPA/CCF units by agitprop, reconnaissance, sabotage and ambush. According to captured documents, the mission priorities were to drain ROK military and civilian manpower from the front areas concentrating on potential porters, great numbers of whom were necessary for operations in the rugged Korean interior, to destroy arms and equipment, to provide military intelligence related information, to cut arteries of communication and transportation, to attack rear echelon installations and to eliminate ROK local government leaders or opinion molders.[17] Directives from the 526th Army Unit left the tactical details up to local commanders.[18] Similarly, logistics responsibility was specifically eschewed by the 526th Army Unit as being a matter best resolved by those most familiar with the local particularities.[19]

The partisans met with mixed success. They were at their best in conducting raids for provisions. They were also tolerably efficient at small ambushes and the cutting of telephone lines. In the area of political murder and terror through the "propaganda of the deed" they were initially successful, but only at the cost of exciting ROK and UNC response. Their propaganda activities did cause some disruptions in the Korean Service Corps porters attached to American units but never any of sufficient magnitude to interfere with the combat capabilities of any U.S. formation. The partisans were not successful at interdicting UNC communications and supply lines, primarily because they lacked the demolitions materiel necessary for the mining of vulnerable rail and road choke points. However, the guerrillas had been a nuisance of sufficient magnitude to require a constant response and an escalating commitment of scarce manpower.

As early as December 1949 the SKLP guerrillas had constituted a sufficiently imposing threat to necessitate a major ROK Army riposte, the Winter Punitive Operation, involving a three division force which comprised nearly 20,000 men in its various assault and support components.[20] One division was detailed to each of the three major guerrilla base areas. These units had not received any specialized antipartisan training.[21] Thus, they employed only conventional infantry patrolling tactics to sweep the Taebaek and Chiri mountains. As operations continued through the spring of 1950 no particularly significant casualties occurred on either side, and guerrilla-initiated incidents decreased in March and ended altogether in May.[22] At the time this was thought to have resulted from the effects of the Winter Punitive Operation; in actuality, the decrease resulted from the shift by NKPA interests away from propaganda, terror and raiding to the lower noise level activities associated with the collection of information and the cessation was necessitated by the preinvasion regrouping.

The UNC commitment of civil and military police units to guard supply lines and rear area installations within the Pusan perimeter was not particularly onerous even given the severe overtaxing of U.S. troops. In a typhoon, a thunder squall is not noticed. The rapid and optimistic advance after the Inchon landing likewise caused no discernible strain upon UNC rear security detachments. South of Seoul two U.S. and two ROK divisions screened the main Pusan–Seoul highway and patrolled the verges of the Chiri. Given the supply-starved and disorganized nature of the SKLP guerrillas, who were attempting to cope with the flood of NKPA stragglers, this somewhat less than imposing UNC force was sufficient to keep the peace. North of Seoul the antipartisan activities were somewhat more arduous, if not more professional in execution. Several police battalions and four newly activated "antiguerrilla battalions," a courtesy title only as no special training or equipment had been provided, engaged the guerrillas straddling the thirty-eighth parallel in central Korea.[23] Above the parallel various tactical reserve units whiled away the time between combat assignments, lackadaisically providing security to the ever-lengthening UNC lines of communication.

U.S. and ROK forces engaged in ad hoc operations against the guerrillas without any central command, control, coordination or intelligence exchange mechanisms. By and large only conventional patrolling techniques were used. One noteworthy exception was furnished by the 25th Infantry Division which employed heavily armed jeep-mounted patrols in constant radio contact with the division artillery's Fire Direction Center or the forward fire control officers. The patrols proceeded rapidly through a sector and, if guerrillas were flushed out, called in the appropriate fire missions.[24] The UNC thought it saw success in what seemed to be a satisfactory number of guerrilla casualties reported reaching as many as 500 killed or captured on a single day.[25]

In the wake of the CCF offensive, rear areas were stripped of combat capable units so that only ROK police and security battalions were available for counterguerrilla operations. "A minimum of forty thousand" partisans were believed to be active in the South Korean mountains in November 1950.[26] The threat continued to escalate, particularly in a 1,500 square mile area in the southeastern portion of the Taebaek mountains. In January 1951, it became necessary to assign the 1st Marine Division, then recuperating from the Chosin Reservoir affray, to the task of confronting these guerrillas in what was dubbed the "Pohang Guerrilla Hunt."

The use of the term "hunt" was well advised for the problem in this situation, as in most where the opponent is a guerrilla, was not so much killing the adversary as finding him in the first place so that he might be killed. A combination of sweeps, search and clear missions and rapid reaction forces was employed with minimal success. Two battalion size attacks were mounted on presumed guerrilla strongholds. The first, on 24 January 1951, had quite encouraging results in that 161 partisans were killed or captured.[27] The other, on 6 February 1951, proved fruitless despite the fact that the guerrillas had been positively identified at the location the previous day.[28] After twenty-seven days of operations the marines had killed 120 and captured 184 supposed guerrillas in exchange for losses of 16 dead, 148 wounded and 10 missing.[29] Despite the disappointingly small bag due to the partisans' creditable evasion tactics, the hunt turned out to have been a success: after a council of war the local Branch Unit commander decided that the area was no longer tenable and a majority of the partisans withdrew, leaving behind a residuum manageable by ROK police and security battalions. Throughout the summer methodical, small-scale search and clear operations served to clear the Taebaek completely for the first time since 1948.[30] By winter the only significant remaining guerrilla concentration was to be found in the Chiri mountain area.

The first major effort to lance the Chiri abscess, Operation RAT-KILLER, employed two of the best ROK divisions, plus another division equivalent in police and security battalions under the command of one of South Korea's most able officers, General Paik Sun Yup. The plan of operations envisioned a three phase campaign commencing on 2 December 1951. Phase I was directed toward the central Chiri massif. While the police and security battalions occupied blocking positions on the most likely escape routes, the two regular divisions assaulted the peak simultaneously from both north and south. By 14 December the ROK troops achieved the summit after having killed 1,612 guerrillas and captured a further 1,842.[31] In Phase II the two regular divisions displaced fifty miles to the northern edge of the guerrilla-infested area, clearing the critical pass above Conju. From 19 December 1951 until 4 January 1952 the ROK forces launched a series of search and clear operations which served to raise the bag of partisans to 8,300.[32] It deserves mention that, after screening, many of these supposed partisans proved to be the proverbial innocent bystanders. For the final phase the ROK forces returned to the central Chiri massif for two regimental size sweeps designed effectively to counter attempted partisan reinfiltration. Phase III and related mopping up activities continued until 6 March 1952. This rescreening was profitable with a final tally of over 9,000 putative partisans killed or captured.[33] It might be noted that an influential and widely reprinted article, bearing the imprimitur of the U.S. Command and General Staff College, provides the following unattributed figures for Operation RATKILLER:

> More than 11,000 guerrillas were killed and more than 10,000 captured including 50 major leaders. Approximately 4,300 of the prisoners were released after screening.[34]

It is difficult to reconcile these casualty figures with those in any other published source.

Following RATKILLER, a series of smaller antipartisan operations were mounted by ad hoc division equivalents of security and police battalions. Three different campaigns lasting until late November 1952 served to eliminate the guerrilla presence in the Chiri.[35] Ultimately, fewer than 1,000 guerrilla remnants were left in the area and they presented no threat to South Korea or the allied forces.[36]

The American appreciation of the Korean War antipartisan experience emphasized the utility of conventional infantry and combined arms techniques in suppressing the guerrilla threat. It was argued that the absence of sufficient numbers of highly trained, conventional forces, as well as a deficiency in tactical and reconnaissance aircraft made the job of defeating the partisans more difficult and prolonged. The fluctuating fortunes of the guerrillas dependent upon the availability of support and supplies from the conventional NKPA and CCF units underscored the importance of external sponsorship for guerrillas and the necessity of severing lines of communication as a tool for defeating the partisan fighters. The atypical nature of the Korean conflict at least as regarded the guerrillas was not noted, but rather the consensus was that Korea served to establish the true nature of the guerrilla threat: not simply adjuncts to a conventional force but the first sign of attack by a conventional force. Thus, the defeat of guerrillas took on a new saliency in the minds of American planners but there was no perceived need to change the basic operational priorities from those of the conventional employment of general purpose, high mobility forces in order to meet and defeat the hostile guerrillas in the field in set-piece battles to those of a more exotic format of combat. Matters of psychological warfare or civil affairs were not seen as having any importance in the suppression of guerrillas. Intelligence collection and dissemination needs were not seen as differing qualitatively from those applying to combat with a conventional force. This conclusion was reached despite the great deficiencies in American intelligence due to the professional incompetence of General MacArthur's intelligence staff. A good example of the American army attitude to Korea and partisans was found in a widely reprinted article which concluded that the existing doctrine was sound and should be taught in service schools.[37]

NOTES

1. U.S. Department of State, *Bulletin*, vol. XIX (June 1949), p. 781.

2. Fred Barton, *Salient Operational Aspects of Paramilitary Warfare in Three Asian Areas*, (ORO-T-228), Chevy Chase, Md.: Johns Hopkins University, Operations Research Office, 1963, pp. 15–16.

3. Ibid., p. 22.

4. ROK Ministry of Education, *Korean War History for Year One*, (Seoul: ROK 1955), p. A67.

5. Ibid., pp. A70–71; Barton, *Salient Operational Aspects*, p. 27.

6. *Korean War History*, p. A74.

7. Ibid., p. A74.

8. Barton, *Salient Operational Aspects*, p. 34.

9. Ibid., pp. 37–38.

10. *Korean War History*, p. A157.

11. Ibid., p. A153.

12. Ibid., pp. A80–86, A95–98 passim.

13. Robert K. Sawyer, *Military Advisors in Korea: KMAG in Peace and War*, (Washington, D.C.: Office of the Chief of Military History 1962), pp. 81–90 passim.

14. Roy Appleman, *South to the Naktong; North to the Yalu*, (Washington, D.C.: USGPO 1961), p. 10.

15. Barton, *Salient Operational Aspects*, p. 29.

16. *Korean War History*, pp. A165–67, and U.S. intelligence appreciations.

17. Ibid.

18. Barton, *Salient Operational Aspects*, pp. 132–33, 162.

19. Ibid., pp. 135, 167.

20. *Korean War History*, p. A16.

21. Barton, *Salient Operational Aspects*, p. 18.

22. Ibid., p. 19.

23. *Korean War History*, pp. A80–81.

24. Anon., *Battleground Korea, the Story of the 25th Infantry Division*, (Atlanta, Ga.: Albert Love 1961), Chap. 5 passim.

25. Appleman, *South to the Naktong*, p. 261.

26. John Beebe, "Beating the Guerrilla," *Military Review*, vol. 35 (December 1955), 6.

27. Lynn Montross et al., *US Marine Operations in Korea 1950–1953: East Central Front*, (Washington, D.C.: USGPO 1962), p. 47.

28. Ibid., p. 53.

29. Ibid., pp. 41–58 passim.

30. *Korean War History*, pp. A161–67 passim.

31. Walter Hermes, *Truce Tent and Fighting Front*, (Washington, D.C.: USGPO 1966), p. 102, n28 citing HQ 5th Army command report December 1951 G-3 section bk. 4, inclusions 1–5, p. 7.

32. Ibid., p. 103, n29 ibid., p. 8.

33. Ibid., p. 103, n31.

34. Beebe, "Beating the Guerrilla," p. 11.

35. Barton, *Salient Operational Aspects*, p. 129.

36. Ibid., p. 135.

37. Beebe, "Beating the Guerrilla," p. 18.

4.
The Philippines, 1946–1954

Considering that the Huk Insurrection which dominated affairs in the Philippine Islands did in fact occur in an archipelago suitably isolated from the potential of external sponsorship for the guerrillas, it is not surprising that the type of guerrilla war found there was not of the partisan type but of the insurgent variety. While direct American involvement in the Huk Insurrection was nowhere near as complete as had been the case in Greece, and the lessons derived by the formulators of military doctrine nowhere near as clear and convincing as those derived from Greece and Korea, this does not mean that the conflict was without significance in the evolution of the American understanding of guerrilla war and how to win it. Unfortunately, observers of this war, both contemporary and more recent, like those of the other insurgent conflict closely watched by Americans, the Malayan Emergency, missed the essential elements of the course and nature of the conflict and emphasized attractive but misleading aspects with potentially disastrous consequences.

While possessed of definite Marxist aspects and loosely correlated with other Asian communist movements, the Hukbalahap (Huks in common usage) was a not new communist organization created out of nothing in the pervasive climate of nationalism which swept Asia in the wake of World War II, as was the case in Indonesia, Indochina or Malaya, but rather was the most recent expression of a tradition of violent agrarian unrest extending several centuries into the Islands' past. Luis Taruc, the military commander of the Huks during their period of greatest success, reflected upon the motives for both the insurrection and his personal commitment to the movement in his prison memoirs:

But what moved me most of all was the plight of my fellow peas-

ants, who for centuries have been the victims of bitter oppression
by feudal landlordism. . . . Thus for centuries, "land for the landless" has been the peasants' cry and the peasants' hunger for land
has been our nation's most pressing problem.[1]

Violent agrarian unrest was endemic throughout the Spanish colonial period with the result that society was deeply polarized along both social
and class lines. The *mestizo* (mixed race) and Spanish planter aristocracy
and their armed retainers opposed the native Tagalog sharecroppers. Out
of this background arose the radical, not to say revolutionary, nationalism
of Luzon, particularly the Tagalog-speaking provinces of Bulacan, Cavite,
Laguna and Pampanga. In these the tocsin of rebellion would sound frequently, first against the Spanish, then against the new American colonial
administration and finally against the Philippine national government.

The Huks directly traced their roots to a collection of vaguely Marxist
labor groups, peasant organizations and other groups which sought to
unite against Japanese aggression in the weeks immediately preceding the
attack on the Philippine Islands by Japanese troops. On 10 December
1941, these groups, under the leadership of the Philippine Communist
Party, pledged support for the allied war effort and urged preparation for
guerrilla war. The government of President Quezon rejected this gesture.

The Philippine government was no longer in a position to object when
the various leftist parties formed the *Huknong Bayan Sa Hapon* (People's
Army Against the Japanese), the "Hukbasahap" or Huks. This politico-
military organization grew to become the largest and most powerful of
the resistance groups in Luzon, if not in the Philippines generally. It was
certainly the only guerrilla movement in the Islands with a political objective larger than that of simple opposition to the Japanese occupation.
No other prewar Philippine political party played a role as such in the
resistance movement.[2] Obviously this placed the Huks at a distinct advantage vis à vis their political rivals in staking a claim for patriotic reward
and public approbation after the war.

The Chairman of the Huk Military Committee was Luis Taruc who,
though an experienced veteran of the prewar organizational struggle, was
only twenty-nine when he became leader of the Huks. He was, and remains, a fascinating and complex character whose personality was central
to the course of the Huk insurgencey from its birth in the resistance to

its virtual death a decade later. He candidly remarked on the communist influence, indeed dominance, in the Huk organization, but convincingly argued that a split existed between the nationalist majority and the pro-Comintern minority, and that he was identified with the nationalist wing of the movement.[3] To see him as a Tagalog Tito does neither Taruc nor the truth a disservice.

When U.S. forces entered Luzon in January 1945, General Douglas MacArthur's headquarters (GHQ SWPA) had collected a considerable amount of information on the Huk organization, strength, leadership and aims. The interpretation given this data was that the Huks were not so much a militant nationalist and anti-Japanese resistance force as they were a communist subversive group.[4] While GHQ SWPA did not see any credible potential for Huk overt resistance to the U.S. forces, it did clearly anticipate that the movement would be a severe, perhaps indigestible, problem during the period of transition from military liberation to the reestablishment of a legitimate civilian government. In the perception of senior GHQ SWPA personnel, most importantly Courtney Whitney, an ultraconservative Manila-based corporation attorney, who had joined MacArthur's staff in the position of Civil Affairs officer, the ultimate aim of the Huks was nothing more nor less than the establishment of a communist regime in the Philippines as soon as the U.S. forces had completed the liberation and were preparing for the final invasion of the Japanese home islands. Even if MacArthur's antipathy for anything smacking of socialism had been less pronounced, any Huk antigovernmental activity would have been quite unacceptable, given the difficulties of mounting the anticipated invasion of Japan.[5] U.S. troops were ordered to look askance at the Huks and to allow no interference from them.

American forces disarmed many Huk units in the vicinity of Manila and in the central Luzon plains. The Civil Affairs officers removed and replaced the local officials installed by the Huks. Finally, in mid-March Luis Taruc and his second-in-command were arrested by U.S. Army Counterintelligence Corps (CIC) officers but were released in a matter of days due, in large measure, to the sizable public demonstrations which ensued upon their arrest, but also because CIC hoped that Taruc would assist in the disarming and demobilization of the remaining Huk formations. Years later Taruc argued that the policy of rigorous repression constituted a serious miscalculation.

When the war ended, the Party leaders said that only under un-
bearable provocation from the reactionary elements would the Huks
take up arms again, in self-defense.[6]

The release failed to cause any further Huk demobilization and the two
leaders were rearrested in April and confined to the Iwahig Penal Colony
with assorted Japanese collaborators and accused war criminals until 30
September 1945. In the meantime, anti-Huk actions were taken by the
American-led police forces, which were comprised primarily of former
right-wing guerrillas and collaborationist Sakdals, who in many cases were
the spiritual if not the physical kin of the victims of the Huk "puppet"
liquidation efforts. During the war the Huks' primary focus had been the
emasculation of conservative prewar opponents: this was accomplished
under the guise of eliminating collaborators with the Japanese. The result
was a chaotic reign of terror far surpassing in brutality even the worst of
the Japanese excesses. Further alienating the Luzon peasants from the
American and Filipino authorities was the refusal of GHQ SWPA to pay
the Huk combatants for their wartime service, as had been done with
other guerrillas. An influential military writer termed this "unfortunate."[7]
He was wrong. So was the other American observer who termed the final
release of Taruc and the other Huk leaders from detention, "a costly mistake."[8]

Further serving to make the political reconciliation impossible was the
announcement by Douglas MacArthur of the "liberation" of Manuel
Roxas.[9] This action raised the thorny question of wartime collaboration
with the Japanese, both in terms of its nature and extent and the character
of consequent American treatment of alleged collaborators. Roxas, a prewar politician of prominence as well as a brigadier in the Philippine Army
and longtime friend of General MacArthur had cooperated, apparently
voluntarily, with the Japanese occupation authorities. While Roxas was
freed from any charges, four equally voluntary major collaborators were
imprisoned along with thousands of smaller fry. This action stimulated the
Filipino President Osmenia, a political rival of Roxas, to acquiesce in
MacArthur's demand that forty-five members of the Philippine Congress
be seated without any further investigation. To the majority of the Filipino
people this sequence reeked of an unacceptable overlooking of malfeas-
ance during an occupation which had cost the lives of tens of thousands.[10]

Further, it appeared as though this craven turning of the blind eye was in response to the urgings of prewar political imperatives, which no longer seemed either pertinent or proper.[11] An addition to Filipino disenchantment was provided by the Philippine Trade Act of 1946, which, when proposed in the American Congress, was widely perceived in the Philippines as being simply a means of freezing the Islands' economy in its prewar colonial pattern.

While all of these grievances were exploited by the communist propaganda mechanism, it must be noted that not only communists were angered and alienated by these specific occurrences as well as their surrounding matrix of general social and economic chaos: inflation, black marketeering, corruption, and other manifestations of structural collapse. It was increasingly obvious to all social strata below the most elite and all shades of political opinion save the most conservative that some drastic changes were overdue. The government was in a state of flaccid paralysis and was rapidly becoming totally discredited. Finally, in January 1946, an open split developed between President Osmenia and Roxas, who bolted the dominant Nationalist Party and organized the sorely misnamed Liberal Party, which in turn nominated him for the presidency in the April 1946 elections.

The communists had been undecided for some time as to the line to be adopted regarding the elections. Finally the decision was made to join the Democratic Alliance (DA), which had been formed by disillusioned moderates, liberals and socialists in the fall of 1945. Generally, DA was nationalistic and reform-oriented; it never came under communist control at the national level, although many of its local affiliates were undoubtedly communist-dominated. The DA was presented by a dilemma with the formation of the Liberal Party but finally decided to support the Nationalists, believing that the introduction of a third party slate would simply insure the election of the hated Roxas.

The Liberal Party and Roxas prevailed nationally, but in central Luzon Osmenia and the DA triumphed, despite a terror campaign on the part of Roxas' supporters as well as armed retainers and elements of the nascent Philippine Armed Forces. The provinces in central Luzon elected six DA Congressional candidates including Luis Taruc. This small number presented a serious threat to Roxas, as they could deny him the congressional majority needed to amend the Constitution; an amendment was required in order to assent to the Philippine Trade Act of 1946. Roxas simultaneously solved his immediate problem and succeeded in creating one of larger dimensions and longer duration. By having his supporters in the Philippine House deny entrance to the DA dissidents, Roxas assured the amendment would be passed, and the Huk Insurrection would be initiated.

The Philippine Armed Forces (PAF) were in no shape to deal with an insurrection. In the months prior to independence the army had to reduce its strength from 132,000 to only 37,000 men, of which 24,000 were members of the Military Police Command (MPC), which was charged initially with the responsibility of dealing with internal security matters, including the rearmed and militant Huks.[12] PAF and MPC alike were woefully underequipped and would remain so for some time to come, considering that as late as June 1948 less than fifty percent of the promised American materiel had been received.[13] The leadership was politically appointed and poor in quality; troop morale was nonexistent. The PAF units were badly distributed, being parceled out according to the requirements of powerful politicians, large landholders and business interests. The other security force components, local and provincial police, were in even worse straits, with the police positions being purely political plums and opportunities for economic self-gratification. The Roxas "mailed fist" anti-Huk campaign of spring and summer 1946 was a renewal of naked, unadulterated terror. As one highly placed government-oriented observer noted:

> The "mailed fist" often was indiscriminately applied to civilian friend as well as military foe. Soon many Filipino farmers and civilians feared the constabulary as much or more than the Huks. This destroyed the respect and confidence in many of the people, not only in their armed forces but in the central government. In many areas of Luzon the people now openly supported the communist troops.[14]

Roxas was hard-pressed to redeem his pledge to crush the Huks in sixty days.

Extermination of the Huks through military measures was the basic Roxas policy. In this he was supported by such rightist worthies as Pampanga province governor, Pablo David, and his successor, Jose Lingad, who was, ironically, a former schoolmate of Luis Taruc. Both governors resolutely imposed the "mailed fist" policy. An immediate and obvious result was that Pampanga became the center of the insurrection led by Taruc who, having been prevented from taking his seat in Congress by Roxas, made directly for the bush. Ranging out from Pampanga with its secure Mt. Arayat base camp, insurgent bands numbering as many as 1,000 men moved freely through most of central Luzon, a portion of which was again known by its wartime name of "Huklandia." This was an apt appellation, for the PAF was outnumbered, outgunned and outmaneuvered at every turn.[15]

The Americans were conspicuously absent during this period of rapid and pronounced deterioration, not simply because of their postwar fixation on European problems and the rapidly developing cold war, but also because Washington was simply oblivious of the Huk Insurrection prior to 1949.[16] Apparently apprehensive of American reaction which might prove erosive of either sovereignty or the political status quo, Manila had not been candid in its requests for military assistance and had provided reports concerning the situation which were obviously duplicitous. Further serving to hinder American concern about the Philippines was the absence of a vocal constituency in Washington. In a real sense, the Philippines were very much of a backburner proposition in which American interests were limited to the rapid settlement of any problems regarding U.S. rights to bases on the Islands.[17] It also deserves mention that there was no American intelligence gathering capability in the Islands other than what the Embassy staff might gather in Manila. The result was that the United States was sublimely unconcerned about the Philippines and temporarily blind to the need to become concerned.

This started to change in 1949. By this time the activities which passed for democratic process in the Philippines had virtually collapsed, while the Huk main force and mass support structure were rapidly approaching their estimated maximum strength of 12,000 combatants and 100,000 active support structure members.[18] The elections of 1949 aspired simultaneously to low farce and high tragedy. Jose Laurel, formerly the collaborationist President under the Japanese, ran as the Nationalist Party standard bearer against the intellectually and morally bankrupt leader of the Liberals, Manuel Quirino. It was a contest between a resuscitated quisling and a failed, discredited and thoroughly corrupt incumbent in a campaign charitably characterized as bestial. Violence, terrorism, vote fraud on a cosmic scale and a pervasive apathy born of fatalistic resignation were all exhibited in this crucial electoral contest from which Quirino emerged a winner without victory, whose only mandate was that of presiding flaccidly over a dissolving government, streaked with individual self-gratification and besotted with rampant venality.

By comparison, the Huks had a definite and seemingly feasible program which could be explained and, more importantly, demonstrated to the population. The insurgent organization was well defined, disciplined and structurally well integrated. In the three province area of "Huklandia" it operated in a fashion which was perceived by the inhabitants and onlookers alike as being fair and efficient. On the margins of this internal state Huk influence and control were being extended by contagious example with the transmission vector being a well-conceived and executed propaganda program supported by a comprehensive educational operation which effectively combined the social goal of reduced illiteracy with the political one of inculcation of Marxist ideology. Further afield, the Huk units were able to prepare the way for future expansion by effectively denying central government control. Ambushes, raids and assassinations were daily occurrences throughout Luzon and extended even to other islands, most notably Negros and Panay.

The insurgent structure followed established practice. The organization was divided along functional and regional lines which, while seeming to emobody the usual security features of cellularly organized conspiratorial groups, served to complicate problems of communications and command efficiency. Depending upon a collection of couriers and easily compromised radio links, the Huk political and military command structure was vulnerable to the security forces. Additionally, the Huk stronghold, "Huklandia," on the slopes of Mt. Arayat was narrowly circumscribed by geography and politics alike. Huklandia comprised an area which was primarily heavily cultivated agricultural plain, well provided by all weather roads and thus wide open to penetration by the PAF. The support base for the Huks was quite small in terms of the Islands' entire population, being comprised almost exclusively of the historically discontented, historically exploited rural proletariat of central Luzon. A government which was capable of effectively dealing with the problem of equitable land distribution would rapidly undercut the Huk mass support base and thus fatally weaken the insurgency. Through 1950 it may be said that the

Huks were not so much winning the insurrection as that the central government was losing it.

The turning point came in 1950 with the appointment of Ramon Magsaysay to the position of Secretary of Defense in the Quirino administration and the development of an exceptionally effective, low-keyed American interest in the insurrection. Magsaysay was the critical man; his personality was the key in assuring the defeat of the Huks. His effectiveness as the leader of a highly successful counterinsurgency effort would not have been as striking, complete or rapid without the development of an acute American interest in the situation and concomitant progress in the formulation of effective methods of cooperation, support and assistance.

Even before the North Korean invasion in June of 1950 had brought Asia very definitely onto the front burner, there was a slowly increasing U.S. interest in the questionable situation developing in the Philippines. Additionally, U.S. military authorities at the Subic Bay Naval Base and Clark Air Force Base, which lay literally in the shadow of Mt. Arayat, had become increasingly anxious about the security of these strategically important facilities as well as about the physical safety of American personnel and Filipino on-base employees. Interestingly, the Filipino government did not seek to bring the matter of the Huks to U.S. attention, even at the highest level as when President Quirino met with President Truman in February 1950.[19] Even with this strange reticence on the part of the Philippine government which was otherwise notably loquacious on matters of interest containing at least the implicit guarantee of U.S. monetary aid, the Americans began showing not only more interest in the Islands but better reporting and better appreciation of the developments.[20]

A momentum of urgency developed through the spring and early summer of 1950, which was greatly enhanced by the opening of a Central Intelligence Agency (CIA) station responsible for the coordination and facilitation of active collection and penetration operations. A resident network of broad spectrum capabilities was developed with impressive speed. The improvements in American capabilities as well as interest may be seen in the more detailed reporting which came out of the Embassy in the late spring of 1950. The Huks are correctly appreciated as having "the serious agrarian reform problem of the Central Luzon Plain" as the fundamental cause of their existence and support.[21] The Embassy's assessment of the PAF was quite accurate and therefore quite unfavorable:

On the basis of the foregoing, it would appear incorrect to assert that the Philippine government demonstrates a willingness and ability to take military steps necessary to contain HMB (Huk) guerrilla units—much less to disarm them. From the military point of view, Philippine armed forces demonstrate at least two defects which may and in all likelihood will prove fatal—unless they are remedied: (1) They appear unable or unwilling to "fix" and wipe out or capture the dissident units they contact and they are not vigorous in the pursuit. (2) The Philippine Constabulary, instead of winning popular support, has in general behaved so that it has alienated the rural population. . . . So long as the Constabulary seize foodstuffs without paying for them, become drunk and disorderly, extract information by inhumane methods, abuse women, shoot up country towns and generally mistreat the populace, just so long will they continue to lose the Philippines to the HMB.[22]

The Embassy also correctly criticized the Joint U.S. Military Assistance Group (JUSMAG) as having within its number only officers with conventional war experience. As a result it was specifically recommended that:

there be assigned to the JUSMAG a substantial number of officers having actual experience in guerrilla and anti-guerrilla operations and particularly in operations involving Communist led forces. . . . Some officers having similar experiences in the recent operations in Greece should also be assigned to JUSMAG in the Philippines.[23]

The Embassy concluded by strongly recommending that the United States not send troops, as such would be to play into the hands of hostile forces throughout the region, although the Chargé recognized that the presence of U.S. units would immediately tilt the balance against the Huks. The Joint Chiefs of Staff, in a thorough review of the options available to the United States in securing its interests in the Philippines, likewise concluded that American troops should not be used, as such would constitute only a "temporary expedient"; and that "remedial political and economic measures" need to be undertaken by the Philippine government to remove the causes of insurrection.[24] General Omar Bradley concluded in this appreciation that the United States should increase JUSMAG at least to its initially authorized strength of thirty-two officers and twenty-six enlisted men as well as increase the local security contingents at the U.S. bases in the Islands, and that the National Security Council be urged to facilitate "prompt and positive political and economic action to arrest and reverse the current political deterioration in the Philippines."[25]

All parties emphatically agreed with the conviction expressed by Magsaysay that the first major problem was to restore the population's trust in the efficiency and fairness of the PAF. It was necessary to convince a hostile or distrustful Filipino society that the PAF was not only able to protect them from Huk activities but also that the armed forces merited trust in the role of social protector. The first task could be undertaken more easily and rapidly than the second.

Magsaysay, working closely with the small, usually mufti-clad JUSMAG, plunged into the task of rehabilitating the armed forces with a will; terroristic tactics, corruption and incompetence were reduced radically, if not eliminated altogether, by a combination of summary discharges, court-martials of the guilty and field promotions of the deserving. Magsaysay traveled constantly as his own inspectorate general, a practice that had a dramatic, salutory effect on the combat efficiency of the army. The assurance of increased, regular rations and pay made possible by American aid and improved administration ended the pervasive and pernicious practice of commandeering which had been so widespread and glaring as to border on open brigandage and markedly improved the morale of soldier and peasant alike.

Structural reorganization recommended by JUSMAG was implemented when President Quirino published Executive Order 389 on 23 December 1950, dividing the country into four Military Area Commands (MAC). In each, the basic tactical unit would be a combined arms formation of battalion strength, the Battalion Combat Team (BCT). These would be switched between Area Commands on the basis of security needs and would be controlled through the Area Commanders by the PAF Chief of Staff, which in practice meant Magsaysay and JUSMAG.[26] Magsaysay personally selected the BCT commanders from the most able officers between the ages of twenty-five and thirty-three. He wanted young, aggressive and energetic field commanders.

The first operational purpose of the reorganization scheme was that of demonstrating to the peasant population of the contested regions that the national government had both the will and the capability to maintain a protective presence. Even though the initial defensive deployment of a BCT in each of the seven contested provinces tied down a majority of the first-line PAF units and even though this type of static defense was anathema to proper counterinsurgency doctrine as perceived by segments of JUSMAG, the temporary degradation of offensive capability was more than amply rewarded by the increase in public confidence. As the new PAF BCTs replaced their predecessors, they were greeted by a chill of distrust or even frank hostility by villagers who had been so maltreated by the Constabulary that they had little but ill will for the government and its soldiers. The operational priorities established for the BCTs in these initial deployments were: gain public trust and cooperation, engage in defensive activities to protect the population against acts of terror or raids, generate exploitable combat information for limited offensive operations and encourage the development of local self-defense volunteer formations. Tight, centralized command and control procedures were employed to insure compliance with these priorities.

The attachment to the BCTs of Civil Affairs officers with expertise in psychological warfare was of great assistance in gaining support from the local population. Civil Affairs officers had as their first job the explanation of the procedures by which citizens could use the PAF Judge Advocate General's office to pursue legal action against PAF personnel and to gain compensation for damages inflicted by the army. This relatively cheap and simply gambit inaugurated a change in opinion, particularly after the first case or two in which a peasant received monetary compensation or had the satisfaction of seeing a uniformed thug punished. When this was followed by the employment of military medical, engineering, transport or manpower resources for civilian projects, positive perceptions of the PAF were quickly reinforced. The genesis of this civil affairs orientation undoubtedly occurred in the fertile brain of Magsaysay; the details, including techniques of administrative monitoring and psychological operations, originated with the Americans.[27]

The *éminence grise* of American psychological warfare in Asia, Paul Linebarger, was being characteristically self-effacing when he wrote in his classic text on psychological operations that most of the psychological warfare doctrines and operational procedures employed in the Philippines were American in origin.[28] There can be little doubt that Linebarger was the foremost authority on psychological operations in Asia, including covert and clandestine activities. His seminars on the subject were justly famous throughout the CIA.[29] There are strong grounds upon which to conclude that Linebarger was not only the motivating force behind the American support for psychological operations, whether directed at civilians or the Huks, but also that he was closely and personally connected with the development of mechanisms for implementing these operations and the civil affairs programs which they supported. Particularly noteworthy in this regard was Linebarger's early and prolonged residence in China and his intimate familiarity with the principles and methods employed by Mao's People's Liberation Army (PLA) for gaining and maintaining popular support. Linebarger firmly believed that the same precepts and experientially tested methods could be combined effectively with Western procedures so as to be turned against the ideological compatriots of their PLA originators.

In a closely related field, improvements were made in the procedures for gathering information from civilians as well as from captured or defecting Huks. American consultants noted a number of substantial deficiencies in the correlation and validation of the raw informational catch so that reliable, useful intelligence could be developed and disseminated in a timely fashion. Also noticed and corrected were grave problems in the basic techniques used to collect information from such critical sources as civilians and defecting Huk guerrillas or mass support base members. Through most of 1951 the only reliable intelligence was developed through American assets and facilities, with the result that it was not available to PAF commanders as useful combat information.

The purpose of combat information is to make effective combat possible, and ultimately the BCTs were not simply signals of governmental resolve or instruments of civil affairs: they were combat units. Their composition, mission and operations must be examined with this simple reality in mind. BCT training and organization were based upon standard American infantry and mechanized doctrine from which few if any concessions to the demands of counterinsurgency warfare were deemed necessary by JUS-MAG.[30] Minor adjustments were made over time on the basis of experience. These were designed to enhance mobility, flexibility in deployment, as well as to emphasize reconnaissance, patrolling and night operations. Each BCT comprised three infantry companies, a heavy weapons company with 81mm mortars, .50 calibre machine guns and 57mm recoilless rifles, a reconnaissance platoon as well as service and transport elements. Normally artillery was not organic but a battery of towed 105mm howitzers was attached, if required by the mission. U.S. officers did not accompany the BCTs in the field as advisors due to the perception that such was not necessary and would serve only to increase the risk of American casualties without compensatory improvements in PAF performance.[31] It might also be mentioned that Magsaysay was convinced on the basis of his own experience as a guerrilla during the occupation period that large sweeps were unnecessarily expensive in resources and counterproductive. Eventually JUSMAG agreed with this contention.

By spring 1951, the BCTs, operating upon the substructure of increased civilian confidence, support and assistance, proved themselves an effective agency for providing not only local defense but for taking the war to the Huks. The improvement in the intelligence system was providing a firm basis upon which to plan and mount offensive operations. More and more often these operations fell upon their intended targets rather than upon empty bush and deserted campsites. The infiltration of the Huk bands by government agents had seriously damaged guerrilla morale while the widespread propaganda campaign had started the process of demobilizing public identification with and support for the insurgents. Gradually through the summer of 1951 the previously victorious and expanding Huk movement found itself increasingly on the defensive and often on the retreat to remote sanctuaries in rugged terrain. Even in Huklandia the motorized PAF units in multibattalion strength had cleared the agricultural flatland limiting the guerrillas to the slopes of Mt. Arayat and the adjacent swamps. By mid-September the American Acting Secretary of State was commenting upon reports that Magsaysay was of the opinion that the "military aspects of the Huk problem" were now so near solution that the time had come to consider other uses for the army.[32] The Embassy correctly reported that this assessment was too optimistic and that the Huks continued to exist as a military problem.[33] But Magsaysay was right about other uses for the PAF troops.

Magsaysay well recognized that neither military pressure nor the small-scale reforms possible within the context of civil affairs would end the insurgency. In order for that to happen, it would be necessary to redress the basic popular grievance which fueled the insurrectionary movement: the inequitable patterns of land ownership. If the army could successfully expropriate the revolutionary rhetoric of "Land to the Tiller" and "Land to the Landless," the ground would be cut completely out from under the Huks. Considering that the Philippine government had not been able or willing to do this in a civilian agency during either the Roxas or Quirino administrations despite the most strenuous of American urgings, and considering that Magsaysay harbored presidential aspirations and was looking forward to the next national elections in November 1951, it is not surprising that he developed in late 1950 a mechanism by which the PAF might undertake a massive project aimed at land reform on a scale which would have strategic impact. The army, using a mixture of funds from American sources as well as "popular" subscriptions, would acquire land upon which would be located planned agricultural communities. The settlers in these communities, the peasants who would acquire title to the lands which they cultivated, were composed of carefully screened and handpicked former Huks, retired soldiers and civilian volunteers. The communities would be initiated, constructed and partially controlled by the army. The PAF would likewise control the propaganda which would be based upon the existence of these communities and the demonstration land reform project which they represented. The program became well known as the Economic Development Corps (EDCOR). This program was in part developed as the result of a close advisor and confidante of Magsaysay, Col. Edward Lansdale. The exact nature of Lansdale's role in EDCOR is still obscure but it was in no way diminished in later years when he became the associate of the man whom the Americans hoped would be the equivalent of Magsaysay in South Vietnam, Ngo Dinh Diem.

Lansdale was later virtually mythologized as an expert on counterinsurgency.[34] He was an effective political operator whose bonhomie and *mano a mano* charisma made him a singularly and strikingly effective advisor to Magsaysay as was officially recognized by the U.S. Ambassador.[35] Further, he was a minor public relations genius whose promotional talents were in no way lessened when dealing with himself as the subject; who was quite capable of cheerfully gathering to his own harvest the fruits of other men's vineyards, a process facilitated, if not obligated, by the semiclandestine nature of many of the operations and American projects in the Philippines as well as the nature of the agencies charged with their conduct.[36]

The EDCOR plan did not exist simply to transfer untilled land to unorganized packets of settlers. Such an approach would have been unproductive. Neither was the approach analogous to the contemporaneous population resettlement scheme in Malaya. Broadly speaking, the intent was that the army would acquire land in areas far removed from the focus of the insurrection such as on the island of Mindinao, 500 miles south of Manila and central Luzon; there to clear the land, construct roads, erect houses and generally prepare the physical infrastructure of a functional agricultural community. Settlers, whether former Huks, volunteers or retired military personnel would be screened, selected and provided a loan as start-up capital as well as necessary hand implements, repayment for which would be on quite liberal terms. The first settlement at Kapatagan covered 4,000 acres which, after deductions for the town site and preexistent claims, provided some 126 allotments.[37] After three months of engineer effort at land clearing and village construction, the first settlers arrived in spring 1951, followed quickly by the rest. The second project at Buldon, Mindinao, commenced in late 1951 and was designed to provide 255 farms.[38] The third, located in North Luzon, did not get underway until January 1954 after the Huk Insurrection had been liquidated. The small number of people who directly benefited from the EDCOR program provided an immense propaganda leverage to the government of stunningly greater magnitude than would have been expected on the basis of simply counting heads.

After mid-1951 EDCOR formed the centerpiece of both government and Huk propaganda. By the use of voice, print media, both white and gray, radio and film, the government showed peasants in contested areas that it had the ability and the desire to provide land to the landless, thus eroding the central appeal of the Huks. Additionally, PAF psychological operations directed against Huk fighters emphasized the possibility, even the probability, of EDCOR settlement, if only they surrendered. The offering of an attractive alternative to life in the bush and combat against the increasingly numerous and effective BCTs had a significant appeal to the marginally ideologically motivated or the frankly conscripted individuals who formed much of the guerrilla main force and almost all of the auxiliary units. The Huks saw immediately the negative effects of this propaganda campaign and countered with an offensive both military and psychological. The military action was a sort of feverish last stab which was not accurately appreciated as such by the Embassy and which did necessitate a temporary increase of the PAF authorized strength by 6,000 men.[39] The propaganda actions portrayed EDCOR as concentration camps complete with electrified fences, machine gun-festooned guard towers and peasants in chains. The Huks stridently claimed that the entire program was an American attempt to shore up a weak and corrupt government. American-initiated public opinion inquiries showed the prevalent peasant reaction to the Huk campaign was that of initial incredulity followed by an increased positive interest in EDCOR. The Huk charges were so out of tune with the films, photographs and reports emanating from the projects that they were not simply rejected but served to give government statements increased credibility. In quick order EDCOR was overwhelmed, but by applicants, not opponents. The Huks had made a number of fatal propaganda mistakes.

As psychological warfare eroded the insurgents' mass support base and fighting morale from within, the armed pressure of the PAF attacked Huk bands and Huklandia from without. By the spring of 1952 the PAF had 26 BCTs in the field each near its authorized strength of 1,047 officers and men.[40] Backed by the elite Scout-Ranger formations as a strategic reserve, the BCTs engaged in a series of cordon and search operations which virtually eliminated all the independently operating Huk squadrons and pushed tightly against the central bastions of Huklandia on Mt. Arayat.

The insurgent response was to avoid contact, disperse to more widely scattered base areas, and to "prepare the Party for a long and bitter struggle, . . . sharpen the political consciousness . . . [and] strengthen the iron discipline of the Party."[41] Immediately, a split developed between those who advocated an intensification of the armed struggle leading to a seizure of power and those who argued for a strategy based upon "military defense and political offense," code words meaning protracted low-intensity guerrilla war.[42] This latter approach, advanced by Taruc and other experienced field commanders, ostensibly prevailed, but on a deeper level served to isolate them from the more militant Moscow-inclined politburo members resulting in an internal schism.

As the Huk high command was meeting and split by factionalism in the hills, the government was holding the biannual Congressional elections. Magsaysay, without any appreciable outside urging, moved decisively to employ the PAF to prevent any recrudescence of the violence, vote fraud and corruption which had characterized previous elections. Reserve Officers' Training Corps (ROTC) cadets were used as poll watchers and judges, while troops intervened to prevent either Huk interference or overly boisterous electioneering by partisans of any political organization. The result was unexpected: an honest and tranquil election even by American standards and an erosion in the strength of the incumbent Liberal Party.

Throughout 1952, the Huks were under increasing pressure as their mass support base shrank and their squadrons were forced to operate without supplies or an intelligence system. Confronted by a military structure capable of rapid and flexible employment and a greatly improved static defense provided by local volunteer formations, the guerrillas were rapidly being reduced to the status of hunted, hungry fugitives, even within the former confines of Huklandia. Guerrilla communications were virtually impossible, given the presence of police barriers on the roads, military patrols on the trails, pseudo-gangs in the bush and untrusting peasants everywhere. By April 1952, it was estimated that forty percent of the insurgent forces active in 1950 were dead or captured, with the balance isolated and without timely or effective coordination.[43] By the end of the year the Huks were reduced to 1,500 mainforce fighters, 2,500 part-time guerrillas and a support base of 33,000.[44] The Huk situation was clearly desperate.

Magsaysay's election to the Presidency on the Nationalist ticket in April 1953 allowed a renewal of the civil affairs component of the counterinsurgency efforts. New land reform legislation and vigorous enforcement of preexisting tenant protection laws served to consolidate further the government's hold upon the peasants. Increased American economic aid allowed significant infrastructure improvements to be made. The crowning feature was the initiation of a land reform project in Pampanga province, the center of Huklandia, in which the expropriated lands were redistributed to peasant communities. This action resembled the Malayan squatter resettlement scheme and, as in Malaya, allowed for the effective separation of peasant and guerrilla. As 1953 progressed, the military made fewer and fewer contacts with insurgent bands with the result that an increasing number of PAF units were redeployed from field to civic action programs.

Conventionally, for insurgencies rarely have tidy terminations, the end of the insurrection came in May 1954 when Luis Taruc surrendered. By this time 15,866 insurgents had surrendered and 4,269 had been captured while the end of the conflict had come too late for the 9,695 who had been killed in action.[45] A few scattered fugitives still roamed the hills.

Several lessons of the Huk Insurrection were eagerly seized upon by American analysts. Others, equally obvious, were overlooked in the rush to the typewriter and map pointer. As might be expected, the points derived from this successful counterinsurgency effort were narrowly tactical in focus although they did emphasize, by and large, the paramountcy of the civilian over the military or at least the civic action over the firefight.[46] The overlooked aspects were those which highlighted the unique contextual, policy and personality features which served to differentiate the Philippine conflict from other Asian guerrilla wars.

The sine qua non for successful counterinsurgency was seen as the demobilization of the popular support base from the insurgents and its reattachment to the central government. The mechanism for performing this task was defined as being the identification and amelioration of major popular grievances. Related to this mechanism was the necessity of rendering more efficient and more humane the instruments of the government which had the most immediate impact upon the population: the armed forces and their security force adjuncts. The army had to be effectively organized, disciplined, supplied and led so that brutality and brigandage under the color of counterguerrilla operations were prevented. Further, the armed forces had a definite utility in civic action programs where their manpower and technical or management expertise and skills might be directly and visibly employed to the direct and obvious benefit of the contested population. The employment of the army in such pacifistic tasks as sanitation, health care, construction and education was not only permissible but a mandatory high priority mission.

Psychological warfare operations were also essential. Image building was as important as nation building in order to convince the residents that a nation was in fact being built courtesy of a determined, dedicated and responsive central government. This problem was one of determining the "most effective way of advising or telling the people just what their government and military forces are doing or can do for them."[47] To this end a dynamic and large-scale white (overt) campaign of psychological operations is necessary to convince citizens that their lives were being immediately and directly benefited by military civic action. It was also important to convince personnel that their nonmilitary work was at least equal to more traditional soldiers' activities. Troops needed persuasion to consider the spade as worthy an implement as the rifle.

Over and above the conduct of domestic propaganda directed at the citizens by their government, it was necessary to conduct aggressive and well-orchestrated psychological warfare against the insurgents, emphasizing that they had no reason for fighting as the government was redressing all genuine popular grievances and to believe otherwise was to allow oneself to be manipulated by nonnational forces, ideologies and concerns. Additionally, it was important to stress that further fighting was futile, given the strength of the governmental security forces. This was combined with hints that fighting was unnecessary because there was a "golden bridge" out of combat, government sponsored alternatives such as amnesty and resettlement after capture or defection. The goal was twofold: separate the hard-core guerrilla from the marginal or unwilling supporter, and sap the will for resistance prior to military operations. The United States provided doctrine, methods and procedures used in the Huk Insurrection which were seen as having been generally correct and effective, with only variations in detail being necessary to cope with other insurgencies in the region.

Although overlooked by most American commentators, the Philippine experience indicated strongly that military operations were best limited to a few, discrete roles. The first was defensive in orientation: the provision of security on a static basis to the population in contested areas so as to convince the peasants that their most basic need, to be secure and safe in their own persons, homes and fields was best met by the government forces and the peasants' best course of action was to cooperate with the security personnel in achieving this goal. In addition, this defensive role would serve to erode the guerrillas' momentum and confidence. After local security had been effected it would then be possible for the government forces to undertake local, limited offensives based upon local intelligence so as to reinforce the stability in the region and develop the symbiotic relations between troops and local population. The effect of this program of static defense and local offensive operations would convince the population of government resolve and deter any further insurgent political mobilization within the contested population.

The second major military mission was more offensive in nature, the interdiction and interruption of guerrilla communications and supplies through active patrolling backed by population movement control measures such as roadblock, curfews and random or spot area document checks. The third mission was completely offensive in nature, the undertaking of conventional operations against identified base areas or the use of search and clear or cordon and search tactics in remote, low-population density areas where guerrilla camps were suspected but not specifically located. Mobile, light infantry of conventional American training and equipment were superficially suitable for all these tasks. However, it was believed that small elite groups could effectively complement larger conventional formations in reconnaissance, deep penetration and "pseudo-gang" missions. These small group missions were not a panacea, but a highly useful adjunct which was all too easy to overlook or underemploy. It bears noting that despite some later special pleadings, the utility of high-lethality weapons and airpower was severely limited. The lengthy and somewhat absurd debate over the use of napalm in the Philippines by the Philippine Air Force might serve to give the opposite impression, but the use of aircraft in the Huk Insurrection after mid-1951 decreased and had virtually disappeared altogether within the next year.[48] Except in a few areas, such as Mt. Arayat, tactical air strikes were not particularly effective.

Intelligence was a centrality to successful counterinsurgency. Without an effective mechanism for the collection, verification, analysis and dissemination of timely and exploitable intelligence, it was impossible to focus either psychological or military operations on a meaningful target. The speed and efficiency with which the Americans deployed and developed their own mechanisms as well as the rapidity with which they fostered an independent Filipino capability in the intelligence field bred an expansive sense of self-confidence which was only marginally justifiable.

Central to the defeat of the Huks was the personality of Ramon Magsaysay. The Americans saw his presence in a powerful position as having been absolutely essential to the rapidity and completeness of the victory. At the time, U.S. officers recognized that his drive, energy, perspicacity and determination could and did constitute an effective nexus for American efforts as well as providing the middle political alternative necessary for the polarized extremes which had precipitated the war. Later American planners would search for another Magsaysay, without recognizing or articulating the essential personal attributes which rendered the original Magsaysay effective in a unique environment. As a result, they were all too ready to mistake virtually any local strongman as a suitable candidate to occupy the Magsaysay ecological niche.

The fact that the United States had both a historic familiarity with the Philippines and effective levers to induce Filipino compliance with American policy decisions was ignored in the postconflict analyses. These factors not only worked against the deployment of U.S. troops, they also contributed to the effectiveness of American intelligence operations and psychological warfare. There was a reservoir of experience and personnel upon which to draw in the formulation and execution of programs. Many American advisors and Embassy personnel had had more or less extensive experience with the Philippine occupation or liberation period. They knew the members of the government down to the local levels. They understood the local customs, forces and rivalries with a degree of familiarity necessary to adapt policy directives and guidelines to meet the exigencies of situation and ego. More fundamentally, the Americans had a significant reservoir of good will to draw upon in dealings with the population, army and government alike. Without these twin familiarities, the job of JUSMAG would have been much more frustrating and much less fruitful.

Assisting powerfully in the execution of U.S. policy desires and programmatic schemes was the reality that the Filipino economy was effectively held hostage by the Americans. Both the public and private sectors were susceptible to complete collapse without continued and massive economic aid infusions. This fact, coupled with the very nature of the ruling classes and their strong symbiotic relation with the U.S. economy, assured a degree of compliance with Embassy and JUSMAG desires which would otherwise have been lacking. In this context it might profitably be noted that the United States dealt essentially with only two significant government personalities during the life of the Insurrection, Quirino and Magsaysay, of which the latter was the more significant. This degree of governmental stability was also undervalued in the assessments of the Philippine experience which was certainly not merited considering the uniqueness of the phenomenon.

The degree of trust and confidence which the mass of the Philippine population placed in the good faith and good will of the United States is persuasively indicated by the failure of Huk anti-American propaganda stressing the neocolonial Wall Street designs to arouse Filipino antipathy to the American presence. Americans were unable or unwilling to accept that others were likely to perceive U.S. motives as being dark and sinister, and thus it was easy to overlook how unique and important a factor it might be that a country's population is genuinely favorable in its view of America.

A final overlooked key point was that the government confronted a single significant popular grievance: land reform was the overriding issue. If it could be addressed at a level sufficient to trigger and support a popular perception that the government was actually moving to resolve this longstanding question, then the ideological, moral and propaganda underpinnings were knocked out from under the insurgency. There was opposition to land reform but not of sufficient magnitude to inhibit the government from establishing EDCOR or following through to a greater extent after Magsaysay's election. Indeed the landholder opposition assured his election. Had the government been presented with additional major grievances, such as anticolonialism, or if issues of less importance such as army corruption and brutality had been left unresolved, the combination would have proven too large for ready or ultimately effective management. Since the problems were attacked sequentially with the most important left to last, the opposition on both right and left was defeated piecemeal.

These unique factors which served to assure the suppression of the Huk Insurrection had little, if any, effect upon the development of the American understanding of insurgent war or the theory of victory in guerrilla operations. There is no reason to believe that the Philippine experience sensitized American decision makers or their advisors to the idea that guerrilla war could develop and continue as an organic manifestation of indigenous political discontent. Neither is there any reason to believe that a close examination of the Philippine Army operations in the course of the Insurrection led military planners to the realization that low-lethality approaches to the fighting of guerrillas were either preferable or possible. Other than in the development of some doctrine concerning psychological warfare or the use of special operations forces such as rangers in the context of guerrilla conflicts, there is no measurable effect of the Insurrection on the making of doctrine. Neither did these realizations arise from American observations of the Malayan Emergency.

NOTES

1. Luis Taruc, *He Who Rides the Tiger,* (New York: Praeger 1967), p. 12.

2. Ismael D. Lupus, "The Communist Huk Enemy" in *Counterguerrilla Operations in the Philippines 1946–1957: A Symposium, 15 June 1961,* (Fort Bragg, N.C.: Special Warfare Center 1961), pp. 11–14.

3. Taruc, *He Who Rides,* pp. 21–23 passim.

4. Interestingly, the deputy controller and cofounder of MacArthur's private intelligence service, the Allied Intelligence Bureau and postwar army intelligence expert on the Far East, Allison Ind, is totally silent on the Huks in his 1958 book, *Allied Intelligence Bureau,* (New York: McKay).

5. For a fascinating personal observation of MacArthur at his most paradoxical, viewing the Huks sympathetically but noting that they were "socialists" and "revolutionary" although he would not send a "punitive expedition" against them see: Roger Olaf Egeberg "General Douglas MacArthur," *Transactions of the American Clinical and Climatological Association,* vol. 78 (1966), p. 169.

6. Taruk, *He Who Rides,* p. 26.

7. Boyd Bashore, "Dual Strategy for Limited War," *MR,* vol. 40 (May 1960), p. 53.

8. Alvin Scaff, *The Philippine Answer to Communism,* (Stanford, CA.: Stanford University Press, 1955), p. 26.

9. Hernando Abaya, *Betrayal in the Philippines,* (New York: Scribners 1946), pp. 59–60; David Berstein, *The Philippine Story,* (New York: Dutton 1947), pp. 204–7.

10. Doris Clayton James, *The Years of MacArthur,* 2 vols. (Boston: Little Brown 1970, 1975), II: 694–98 passim.

11. Ibid.

12. Philippine Armed Forces, "Annual Report of the Chief of Staff, 1946," (Manila: unpaged mimeo).

13. Philippine Armed Forces, "Annual Report of the Chief of Staff, 1948," (Manila: mimeo), pp. 22–23.

14. Bashore, "Dual Strategy," p. 54.

15. Philippine Armed Forces, "Intelligence Summary." Tarduc: G-2, MPC 14 October 1946.

16. See U.S. Department of State, *Foreign Relations of the United States, 1949: The Far East and Australasia,* vol. VII, pt. 1 (Washington, D.C.: USGPO 1975), pp. 591-600.

17. Ibid., pp. 592-93.

18. Philippine Armed Forces, "Intelligence Summary." Manila: HQ G-2, 30 June 1949.

19. "Memorandum of Conversation" dated 4 February 1950, reprinted in U.S. Department of State, *Foreign Relations of the United States, 1950: East Asia and the Pacific,* (Washington, D.C.: USGPO 1976), pp. 1412-16.

20. See Ibid., pp. 1428-32.

21. "Telegram from the Chargé in the Philippines to the Secretary of State" dated 7 April 1950, reprinted in ibid., pp. 1433-38.

22. Ibid., pp. 1435-36.

23. Ibid., p. 1437.

24. "Memorandum by the Joint Chiefs of Staff to the Secretary of Defense" dated 6 September 1950, reprinted in *Foreign Relations, 1950,* p. 1487.

25. Ibid., p. 1489.

26. Uldarico Baclagon, *Lessons From the Huk Campaign in the Philippines,* (Manila: M. Colcol 1956/1960), p. 7.

27. "Telegram from the Ambassador in the Philippines to the Department of State" dated 15 February 1951, reprinted in *Foreign Relations of the United States, 1951: Asia and the Pacific,* pt. 2, (Washington, D.C.: USGPO 1977), pp. 1510-11.

28. Paul Linebarger, *Psychological Warfare,* 2nd ed., (New York: Hawthorne 1954), p. 260.

29. An interesting account of Linebarger's seminars and their impact upon operational members of the intelligence community is to found in Joseph B. Smith, *Portrait of a Cold Warrior,* (New York: Putnams 1976), pp. 86-99.

30. Foreign Military Assistance Coordinating Committee files in Lot 54 D 5 of the State Department Archives. See also the MDAP Progress Reports filed under 796.5-MAP and 796.5 MSP.

31. "Telegram from the Chargé in the Philippines to the Department of State" dated 15 June 1951, reprinted in *Foreign Relations, 1951,* p. 1549.

32. "Telegram from the Acting Secretary to the Embassy in the Philippines" dated 17 September 1951, reprinted in *Foreign Relations, 1951,* p. 1565.

33. "Telegram from the Chargé to the Department" dated 17 September 1951, in ibid., p. 1566.

34. Lansdale is the model from which Eugene Burdick took the central character of Colonel Hillendale in the highly popular and undeservedly influential novel *Ugly American.*

35. "Memorandum by the Ambassador to the Secretary of State re: Lt. Col. Edward Lansdale" dated 19 September 1951, reprinted in *Foreign Relations, 1951,* pp. 1566-67.

36. See Edward Lansdale, *In the Midst of Wars*, (New York: Harpers 1972). The same tone permeates his earlier professional writings and symposia appearances such as, "Civic Action Helps Counter the Guerrilla Threat," vol. 17 (June 1962), 50–53 or *Counterinsurgency—A Symposium* 16–20 April 1962, later published and publicly available as Rand Document R-423 ARPS, (Santa Monica, Ca.: Rand 1963). A less flattering opinion of Lansdale was held by Maxwell Taylor and McGeorge Bundy who with Presidential approval refused to have him as a part of the senior staff in Saigon in 1964. See LBJ/NSF/CF/VN/8/M17/123 & 123A.

37. Scaff, *The Philippine Answer*, p. 41.

38. Ibid., p. 45.

39. *Foreign Relations, 1951*, pp. 1560–90 passim.

40. JUSMAG, "Semi-Annual Report" 1 July 1952.

41. Taruc, *He Who Rides*, p. 100.

42. Ibid., pp. 101–2.

43. Philippine Armed Forces, "Estimate of the Situation." Manila: HQ G-2, 30 April 1952.

44. Tomas Tirona, "The Philippine Anti-Communist Campaign," *AUQR*, vol. 7 (Summer 1954), p. 52.

45. John Beebe, "Beating the Guerrilla," *MR*, vol. 35 (Dec. 1955), p. 9.

46. An outstanding example of the narrow tactical focus as well as the at least verbal homage paid to the centrality of the civic action and psychological operations' side of the Philippine counterinsurgency campaign is Lansdale, *Counterinsurgency*. More narrow in its focus and outrageous in its conclusions concerning the Philippine experience is A. H. Peterson et al., *Symposium on the Role of Airpower in Counterinsurgency and Unconventional Warfare*, (Rand 3652-PR. Santa Monica, Ca.: 1963).

47. Robert H. Slover, *Symposium: The US Army's Limited War Misson and Social Science Research*, 26–28 March 1962, (Washington, D.C.: American University [SORO], 1962), p. 52. Slover was Deputy Chief, Plans and Doctrine Division, Office of the Chief of Civil Affairs at the time of this symposium.

48. *Foreign Relations, 1951*, pp. 1549–93 passim.

5.
The Malayan Emergency

Like the Huk Insurrection, the Malayan Emergency of 1948–1960 constituted an insurgency. Like the Huk conflict, the Malayan war contained a strong Marxist flavor; it was of a protracted nature and its suppression was accomplished not so much by military measures as by a judicious mixture of civil reforms and police activities in which the British Army and other security forces operated in a support role. The Malayan Emergency was often cited by American planners and decision makers, but it was rarely understood. American observers noted the long duration of hostilities and commented upon the successful program of separating civilians from insurgents. They occasionally mentioned the fact that the insurgency was confined to the Chinese residents of Malaya, a minority of the population which was easily separated from the ethnic Malays who constituted the majority. Americans also referred to the fact that the British were not faced with any significant amount of external assistance to the guerrillas. Conspicuously absent from American perceptions were such centralities as the comprehensive nature of the local British intelligence capabilities, the exceptionally low lethality of the conflict or the long British tradition of using the military to aid the civil power. Also overlooked was the fact that the British enjoyed de facto sovereignty in Malaya or that they were able to effectively combine civilian and military command in the same organization.

Conventionally, the Malayan Emergency, or the "Anti-Bandit Campaign" as it was initially called, commenced in June 1948. This is misleading, for, like the Huk Insurrection, the formal start of the insurgency was simply the most recent stage in a long-lasting conflict whose roots extended some distance into the past. The Malayan Communist Party

(MCP), an almost exclusively Chinese organization, had existed since the 1920s and its armed component, the Malayan Peoples' Liberation Army (MPLA), had first taken to the bush in opposition to the Japanese during World War II. In the role of protector of the people during the war, it had spent more time and energy on the liquidation of political rivals than on conducting partisan operations against the occupying troops. By war's end, it had established itself among the Chinese population as a legitimate political force with a claim upon popular support. It had also been thoroughly penetrated by British intelligence and had become riven by factions, one of which supported long-term political organization and the seizure of power through legitimate means, while the other argued for immediate use of armed means to force the British imperialists and their Malay stooges out of the country. The second group won out. The situation in the spring of 1948 seemed to favor a strategy of violence. The MCP, under its new General Secretary Chen Peng, clearly believed that immediate armed insurrection would not only improve the hold which the Party had upon the Chinese community, which was split between the supporters of Mao and those of Chiang, but would also take advantage of perceived British weakness. Chen Peng argued that the withdrawal of Britain from India provided proof that the Empire was in full retreat and would not fight to maintain its hold on Malaya.

Much of Chen Peng's analysis, as presented to the Plenary Meeting of the Central Committee in May 1948, was accurate. The British presence east of Suez was contracting. The British were withdrawing troops from foreign postings, even Palestine. The British public was war weary and preoccupied with domestic concerns. The British economy was in a shambles.[1] However, he misinterpreted this last point entirely. Malayan tin and rubber were critical sources of hard currency income to British firms and government alike. As Europe struggled to rebuild, as American aid for this increased and as the recession in the United States ebbed, prices for these twin pillars of the Malayan economy increased. In short, the critical needs of the British economy dictated that Britain maintain its hold on Malaya. Further, the reduction of British commitments in India, Burma, South Africa and Palestine served not so much to indicate that imperial will had decayed completely but rather that the resources available to maintain the imperial writ in Malaya had increased. Government capabilities matched economic inducements; the British would contest the MCP, should the latter initiate the struggle.

The British could count upon domestic popular support for the conflict being reinforced by the cold war, a recent development about which Chen Peng was only dimly aware. Insurgency in the days before electronic media and communications satellites bred a remarkably provincial attitude. The British, in short, were better prepared for a protracated conflict than were the Chinese insurgents.

The British, while neither seeking or even expecting war in Malaya, were in a good position to fight one of a lengthy nature with a well-trained and -equipped professional army, backed by a public and government motivated by a combination of economic considerations and ideological commitment. The Malayan Communist Party was spoiling for a fight, but was ill-prepared for one; they expected a virtual walkover without serious contest from the British.

An examination of the MCP documents captured early in the insurgency clearly shows the simplistic views taken by Chen and his military deputy, Lau Yen, who was alleged to have been a keen student of Mao.[2] The insurrection was to consist of three distinct phases: the crippling of the British planters and tin miners through harassment, while increasing guerrilla strength through the capture of arms and equipment from police posts; the forcing of the government security forces out of the countryside, confining their presence to the main roads, strategic points and urban centers; the establishment of "liberated areas" in insurgent-controlled territory which would then expand inexorably until they encompassed all Malaya. The emphasis was to be placed on economic targets, crippling the imperial resources while strengthening those of the insurgents.[3] The opening act of the Emergency was intended to accomplish this goal: on 16 June 1948, three rubber plantation managers were murdered. Two days later a State of Emergency was declared and the war was on. Neither belligerent was prepared for actual war as was clearly demonstrated in the first few months of conflict.

The basic requirements of the guerrillas were security, intelligence, rice, weapons and ammunition. The jungle could provide security, the caches, weapons and the squatter communities, rice and intelligence. The guerrillas moved without delay into the jungle strongholds of World

War II and attempted to reestablish the necessary base camps. Because of inexperience, a pervasive underestimation of British capabilities and the necessity of minimizing logistics channels, the insurgents elected to build large camps capable of accommodating as many as one hundred men. It must be emphasized that these camps, like their smaller and more remote successors, were totally dependent upon Chinese civilians, known to the British as "squatters," for their daily food supplies. While occasional dumps holding 2,000 man/days of rice were established, the official goal was 1,000 man/days of rice in reserve at every camp; the reality was that the guerrillas habitually had extremely scanty reserves, necessitating a daily battle of wits between squatter porters and the security forces.[4]

The handling of the squatters by the British was central to the successful ending of the Emergency. The mechanisms developed by the British for dealing with the squatters, particularly for assuring the complete severing of communications between them and the guerrillas, were admired by Americans and the attempt was made to apply these techniques to Vietnam. An examination of the squatters and their communities would not be amiss. Chinese rural communities were of relatively recent formation in Malaya but had become common in many parts of the peninsula, particularly along the west coast.[5] These communities had several features in common. They were a spontaneous establishment, before World War II, on lands not originally dedicated to that purpose, usually forest preserves, Malay reservations or abandoned rubber groves, with the result that the squatters tended to be an embarrassment to the government. The squatter economy had been so successful that the profit motive had supplanted fear of the Japanese as an inducement to keep the communities going after the end of World War II. By making a cash profit on crops of rice, tobacco and vegetables, as well as pigs, chickens and cattle, the squatters were able to successfully counter requests for their relocation unless such were accompanied by compensation, coercion or both. The squatter communities had not been absorbed into the local Malay governmental infrastructure because these Chinese communities were embedded in rural areas generally regarded as Malay by both the natives and the British.

The squatters had no title to their land. As a result of this, they were leery of all government representatives, particularly the police. When the long existing Malay–Chinese antipathy is added to the social outcast status of the squatters, it is not surprising that they readily cooperated with the insurgents, allowing the MCP to organize a clandestine but quite formal and efficient support, logistics and intelligence organization, the Min Yuen, among them. At the same time, they turned a black and distrustful face toward an increasingly overreaction prone government whose security forces in the weeks following the Declaration of Emergency tended to turn to collective reprisals in districts where guerrilla actions occurred.

The strength of the forces available to the government at the outset of the Emergency varies according to the source consulted. Not counting formations held in Singapore and therefore not available until September 1948, when it became obvious that insurgent activities in that city would be so sporadic and of such low intensity that a police rather than a military response would be merited, the government could field only eleven understrength battalions with an aggregate strength of less than 4,000.[6] This low troop strength did not breed confidence among the exposed civilian population, with the result that there was a constant and constantly growing call issuing from the collective throat of the plantation and mine operators for static guards, be they military, police or private paramilitary. Neither the military nor the 9,000 regular Malayan police were in a position to answer even a fraction of the demand.

A response to this demand was quickly formulated and a force of Special Constables (SC) was authorized. Originally envisioned as having a strength of 10,000 to 15,000, approximately 23,500 were recruited by September of 1948.[7] The recruits were overwhelmingly ethnic Malays and only very rudimentarily trained at best. Organized as static guard detachments and officered by a motley array of seconded civilian bureaucrats, police reserves, and, ultimately, redundant NCOs of the Palestine Police, these representatives of the rabble in arms were dispatched to stand watch at rubber plantations, tin mines and high-value infrastructure targets. Over time the SC became an effective defense force but at the outset they served primarily as a mechanism for assuring deteriorating relations with the Chinese community.

As the security forces, including the substantial number of Special Constables, were not able to deal with the squatter communities and the necessity of separating them from the guerrillas, the British sought new ways to accomplish that task. In December 1948 a special committee was appointed to investigate the squatters and their situation in regard to the insurrection. The committee's report, presented in early 1949, contained conclusions and recommendations of seminal importance to British policy formulations as well as gambits later played by the Americans.[8]

The problem was considered as twofold, having both a short-term security aspect and a long-term one of land use and tenure policy. The squatter areas, it was determined, served as excellent cover for guerrillas, and it was highly probable that a significant number of squatters were active part-time fighters. Owing to the lack of administrative integration and their remote geographic location, squatter settlements were of necessity highly susceptible to guerrilla pressures to provide food, shelter and intelligence. However, the report noted, the squatter communities often rendered a definite service to the Federation in the production of foodstuffs beyond what was needed for immediate community consumption. An example was derived from Jahore, where it was estimated that the squatters cultivated 40,000 acres and supplied fresh produce to both Jahore and Singapore. It was essential to insure that appropriate agricultural methods were employed to prevent land spoilage and ultimate reversion of the land to secondary jungle. Where squatters were located on land unsuitable for agriculture, they ought to be resettled.

Recognizing that displacement of any kind, however carefully conducted, could not be accomplished without causing hardship to the people concerned, the committee made definite recommendations regarding resettlement policies. The salient features were:

1) To settle the squatters, wherever possible, in the same areas which they already occupied.
2) To resettle squatters in alternative suitable areas when the settlement in existing areas was not possible.
3) To repatriate squatters who refused to accept settlement on the terms offered.[9]

However, the most critical proviso was the final paragraph which insisted that the new settlements be provided not only with public services and educational facilities, but with law enforcement and security installations as well, so as to inculcate a "proper respect for law and order."[10] Although all the recommendations embodied in the report were not to be fully and effectively implemented for another year, it contained all the elements central to severing the guerrilla–squatter communication, isolating the insurgent population and providing powerful inducements to those of an insurrectionist bent to forgo revolution in order to achieve personal success and reap its attendant material rewards.

While the question of the squatters was under consideration, the war in the field continued. The guerrillas conducted an ongoing campaign of small actions directed against civilian targets and isolated police posts. The insurgents did not have the command skills to collect more than a few dozen men for a brief raid. When they made an attempt at something more grand, they lost. Their larger formations were ponderous and slow-moving, with the result that they were often detected in the open with disastrous results, particularly if the ground defenders were assisted by a Spitfire or two. British reinforcements were arriving in significant numbers following late fall 1948. As had been the case in Greece and the Philippines, small elite units were aggressively employed in an effort to buy time during which the defender's numbers might be built up. These were collectively dubbed Ferret Force and were composed of specially selected small teams of British, Gurkha and Malay soldiers trained in bushcraft and jungle warfare. Often these units were led by former British long-range penetration force officers to whom the jungle was not hostile but a most friendly ally. Their mission was to effect long duration deep penetrations of guerrilla jungle sanctuaries and locate guerrilla camps in order to direct security forces in for the kill. Ferret Force not only caused physical casualties to the insurgents, it caused a galloping sense of insecurity to afflict the insurgents. Previously, the jungle had been a friendly environment, nurturing and protecting the guerrillas. Now it had become a hostile place, thick with sudden peril and death. From the elusive master of the bush, the guerrilla had fallen to the level of a hunted animal. However, British authority at the highest levels in the country, with the complete support of the War Department traditionalists, killed Ferret Force.

Ferret Force survived long enough to buy sufficient time for heavy British reinforcements to arrive and for the police intelligence office to gain a firm handle on the number of Malayan Races Liberation Army combatants (MRLA; better known as MPLA) and Min Yuen mass support base auxiliaries as well as on the reservoir of potential active and tacit supporters. This was a question of some importance as the number of active guerrillas and their supporters in the community would affect not only the number of troops needed, but also the way in which the matter of squatter resettlement would be handled. In the spring of 1949, the government believed that there were between 3,750 and 4,500 active guerrillas in the field, of which 10 percent were female and virtually all were Chinese.[11] The MCP itself had fewer than 3,000 full-fledged members, some of whom were MPLA guerrillas. The number of Min Yuen were figured notionally at the rate of ten per combatant.[12] It must be emphasized that there was an accurate British system which accounted for all armed guerrillas captured or killed with an elaborate cross referencing system which listed known and suspected armed insurgents. The result was that the combatant strength estimates might be considered quite accurate. The same type of quality control was less obvious regarding the Min Yuen and absent with respect to suspected and potential sympathizers.

Three regulations, 17D (January 1949), 17E (May 1949) and 17F (August 1949), formed the basis for repatriation, resettlement and regroupment.[13] Under the color of Regulation 17D, the government detained 6,343 persons between January and October 1949.[14] Of this number, 740 were forcibly repatriated to mainland China.[15] It should be noted that the change of government in China in late 1949 restricted the utility (or deterrent effect) of forced repatriation. Regulations 17E and 17F enabled the government to resettle or regroup the squatter population. Resettlement, as the term implies, empowered the government to compel the removal of squatter families to areas at a distance from their previous homes. Regroupment was a polite euphemism for a process long known to the British as reconcentration and first practiced by them a half century earlier during the Boer War. Normally, it involved the relocation of squatters from the jungle perimeter of an estate or reservation to a central location where they might be more readily kept secure and under surveillance. The twin processes commenced rather slowly and by March 1950 only 4,465 individuals had been resettled and 2,396 regrouped.[16] Additionally, 11,683 had been given legal title to lands previously used without title, a process called "settlement" and constituting another species of land reform.[17] This left some 300,000 squatters still outside government control.

The slow pace of attacking the squatter problem received sudden acceleration in April 1950 with the appointment of Lt. Gen. Sir Harold Biggs as the new Director of Operations, with a mandate to prosecute the Emergency by coordinating the efforts of the civil administration and the security forces.[18] He confirmed that there was no single, simple, quick way to end the Emergency. The killing of guerrillas was not sufficient, as ample replacements were available. The path to success required the breaking of guerrilla morale and the severing of Min Yuen supply routes. This could be accomplished only through the removal of squatters to areas under effective government control.

The Biggs Plan was predicated upon the establishment of a military framework on the jungle verge serving to protect populated areas and lines of communication against guerrilla molestation and capable of destroying the insurgents impelled to make the attempt. Simultaneously, the troops would constitute a *cordon sanitaire* blocking the guerrillas from the Min Yuen and MCP cells. The police forces would dominate the populated areas, disperse communist networks, provide local security and, by use of the British Police's Special Branch sources and methods, gain combat information and broader intelligence from a population rendered more cooperative by the new sense of security. In developing this approach, with its emphasis upon the inculcation within the Chinese rural population of a sense of government presence and security from guerrilla pressures, Biggs was working on a correct apprehension, as the MPLA had been employing great and growing quantities of terrorism to compel proper attitudes on the part of the uncommitted or irresolute components of the Chinese community.[19]

The new approach was initiated on 1 June 1950 and went ahead at a steadily accelerating pace. A measure of the speed and effectiveness with which this program was prosecuted is provided by the following figures. In the state of Jahore, between 1 June 1950 and 31 May 1951, 66,000 individuals were resettled.[20] However, this impressive number was attained only at the sacrifice of "desirable features" in the New Villages.[21] By the end of 1952 some 423,000 individuals, 85 percent of them Chinese squatters, had been resettled in 410 New Villages under government control.[22]

The efforts for resettlement were concentrated in the west coast states which had been the prime area of both squatter communities and guerrilla incidents.[23] Tactical mistakes were made in the execution of the accelerated resettlement and regroupment program which were noted by American observers.[24] However, most Americans agreed with British analysts in the conclusion that the program was an unalloyed success and provided a proper paradigm for future insurgent arenas.[25] Two significant costs of resettlement ignored by laudatory writers might be noted: food production and acreage under cultivation declined; food prices in the cities rose.[26]

The progress in resettlement and population appears now to have been impressive, just as it did at the time. The military and security activities of a more traditional nature do not seem to have been so. The scale and scope of action was exceptionally small; such that the military aspects of the Malayan Emergency constituted the lowest of low-intensity conflicts, being less violent than either the Greek or Philippine conflicts. An official Malayan government publication, totally bereft of logical motive to minimize the seriousness of the threat, reviewed 200 insurgent operations for the period 1948–1950.[27] The following represents a summary of the data contained therein:

Type	Number	Percent
1) Raids		
A) Target: economic	50	25
B) Target: security	12	6
2) Road Ambushes	32	16
3) Murder	31	15.5
4) Robbery	22	11
5) Sabotage	22	11
6) Terrorist Bombings	11	5.5
7) Contacts with security forces (guerrilla-initiated)	20	10
TOTAL	200	100

The largest insurgent force involved in a single action was estimated as having been in the neighborhood of 300 men.[28] The smallest were of one or two men with the average force calculated to contain fifty-six men.[29] Neither the rate nor the scale of operations was notably large.

This impression is not altered by examining the record of the 1st Battalion of the Green Howards which was deployed in Malaya from September 1949 to the first week of October 1952, covering the period during which the military activity of the Emergency was at its height and including the period of the Biggs Plan's initiation. In this three-year period the personnel of the battalion engaged in sixty-one fire-fights with MPLA guerrillas.[30] In the course of these contacts, 96 hostiles were positively killed and 7 captured for a total attrition of 103 guerrillas.[31] The record single contact "bag" was seven in an ambush on 12 June 1952.[32] The record monthly total occurred in August 1952 when thirteen guerrillas were killed and four captured.[33] A sense of perspective might be achieved by contemplating the fact that, of thirty-five months in the country, fifteen passed without the battalion killing or capturing a single insurgent. Forty-three percent of the unit's deployment passed without issue. While other units undoubtedly saw greater results, it is equally true that still others saw fewer. It should be noted that the record number of positively confirmed guerrilla deaths inflicted by all security forces in a single month was 110 in June of 1952.[34] The Malayan Emergency was a very small "small war" despite the impressive number of British, Commonwealth and indigenous security forces ultimately deployed against the MPLA.

One legacy of the Emergency was a remarkable amount of specious and pernicious claptrap concerning "tie-down ratios." This figure purports to define the number of security force personnel necessary to defeat an armed insurgency. Typically these ratios were based upon the Malayan experience and ran in the range of 10:1 or 12:1, although the figure of 20:1 is also encountered even among defense planners and military leaders who ought to have known better. In view of the almost mystical appeal which the tie-down ratio exercised upon later American analysts and policy makers, it deserves a close scrutiny in the Malayan environment.[35]

Since the year 1952 marked the turning point in the Emergency as well as the time of maximum "bayonet strength" on both sides of the hill, it presents an opportunity to examine the question of the validity of the tie-down ratios. According to Special Branch wanted lists there were approximately 5,000 identified armed insurgents operating in the field in June 1952 when Biggs handed over to his successor, General Gerald Templar, who would serve not only as Director of Operations but as High Commissioner as well.[36] The Combined Intelligence Staff estimated the figure somewhat higher, in the vicinity of 6,000.[37] In any event there is no doubt that since the first year of the Emergency the MPLA had been able to maintain an effective fighting force in the field of 5,000 plus. Against these the government fielded a regular military establishment of some 25,000 British personnel (all branches), 10,500 Gurkha infantrymen and 5,000 Commonwealth troops, primarily infantry and support units.[38] These were augmented by 3,500 troops of the Malay Regiment.[39] Police forces included 25,000 regulars and 39,000 Special Constables.[40] The final component would have been the 180,000 member Home Guard.[41] In round numbers, the 6,000 guerrillas were confronted by a security force aggregating some 207,500 personnel. This provides a ration of 49:1. Obviously, a more detailed analysis is indicated.

As is carefully noted by an uncritical supporter of the security forces, only one Home Guard in ten was provided with a weapon.[42] The resulting effective strength of 18,000 was dedicated almost exclusively to the static defense of ethnic Malay kampongs (villages) where there was little chance of even the most accidental contact with the Chinese MPLA guerrillas. Other than the 3,000 members of the Jungle Field Force, all regular police and SC personnel were deployed in populated areas on normal local security, plant protection, police and intelligence collection duties. They were not an aggressive detail, searching out mainforce guerrillas in the bush. Among the mobile military forces there were twenty battalion equivalents up-country. Subtracting support troops, base security units and allowing for normal shortfalls from authorized strength as a result of leaves, illness, personnel in transit and so forth, the effective maneuver strength of those formations would not have exceeded 7,500 officers and men. Adding an equivalent proportion of the Malay Regiment troops, it may be seen that the security forces had a probable maximum maneuver strength of 11,000 men, scarcely a 2:1 superiority. This ratio correlates comfortably with the contact and neutralization figures cited earlier.

It is important to note that the strength which counts in insurgent war is that which can aggressively seek and counter the guerrilla. Static forces have a value in that their presence may, under virtually ideal conditions, deter the guerrillas from making an attack or, in the event that they do launch an attack, detain them in combat long enough for a reaction force of mobile troops to arrive and counterattack. The only ratios which matter are those that are achieved locally by the side which gains the initiative of attack or escalation dominance on the defense. Overall ratios are meaningless exercises in statistical thaumaturgy.

Templar did not inherit the bloated and ponderous force implied by the spurious tie-down ratios. Rather he found himself in possession of a remarkably efficient security instrument of modest but appropriate size. The chief reason for that efficiency was an almost unnoticed Biggs formulation, a system of command and control which tightly integrated civil, police and military commands not only at the Federal level but at the subordinate state and district levels as well. This remarkable breakthrough in the usual jungle of liaison failures fraught with conflicting organizational values and loyalties was unfortunately overlooked when the Americans first evaluated the Malayan Emergency. It merited close inspection.

Setting up shop in the Federal Police Headquarters, Biggs had established a War Council (later called the Emergency Operations Council) consisting of the Federation Chief Secretary, the Commissioner of Police and the commanders of the ground, naval and air forces. Biggs presided with the High Commissioner's authority. Duplicate bodies were established at the state and district levels: the State War Executive Committee (SWEC) and the District War Executive Committee (DWEC). In all cases the chair was held by the chief civilian administrator. The rationale for this was simply that the primary British task was that of reasserting the legitimate political administration. Operationally, this implied a paramountcy for civil authority and police power, with the military and paramilitary forces being subordinated to a role "in aid of the civil power." Civilian administrators were perceived as having a better sense of community dynamics, popular dissatisfactions and public attitudes than did their military colleagues, thus the civilians could better determine when a military presence or a specific operation would be more likely to hinder than to help in the development of public support.

As the three principal committee members were of command rank, operational decision making was facilitated, as there was no time lag such as would result from staff officers referring proposals to their principals. Similarly, intra-service and inter-service rivalries and frictions were minimized, while clear areas of authority and channels of communication were maintained. Supporting the three full members were a number of specialist officers: propaganda, food control, Home Guard, and, most important, the Special Branch chief and his deputy from Military Intelligence.

The Special Branch of the Federation Police constituted the primary intelligence production organ of the security forces. Military Intelligence was subordinate, so much so that the state or district Military Intelligence officer was responsible to his Special Branch superior and not the army. He could not release intelligence products to the army without Special Branch authorization.

The stance taken by Special Branch toward its insurgent adversaries in the Emergency is noteworthy. Simply, the MCP, MPLA and Min Yuen were seen as criminal syndicates not unlike the Tongs (Chinese secret gangs) of earlier years. Thus, the meticulous, methodical approach of collecting individual dossiers on known and suspected insurgents represented nothing more nor less than a carrying forward of tested police practice. This exceptionally painstaking manner of ascertaining and verifying the informational catch extended even to the regulations requiring the physical identification of killed insurgents via photographs, fingerprints and descriptions. Normally military units were required to carry guerrilla corpses to Special Branch officers in order that the master wanted lists might be properly and accurately adjusted. A collateral bonus was that British body counts were accurate and not exercises in speculative necrology.

By any standards, the intelligence product generated by Special Branch from its massive, manual system was highly accurate, totally reliable, remarkably timely and readily exploitable by the security forces. However, this was possible because the number of target individuals was quite small and Special Branch personnel had decades of experience in the Malayan cockpit. Of course, no intelligence product, regardless of substantial merit, has any utility unless it can be exploited quickly, vigorously, appropriately and without interorganization jurisdictional disputes. The elegance of the SWEC/DWEC system lay in its ability to assure a high level of operational efficiency. An example of this might be seen in the policy of "clearing" operations. No military or police unit could initiate an active, aggressive or nonroutine mission without clearance by the DWEC of cognizance. This assured that military operations would not impede civil affairs tasks or "blow" police sources. Likewise, it insured that police patrols would not ambush military counterparts or vice versa. In short, it constituted an effective coordination mechanism with a proper sense of perspective.

The critical venue for coordination and exploitation was the short daily meeting of the SWEC/DWEC operations subcommittee generally called "morning prayers."[43] In attendance was the basic triumvirate plus the

Special Branch Chief and his Military Intelligence deputy. The sermon would consist of a briefing by the Military Intelligence man on the operations and events of the preceding twenty-four hours. The commanders would then decide whether to modify or continue ongoing activities or to exploit some new opportunity, perhaps arising from a newly surrendered guerrilla or newly captured documents.

The presence of a battalion or brigade commander allowed immediate decisions to be made with such effect that it was not uncommon for a captured or surrendered guerrilla to be leading an army patrol against his erstwhile comrades at their jungle camp within hours of his apprehension. Occasionally, the turnaround time was so short that the target insurgents were unaware that one of their group had defected or been captured. Similarly, it was not unusual for company-sized cordon and search operations to be mounted within an hour or two of "morning prayers."

These meetings allowed civil affairs programs to be fine tuned in real time, particularly when representatives of the ethnic communities participated, even unofficially. Military, medical, engineering, communications and transport assets could be brought to bear upon time-sensitive situations or psychological warfare and propaganda operations could be adjusted to minimize adverse popular reaction when extreme policy measures, such as those associated with the food denial program, were necessitated.

Sir Gerald Templar arrived shortly after High Commissioner Henry Gurney had been killed in an audacious guerrilla ambush. He arrived in the country as a dictator, combining supreme civilian and military command. Having been Military Governor in the British Occupation Zone of Germany as well as both Director of Intelligence and Director of Operations at the War Department, he was not only aware of the situation in Malaya and the exigencies of military government, he also had firm intentions concerning his course of action, namely that ". . . Malaya in due course should become a self-governing nation."[44]

From the outset, Templar maintained that the fighting of the war and the civil administration of the country were "completely and utterly interrelated."[45] The suppression of the insurgency was simply the obverse of bringing a new independent nation into existence. His stated goal was the creation of a way of life, ". . . not necessarily the British way, nor the American way; it must be the Malayan way of life."[46] He was notoriously impatient with the notion of "independence before breakfast" and characterized the insurgency as ". . . a disease that was still with them and potentially still virulent."[47] In a more blunt fashion, he said to reporter Homer Bigart, "I'll shoot the first bastard who says this Emergency is over. There are probably as many communist terrorists in the jungle as there were two years ago."[48] His operational goals were the development of a government able to prevent the type of racial violence exhibited in India on the heels of independence while assuring the alleviation of insecurity and poverty in the kampongs and New Villages alike. To gain these ends he saw no need to modify significantly the plans, policies and mechanisms emplaced by Biggs, merely the need to prosecute and employ them with greater vigor, not to say ruthlessness.

The near completion of the resettlement-regroupment policies enabled Templar to fix upon a rigorous program of food control in order to increase the pressure upon the insurgents. Gradually during the third quarter of 1952, the emphasis upon denying food to the MPLA in the jungle was increased. The selling of food by village stores was very tightly controlled. Merchants were required to puncture tinned goods at the time of sale and to maintain scrupulous records of purchasers and amounts. Rice was cooked at central locations under police supervision. In some villages all citizens were fed communally. Food transport was by sealed military vehicles travelling in heavily guarded convoys.

The food control program ultimately reached such a level of thoroughness that every man, woman and child was physically searched every time he left his village or the rubber plantation upon which he worked. Not only people but vehicles, including all bicycles as well, were searched for foodstuffs as well as other commodities such as medicines which were of value to the guerrillas. As one battalion commander noted, the searching of every one of the 50,000 inhabitants of his unit's tactical area of responsibility as well as the thousands of vehicles using the main road daily constituted a herculean task.[49] It is also obvious that the food denial program would have been impossible without the effective SWEC/DWEC system as a careful coordinator between the civil affairs, psychological warfare and police authorities. But, in the final analysis, it was the troops who bore the brunt of a very unpleasant task.

It is not easy to turn one's battalion into a cross between a body of high class customs officials and police detectives but what I saw that morning confirmed everything that has been said about the adaptability of the British soldiers.[50]

This was an accurate assessment, thanks to tight subunit control and greatly facilitated by the British policy of maintaining units in the country for multiple year tours.

The rapid effect of the stringent food control and denial program was indicated by two indices. The first was that of diminishing contacts with the MPLA guerrillas by the civilian population as indicated by the drop off of information about the insurgents received by police and intelligence personnel from sources within the villages. An example of this is the experiences of a Fijian battalion, which arrived in the Batu Pahat district, long a center of insurgent activity, replacing a company of Gurkhas. Almost immediately they killed ten guerrillas but credited not a single contact as having resulted from the exploitation of prior information.[51] This type of meeting engagement replacing the exploitation engagement as the norm coupled with a decrease of guerrilla-initiated incidents to signal that the war had entered a new phase.

Previously, the interaction of guerrilla and citizen in the context of food acquisition had resulted in a two-way flow of information from which both the security forces and the insurgents had derived benefit. With rigid food controls these interactions were diminishing, as the citizens evaded meetings and the guerrillas faded deeper into the jungle, hoping to grow or obtain food from the aborigines. The second index was the sudden spotting by reconnaissance aircraft of neat, orderly gardens in jungle clearings. Unlike the aboriginal Malays who planted haphazard hodgepodges, the Chinese were quite methodical in their cultivation.

Immediate counter measures were taken. The RAF sprayed the suspect plots with powerful herbicides. This had only a palliative effect as the defoliants were not always strong enough to kill the crops. As a result, troops backed up the operation by hiking into the plot and physically uprooting the subversive vegetation. Driven by hunger, the MPLA units now attempted to extort food and shelter from the aborigines. In this they were initially successful, as the security forces maintained no permanent presence deep in the bush. Perhaps as much as one half of the aboriginal population gave some degree of assistance to the guerrillas. As a counter the government inserted Special Air Service (SAS) and Royal Marine Commandos by air. These established jungle posts throughout the aboriginal areas. Initially maintained by airdrop and helicopter, these posts were later placed on a more permanent footing with the construction of airstrips, replacing the specialist formations with units of the field police. As the government extended protection and elementary medical care and education to the aborigines, the guerrillas were forced out from this area.

Despite the diversion of military units from aggressive patrolling to static food denial tasks, the eighteen months following Templar's assumption of control had proven disastrous militarily to the insurgents, with 846 having been killed and 66 captured by the security forces.[52] An additional 370 had surrendered.[53] To this must be added an unknown, but not insubstantial, number who died in the bush of malnutrition, illness and untreated wounds. In any event, Special Branch now listed the MPLA strength at less than 4,000.[54] At the same time the number of suspected subversives in administrative detention fell sharply from 5,492 to 2,225.[55]

The time had come for Templar to produce a carrot sufficient to match the stick which had so far proven so effective. This was accomplished in mid-September 1953 when he declared a 220 square mile area in Malacca containing 160,000 residents as the peninsula's first "white area." All Emergency restrictive regulations were terminated. The inhabitants could proceed about their lives without the irritations and hindrances of food controls, curfews, police identity checks or searches.[56] In January the white area was extended, with portions of three more states being declared white in quick succession. Shortly thereafter, with portions of five states in the white category, Templar turned over his office and command to his successors. The two years of his "dictatorship" had turned the tide conclusively against the insurgents and, in equal measure, in favor of independence.

The success of the white areas led the British to announce a timetable leading first to a new constitution and subsequently, in mid-1955, to elections and a large degree of autonomy. It was widely perceived that autonomy would be rather speedily followed by independence. The stated proviso was the continued success of the counterinsurgency program and the expansion of the white areas. Progress through 1954 was eminently satisfactory; the resettlement program was virtually complete. The first wave of New Villages had become economically viable and politically stable, well tied into the governmental infrastructure. The careful avoidance of "refugee generation" policies and the restriction of airstrikes and artillery fire to remote jungle areas had served to assist in the provision of a stable and settled population in place of the former squatter communities.

Insurgent strength had been whittled down to under 3,000 in widely dispersed bands. At last attrition was running far ahead of guerrilla recruiting. The small groups of fugitives, malnourished and ill, were constantly harried by deep penetration "hunter-killer" platoons, This pressure, coupled with a very generous government surrender policy, produced a satisfying stream of defectors, even of senior and deeply trusted personnel. Residual party discipline could be maintained only by an escalating reliance on terror.

In response to this deteriorating situation the MCP essayed a peace offensive on the eve of the Malayan elections coupled with the first face-to-face meeting of MCP and the new Malayan government leaders. Neither came to any result. The deployment of a multi-racial Malayan National Army of 9,000 men in 10 battalions in July of 1956 proved to be both a powerful symbol of emerging Malayan independence and a competent internal security force. Another MCP ploy at negotiations was contemptuously rejected by the Malayan government which smelled victory. By July 1957 30,000 of Malaya's 51,000 square miles had been declared white; two months later Malaya became independent and started upon the job of effecting a final mopping up of the guerrilla remnants, a task which occupied another two years.

Several points of particular importance are to be seen in the Malayan Emergency. The British military mission was essentially constabulary in nature. The period of big battalion operations, massive sweeps and the like came early in the Emergency and was of short duration. Essentially, the year 1949 might be seen as the era of large, semitraditional military operations. After that, save for brief recrudescences, British troops were employed to aid the civil power and acted much like field, even beat, police. After the era of the big battalions, the typical military activities were small subunit patrols and ambushes, cordon and search operations, direct support of the police in tasks such as food and resource denial, road blocks and body or vehicle searches and direct implementation of civil affairs policies, most notably those of resettlement and regroupment. In the original words of Templar, the government's main thrust was that of winning "the hearts and minds of the Malay as a people."[57] Some operational implications of this mission definition should be briefly noted. The offensive use of airpower was sharply restricted. Tactical air support was limited to occasional close air strikes carried out by single engine propeller-driven fighter-bombers. These were executed only in remote locations, generally aboriginal areas, under rules of engagement that required positive visual identification of targets and positive clearance by the SWEC of cognizance. Artillery fire was similarly restricted. Routine harassment and interdictory fire missions were virtually unknown. In fact, most artillery units spent more time acting as infantrymen than in serving the guns. Armored vehicles were conspicuously absent, being employed only in convoy security or road block support capacities. The principle of minimum force governed all military actions. The success of this policy may be seen in two key lacks: the absence of press complaints regarding extreme, hasty or overreactive military actions; the absence of even implicit complaints concerning overly restrictive rules of engagement in the writings of former British officers. Both indicators stand in stark opposition to their counterparts arising from the Cypriot, Palestinian and Kenyan conflicts.

Units and individuals ordered to Malay remained in the country for multiple year tours of duty. This must be underscored. National Service conscripts serving with Malayan units normally completed a two year tour there, while regular troops and officers spent three years in the country. As a result units gained a high degree of coherence and operational competence predicated upon prolonged experience in the country.

The British Army had a long history of constabulary employment in aid of the civil power. Many officers and senior NCOs had personal experience going back to the interwar days with constabulary duties in the Middle East. British training of junior officers gave an emphasis to operations in aid of the civil power far transcending any equivalent in other countries. The predominantly professional long-service British Army trooper considered constabulary missions to be a normal part of an active soldier's career, which had salutary effects upon his efficient and good-natured handling of difficult, distasteful police tasks such as the strip searches of the food denial campaign.

The same set of factors facilitated the close and often critical cooperation between the army and the Federation police. It is not stretching the point to say that the police controlled military operations within the SWEC/ DWEC structure. Police supremacy was guaranteed by Special Branch's exclusive control of the intelligence collation and distribution mechanism. Given the half century of police experience in Malaya, this reality is readily understandable and represented the best possible use of government assets. Special Branch officers were intimately familiar with the MCP, its personalities, supporters, methods and goals. Equally, they were familiar with the Chinese, Malayan and Indian communities, as well as with the complex interactions between these disparate elements. They had a number of agents in place as well as the documentary matrix in place necessary for the quick cross checking and verification which converts raw informational catch into finished intelligence product. No military intelligence system, no matter how capable its individual members might be, could have hoped to duplicate this experience-dependent efficiency and reliability.

The long experience of the Special Branch and other police components in the intricacies of the Malayan–Chinese affairs was duplicated by the entire British civil administration. The Malayan states, despite the artifices of legal technicalities, constituted a British colony. The full and effective sovereignty enjoyed by the British cannot be overemphasized. Although this would appear to constitute an advantage for the insurgents and their call for an end to colonialism, such was not the case. Anticolonial propaganda was mitigated, if not obviated completely, by the ethnic antagonisms as well as the soothing mood music regarding autonomy and independence played by the British psychological warfare specialists.

Correctly perceiving that economic and personal security concerns initially outweighed the intangibles of independence, the British civil affairs officers attacked these first. Later, Templar linked the growth of the white areas and the progressive granting of autonomy leading to total independence. An external regime or group of foreign advisors would have been hard pressed to duplicate this British approach. Similarly, a purely advisory British presence would not have been able to integrate effectively the civil and military components in implementing critical programs such as resettlement and food denial. It merits reiteration that the government's counterinsurgency effort achieved the peak of effectiveness during those two years that one man served simultaneously as military commander and civilian High Commissioner. As has been seen, the rewards of this ultimate integration were not long in coming.

Britain had a critical, tangible national economic interest at stake in Malaya during the first few years of the Emergency. This facilitated both the decision to resist the MCP insurrection and the mustering of the will to continue the struggle. Without the compelling need for hard currency income from trade in Malayan products, it is doubtful that the Labour government would have committed British troops to the struggle, given the pervasive climate of withdrawal east of Suez. It was fortuitous that the cold war and the Korean War served to lower potential public scrutiny and criticism of the Emergency. But this agent of fortune in no way enervated the initial factor governing British reaction to the insurgency: there was sufficient, definable national interest of sufficient value to merit the expense and unpleasantness of troop commitment. Arguably this national interest would not have served to support a large casualty list, but the government was fortunate in that only 519 British and Commonwealth troops were killed in the 12 years of the Emergency.[58] In the same period 6,710 guerrillas were killed.[59]

The Malayan Emergency was a unique conflict in which the small scale and slow tempo combined with the professionalism and long experience of the security forces to lower the body count and replace purely military measures with military activities in support of a civilian authority and a civilian oriented program. The programmatic emphasis was misunderstood by later observers as were the central features of ethnic strife and centralized British authority which went so far to explain the ultimate success of the government.

NOTES

1. Central Political Bureau, MCP, "Strategic Problems of the Malayan Revolutionary War," (Singapore: n.p. 1950) passim.

2. Quoted in Gene Hanrahan, *The Communist Struggle in Malaya* (New York: Institute of Pacific Relations 1954), pp. 63–64.

3. MCP, *Strategic Problems of the Malayan Revolutionary War,* (Singapore: n.p. 1948), pp. 9–10.

4. Ibid., p. 29.

5. Raymond Firth, *Report of Social Science Research in Malaya,* (Singapore: Institute for Social Science Research 1948), pp. 31–32.

6. Department of Information, Federation of Malaya, *Communist Banditry in Malaya,* (Kuala Lumpur: Government Printing Office 1951), p. 21.

7. Ibid., p. 18.

8. Federation of Malaya, Legislative Council Minutes and Council Papers, *Report of the Committee Appointed to Investigate the Squatter Problem,* (Kuala Lumpur: Government Printing Office 1949).

9. Ibid., p.4.

10. Ibid.

11. Hanrahan, *The Communist Struggle,* p. 66; Federation of Malaya, *Communist Banditry,* pp. 25–29ff passim.

12. Federation of Malaya, *Communist Banditry,* pp. 25–29 passim. Compare with Miller's absurd assertion concerning Min Yuen strength: "a conservative, very conservative estimate is 500,000." Harry Miller, *The Communist Menace in Malaya,* (New York: Praeger 1954), p. 104. The lowest estimated figure is 10,000 in Lucien Pye, *Guerrilla Communism in Malaya,* (Princeton: Princeton University Press 1956), p. 98. This is certainly too low by half.

13. Federation of Malaya, Legislative Council Minutes and Council Papers, *The Squatter Problem in the Federation of Malaya,* (Kuala Lumpur: Government Printing Office 1950), pp. B90–B91.

14. Ibid., p. B90.

15. Ibid. Hanrahan states that 10,300 were deported in 1949 but gives neither breakdown nor documentation, *The Communist Struggle,* p. 65n.

16. Federation of Malaya, *The Squatter Problem,* p. B102.

17. Ibid.

18. Federation of Malaya, *Annual Report*, (Kuala Lumpur: Government Printing Office 1950), p. 3.

19. Hanrahan, *The Communist Struggle*, p. 67.

20. Federation of Malaya, Council Paper #23, *Resettlement and Development of New Villages in the Federation of Malaya*, (Kuala Lumpur: Government Printing Office 1952), p. 317.

21. Ibid., p. 312.

22. Central Office of Information, *The Fight Against Communist Terrorism in Malaya*, (London: HMSO 1953), p. 20.

23. Ibid.

24. Kenneth Pelzer, "Resettlement in Malaya" *Yale Review* vol. 41, (March 1952), p. 398.

25. Milton Osborne, *Strategic Hamlets in South Vietnam*, (Ithaca, New York: Cornell University Department of Asian Studies (mimeo) 1965), pp. 15–16.

26. Victor Purcell, *Malaya: Communist or Free?*, (Stanford: Stanford University Press 1954), pp. 78–79.

27. Federation of Malaya, *Communist Banditry*, pp. 29–105 passim.

28. Ibid.

29. Ibid.

30. J. B. Oldfield, *The Green Howards in Malaya (1949–1952)*, (Aldershot: Gale and Polder 1953), pp. 188–90.

31. Ibid.

32. Ibid., p. 190.

33. Ibid., p. 191.

34. Ibid.

35. "Memorandum to McGeorge Bundy from Chester Cooper regarding Vietnam" dated 10 March 1965, LBJ/NSF/CF/VN/14/M30/130; see also "Telegram from Ambassador Taylor to Secretary of State" dated 7 March 1965, LBJ/NSF/CF/VN/14/C30/111 in which the Ambassador and former Chief of the Joint Chiefs of Staff Maxwell Taylor uses the phrase "historical examples in recent past suggest need of superiority of counterinsurgency forces of order of 10–20:1."; "Memorandum to the President from Secretary of Defense Robert McNamara regarding recommendations for additional troop deployments to Vietnam" dated 20 July 1965, LBJ/NSF/AF/4/12/38.

36. Federation of Malaya, *Annual Report*, (Kuala Lumpur: Government Printing Office 1953), p. 3.

37. Ibid., p. 4.

38. Ibid., p. 10.

39. Ibid.

40. Ibid., pp. 25–29 passim.

41. Ibid., p. 35. Compare with Hanrahan, *The Communist Struggle*, p. 24 who gives the figure as 225,000 without attribution.

42. "Noll," "The Emergency in Malaya" *Army Quarterly*, vol. 68 (April 1954), p. 50.

43. See M. C. A. Henniker, *Red Shadow Over Malaya*, (London: William Blackwood 1955), pp. 33–35, for a good description of a morning prayer meeting.

44. Federation of Malaya, *Annual Report*, (1953), p. 4.

45. Legislative Minutes, "High Commissioner's Speech, Meeting of the Sixth Session, Legislative Council, Federation of Malaya" 18 March 1953.

46. Ibid.

47. Ibid.

48. New York *Herald-Tribune* 15 April 1953.

49. Richard Miers, *Shoot to Kill*, (London: Faber 1959), p. 59.

50. Ibid., p. 160.

51. London *Times* 16 January 1953.

52. Federation of Malaya, *Annual Report*, (Kuala Lumpur: Government Printing Office 1954), p. 18.

53. Ibid.

54. Ibid., p. 20.

55. Ibid., p. 27.

56. Ibid., p. 100.

57. Federation of Malaya, *High Commissioner's Semi-Annual Report (19 November 1952)*, (Kuala Lumpur: Government Printing Office 1952), p. 12.

58. Edgar O'Ballance, *Malaya: The Communist Insurgent War 1948–1960*, (Hamden, Conn.: Archon 1966), p. 177.

59. Ibid.

6.
The Banana Wars, 1915–1934

The U.S. Marine Corps had far more experience with counterinsurgency than any other American armed service during the eighteen year period of interventionary pacification known colloquially as the "Banana Wars." Having said this, it is important to understand that this experience had little effect upon the state of American counterinsurgency doctrine in the early 1960s, as it had been largely excised from the institutional memory of the Corps and the military community generally. However, it still merits examination as the period of marine operations represented a reservoir which was available, even if not fully or properly tapped. Moreover, the lingering traditions of the Banana War period exercised a considerable effect in the noninstitutional methods of instruction and indoctrination in the tight little tribe of the Marine Corps, such that the exploits of Company M under the command of the legendary "Chesty" Puller could, and did, become the direct progenitors of the innovative, if short-lived, projects of the marines in South Vietnamn.

The marine involvements in Haiti and the Dominican Republic, while having aspects of civil development and an emphasis upon the training of local troops in the skills of internal security were, essentially, without effect in the development of counterinsurgency doctrine or the American understanding of guerrilla war. The same was not the case with the intervention in Nicaragua in the late 1920s and early 1930s. The Nicaraguan conflict involved the marines in a lengthy counterinsurgency campaign, in which the results were not clear cut, nor the experience without a large component of frustration. Further, the conflict was well assimilated by the Corps in a major doctrinal work, *The Small Wars Manual* issued in 1940, just in time to be made quite irrelevant by the outbreak of World War II.

Although the eight years from 1925 to 1933 constituted the most important period of marine involvement in Nicaragua, it was not the first time the Corps had been dispatched to that country with a mission of internal security and stabilization. Sporadic interventions had occurred since 1912 in pursuit of a consistent American policy of encouraging internal order and regional disarmament in order to assure the absence of threats to the flanks and sea-lanes of the Panama Canal. Unfortunately, the schismatic nature of the Nicaraguan political structure which combined aspects of family feuds with disputes over turf and influence, as well as the heavily politicized nature of the Nicaraguan military, combined to prevent stability of a long-term sort. Additionally, local political rivalries were on occasion boisterous enough to place foreign lives and property at risk, thus necessitating intervention. As part of the background noise to these periodic outbursts of rhetorical and physical violence, the rural peasantry was rife for insurrection against the landowning oligarchy which controlled both politics and the economy.

In 1925 the combination of incipient insurrection, violent internecine political rivalry, increased levels of Mexican governmental aid to one of the contending factions and continuing danger to foreign citizens convinced the U.S. State Department that only American intervention could restore order and tranquility. President Calvin Coolidge concurred in this opinion after rebel forces in eastern Nicaragua had the temerity to sack American business properties. In quick order, parties of marines and sailors were landed.

In the first two months of 1927 approximately 2,000 marines landed in Nicaragua, commencing with the landing of the 5th Regiment.[1] One battalion moved on 1 February at the request of President Diaz to defend the capital of Managua.[2] After this, the marine detachments moved methodically and systematically to occupy all the major cities and provide neutral zones around each.[3] The size and distribution of the marine force served to convince the major contending factions to seek negotiations even though the American troops had undertaken no offensive operations.

Negotiations did ensue with Secretary of State Henry Stimson acting as President Coolidge's personal as well as professional representative. The Liberals held the military ascendency in the rural districts. Balancing this, the Conservatives controlled the cities and the seaports, at least as long as the marines stayed. As the negotiators swatted mosquitos and hammered out an armistice agreement on the banks of the Tipitapa river in mid-May 1927, marines took up peacekeeping positions between the contending forces. It seems safe to infer that the troops kept their weapons not only loaded but pointed impartially in both directions.

Although reinforced by another regiment (the 11th), the marines undertook no offensive operations against any of the factional forces or dissident bands, as this would have violated American policy as it was understood by the field commanders.[4] As the Nicaraguan National Guard (GNN) proposed and authorized several years earlier had not yet been formed in any effective fashion, marine operations were passive in nature, being limited to the collection of firearms from anyone who cared to surrender them. It was during this period of uncertain policy and military passivity that the new generation of guerrilla leaders led by the most famous of the insurgent commanders, Augosto "Caesar" Sandino, started operations. Other leading insurgent figures included the infamous former cattle rustler and recent convert to Marxism, Pedro Altamirano, the Nicaraguan bandit leaders turned patriotic freedom fighters, Colindres, Salgado and Ortez, as well as the expatriate Mexican Marxist, Platas.[5] In a flush of totally unjustified confidence in the efficacy of unenforced treaties, the Navy Department reduced the 3,300 man expeditionary force to 1,500 troops at the end of July.[6]

Contemporaneously, the first effective *jefe* (chief) of the GNN, Colonal E. R. Beadle USMC, was appointed along with his "very able" Chief of Staff, Colonel Samuel Harrington.[7] Two competent appointments alone have never made an effective military force and the present case was no exception. The essential administrative and regulatory infrastructure had to be created, training manuals written, doctrine developed, and last, but most assuredly not least, reliable men recruited. Never before had Nicaragua been served by a nonpolitical military force. While the officer cadre would be furnished by seconded marine officers and NCOs, the nonpartisan nature of the GNN effectively prevented tapping the most readily available sources of semitrained manpower, the disarmed factional forces. The reduction of the marine force worsened the problem of developing a politically neutral GNN as it caused a demand for GNN detachments to assume static defense duties and to mount punitive expeditions against the so-called bandits. There was no alternative to the enlistment of Conservative partisans, much to the detriment of the new Guardia.

The first contact between the marine-officered GNN and the guerrillas of Caesar Sandino, the Sandinistas, came at daybreak 16 July 1927 at the initiative of the guerrillas.[8] The Ocotol outpost, manned by a combined detachment of thirty-nine marines and forty-seven Guardia was attacked by an estimated four hundred insurgents under Sandino's personal command.[9] The assault was repulsed, due in part to the timely arrival of effective close air support in the form of marine scout-bombers.[10] A large, combined relief patrol arrived at Ocotol on 21 July and engaged in energetic but issueless patrolling in the vicinity for a period of several days.[11] This action represented the entire war in miniature as all the tactical features were present including the use of aircraft for observation and ground attack missions in support of the ground forces, a completely new development in both tactical air doctrine and the practice of counter-guerrilla war.

Despite this initial indication of Sandinista resolve, aggressive will and tactics, the U.S. officer commanding in Nicaragua, General Logan Feland, did not alter his previous perception of Sandino as being nothing more than an ordinary bandit and pursued operations against the insurgent stronghold of El Chipote in a regrettably dilatory fashion, only partially justified by the dearth of useful intelligence as to the precise location of the base.[12] Flushed by the success of the dive bombing attack at Ocotol executed by the aircraft of VO-1M (Scout Bomber Squadron One), Feland, in effect, declared a victory and the ending of the insurgent challenge. He was five years too early.

The marines finally obtained reliable information concerning the location of El Chipote quite serendipitously during the course of a search and rescue patrol and it was decided to mount a major search and destroy operation against the Sandinista base camp.[13] It was estimated that between 200 and 500 guerrillas armed with rifles and machine guns were located at El Chipote.[14] An air strike was briefly contemplated but was rejected in favor of a combined air–ground operation despite communications and liaison difficulties. Two columns totaling 148 enlisted marines, 20 guardia and 6 marine officers marched on El Chipote.[15]

Both patrols had contact with Sandinista forces on 30 December 1927 prior to their final linkup preparatory to the attack on El Chipote. The smaller combined marine–GNN patrol met the more determined resistance, suffering seven fatalities and eight seriously wounded.[16] Forty-three marines under one of their own officers were dispatched to reinforce the stricken patrol, and a successful linking of the separate columns occurred as planned at Quilali, where an improvised landing strip allowed the wounded to be evacuated by air to the Managua field hospital, another first for an American combat force.[17]

The 200 troops left Quilali on 8 January 1928 to establish blocking positions on the approaches to El Chipote. In this they were joined by a GNN and marine detachment from Ocotol which, with later reinforcements, raised the total strength of the investing force to approximately 400.[18] Originally the ground forces were to undertake an assault, but the Sandinista attacks on 30 December had caused a rapid revision of the plan, for the marines, as the Division of Operations writer later remarked: "made an error in underestimating the bandit combat strength."[19] Now the marines' flying artillery would take the lead with the ground troops moving in to mop up and occupy.

The troops were to patrol aggressively, causing the guerrillas to retreat to the upper slopes of the El Chipote hill where "they would be subject to attack by our air service."[20] On 14 January the desired air attack took place, dropping fifty pound bombs and strafing exposed buildings. The commander of the two aircraft strike force reported the results as having included at least forty-five rebel dead.[21] The air attack did not succeed in dislodging the Sandinistas, which led the Division of Operations to comment somewhat dryly "aerial reconnaissance alone should not be accepted as evidence of the nonexistence of enemy forces."[22]

After the initial indication of continued guerrilla resistance, the marines executed a slow, careful, if not ponderous and timid, concentric advance, at the end of which they reached the summit unopposed on 26 January 1928.[23] The guerrillas had long since left. The final results were disappointing and totally out of proportion to the time, manpower and effort expended. The Sandinistas remained in the field.

After this major operation had proven to be a dry hole, the war continued in a never ending series of small guerrilla raids and equally unending marine–GNN patrols. Such actions as occurred were small-scale, occasionally bloody and always without real result. As the raiding and patrolling went on so also did the development of the Guardia, which was expanded and put on a regular basis.[24] As the insurgency had not ended and the infant GNN lacked the ability to take the field against the guerrillas, the marine presence was reinforced to a level of 2,500 in the spring of 1928.[25] Marine Corps Commandant Lejeune believed that even this augmented force was probably too small to combat effectively an organized, mounted and popularly supported insurgent group such as the Sandinistas.[26]

Lejeune's assessment was pessimistic but not unduly so. Despite the fact that unending marine pressure had put the guerrillas on the defensive, the Sandinistas were in no danger of extermination. Aggressive and extended 11th Regiment patrolling activities, coupled with marginally useful cordon and search operations through the summer of 1928, helped to make the northern province of Neuva Segovia less hospitable to the Sandinistas.

In large part this was possible because the marines were showing an increased ability to use aircraft in conjunction with the ground patrols. One battalion commander commented: "aviation played a big part in all this preliminary work and an even greater part when operations started."[27] Aircraft played an important role in reconnaissance and liaison; to a lesser extent they demonstrated a utility for direct attack missions and close support of ambushed columns or supply trains.[28]

Even with air reconnaissance and support the marines did not have things completely their way during the Neuva Segovia campaign. The insurgents were well armed, competently led and intimately familiar with the local situation and terrain. The initiative lay entirely with the guerrillas who could elect to seek, accept or refuse contact with the marine–GNN patrols.

Because of the continuous marine–GNN pressure, Sandino gradually shifted the focus of his forces away from the northern and western sections of Nicaragua into the eastern provinces where there were fewer security forces and an abundance of foreign-owned mines and businesses from which revolutionary expropriations might be made. The pickings were temporarily easy as the primary security forces were private police of uncertain quality. While beneficial economically, this tactical shift served to reduce the Sandinista impact upon the political process in Managua.

While Sandino was engaged in the east hijacking mines and generally raising merry but ineffectual hell, the marines were initiating a series of critical operations aimed at securing the Nicaraguan–Honduran border, thereby interdicting supposed guerrilla supply lines and discomfiting insurgent base areas. The key element here was a series of patrols along the Coco river which were in part intended as reconnaissance and in part oriented toward the establishment of permanent posts in the interior.

Command of the riverine forces was given to Captain Merrit Edson, an experienced, energetic and imaginative marine, whose name would later be linked with the development of the World War II Raider Battalions. Working from a base at Caboyracias a Dios, Edson's first patrol chugged up the muddy reaches of the lower Coco in a sixteen-foot flat-bottomed boat powered by a salvaged Model T engine on 5 March 1928.[29] Edson and his men overcame balky engines, floods, snags, rocks, bottomless mud and Sandino resistance to establish control of the Coco river.

Ultimately Edson's marines would convert control into dominance, in large measure because of the assistance of the Indian tribes of the Coco river flood plain with whom Edson was able to establish good relations and capitalize upon their inherent dislike of the ethnic Nicaraguans.[30] Edson was able to convince both major Indian tribal groups on the river, the Misquitos and the Sumas, to provide support manpower and combat information to the marines. Once he had been able to lighter a radio upstream to the river patrol's inland base at Muswasto, Edson was able to expand his area of influence by arranging for the shipment of food and other supplies to his Indian clients as well as pass on information of a time-sensitive intelligence value.[31] By June he was in a position to identify and interdict guerrilla trails and call in airstrikes on guerrilla encampments. He was also ready to plan aggressive pursuit along the guerrilla routes deep into the hinterland. The naval officer commanding the area who was located afloat in the cruiser *Denver* vetoed the idea, but even eight years later Edson maintained: "I believe that we could have delivered a blow which would have been more effective than the one we eventually struck in August of the year; that we might have completely disrupted Sandino's forces."[32]

One possible reason for the naval officer's negative reaction to Edson's aggressive design was the constant problem of supplying the isolated river posts. As Edson himself reported, the transportation of supplies was an unending cause for worry, with one outpost garrison being reduced to less than a week's store of food.[33] The problems of transportation and normal supply demands complicated Edson's task of stockpiling enough supplies to support a limited advance on the village of Poteca, a major insurgent logistics center and base camp, which had been approved by his commander.

When the necessary supplies had been collected, Edson and forty-six men cleared Bocay village, heading upriver against a reputed 450 Sandinistas at Poteca. The expedition caught the insurgents by surprise, as they had assumed the river would preclude any American advance. Captured correspondence showed that Sandino had no idea that the marines had moved so far across his rear and routes to his northern sources of supply.[34] After two guerrillas escaped from a patrol, the advantage of surprise evaporated and the marines retired downriver to rest and regroup. The advance upriver was renewed later with heavy and sporadic fighting. Although the actions seemed to be inconclusive, they upset Sandino's plans for leaving the eastern provinces and returning to the political heartland of Nicaragua to the northwest. As was later determined from the debriefing of the captured Sandinista Chief of Staff, Jiron, the effect was far more valuable than the fourteen guerrilla fatalities and five prisoners credited to Edson in the final taking of Poteca on 17 August 1928.[35] Between the Coco patrols and the activities of the 11th Marine Regiment, the guerrillas in the East had become isolated, demoralized, and politically ineffectual. But, they were far from defeated.

The marines had done the most which might be expected of any military force in a counterinsurgency environment. They had bought time—time in which indigenous security and governmental structures might be developed sufficiently to cope with the insurgent threat. The GNN would have to be rapidly developed into an effective fighting force, for there were simply too few marines to provide both static defense and the offensive patrols necessary to defeat guerrillas. At the time of the 1928 election the GNN numbered some 173 officers and 1,632 men, sufficient to provide either municipal police forces or to operate behind a marine shield in the less demanding areas of the North or East, but not both.[36] Unfortunately there was no essential agreement between the new Liberal administration of General Jose Moncado and the U.S. Navy theater commander as to which of the tasks would have the higher priority. The Liberals and the Legation wished to see the Guardia walking a beat in Managua while the

American military commanders wanted to commit the GNN to the counterguerrilla patrols.

On the positive side, the Guardia was gaining both competence and the confidence of the citizenry. On the negative side, training had become uneven, particularly so as portions of each Guardia company were permanently assigned to police duties and the balance to field assignments. All too often the former group fell under the pernicious influence of personal political loyalties and the omnipresent opportunities for graft. The lesson was clear but unheeded: the same force cannot combine effectively law enforcement and military duties without exceptional training and leadership. Although not appreciated at the time, political gangrene had already set in.

The manpower shortage caused the marines to experiment with an auxiliary unit, the Voluntarios. A motley eighty-eight man group of Indians and Nicaraguans ranging in age from seventeen to fifty years, the first Voluntarios enlisted for six months as auxiliary troops in Nueva Segovia.[37] They constituted a formation of surprising military utility, being able to patrol 112 days out of 128.[38] Their capability was dramatically demonstrated by the capture of Sandinista Chief of Staff Jiron. But they demonstrated with equal drama the dangers inherent in an undisciplined irregular force when, over the protests of their nominal marine commander, they held a summary court-martial of Jiron and speedily executed him.

Essentially the Voluntarios constituted a pseudo-gang and, as such, would have been fully useful only under very tight command and control. Employed in reconnaissance, ambush and deception roles, pseudo-gangs can and have been highly useful adjuncts to other, less unconventional, counterinsurgency units. However, pseudo-gangs have an unfortunate tendency toward brigandage or wanton conduct which must be forcefully checked before the resultant harm outweighs the possible good.

Further expedients would have to be undertaken and continued degradation of combat effectiveness accepted as the Navy Department ordered the withdrawal of the 11th Regiment at the end of 1929, reducing the strength of the marine force to 1,500 men. This force was concentrated in Managua and the other large cities with substantial American and European national populations. While obviously deployed to protect the lives and property of foreigners, to the jaundiced eye of the cynical observer it was equally obvious that the deployment served to protect the Conservative Congress from the Liberal President and vice versa. In any event the war against the Sandinistas was again at a stalemate in early 1930.

The stalemate was threatened in May 1930 when Sandino was wounded in the hip by a marine bomb fragment which forced him to retire from active field command. He established a new headquarters back in his old stamping ground by the Coco river, from which he directed the activities of his subordinates by courier.[39] The Sandinistas prepared to engage in protracted conflict directed against the lucrative economic targets of the coffee region, as well as the GNN outposts and patrols. In response to this threat and also with an eye toward the upcoming 1930 elections, Liberals and Conservatives alike agreed to increase the size of the Guardia, such that by 1 October 1930 its total personnel numbered 2,256 and its annual budget was $1,116,000.[40] This should have been enough to give the GNN an advantage over the Sandinistas.[41]

This was not to be. Using the economic depression as a justification, but with internecine political rivalries as the actual motivation, the Nicaraguan government forced a reduction of the Guardia on 1 November 1930 to a level of 160 officers and 1,650 men.[42] Of these men, 1,000 were stationed in Nueva Segovia and 650 in the rest of the country.[43] The GNN was primarily dedicated to static protection of foreign-owned properties and major ranches.

In the fall of 1930 the GNN attempted to mount major coordinated search and destroy operations in the Segovia and Jinotega areas. Three such operations, each involving five separate columns, were undertaken between August 1930 and January 1931.[44] In each case casualties were inflicted on the insurgents but the results simply were not worth the resources committed. The command and control structure of the Guardia, the communications technology available to it and the intelligence apparatus employed by it were simply not up to the job of destroying the guerrillas. Miles were marched; shots were fired; food, shoeleather and energy were exhausted without significant result. As the official marine evaluation of the Nicaraguan experience later commented, ". . . there were never sufficient Guardia available to attempt to cover a general offensive in the enormous territory that had to be covered. . . ."[45]

The bright spot in the GNN picture throughout 1931 was Company M which, under the energetic command of Louis B. (Chesty) Puller, operated as a wide-ranging deep penetration unit throughout the Jinotega area. Averaging two marine officers and thirty GNN enlisted men, Company M held a purely offensive brief, which meant that it could respond to any threatened sector without the degradation of defensive capabilities elsewhere. Heavy in automatic weapons and grenade launchers, physically tough, confident and aggressive to a fault, Company M became the terror of the Sandinista contingent under the command of Pedron.[46] The insurgents dubbed Puller the "Tiger of the Mountains," the result of having been bested by his troops in some twenty engagements.[47] The most accurate assessment of Company M was the acknowledgment years later that, given the limited resources of GNN, the best method of combating guerrillas would have been the creation of several, perhaps as many as eight, similar formations.[48] It is instructive to note that not too long after tearing up the bush with Company M, Puller became the Chief Instructor at Basic School. One of his first officer-pupils was young Second Lieutenant Lewis Walt, later the commander of III Marine Amphibious Force and the first commander of I Corps in South Vietnam.[49] This is a genealogy worth noting.

Company M was a sign post destined not to be followed. On 13 February 1931, the State Department announced officially that all marines would be withdrawn from Nicaragua following the elections of November 1932. The marines now had to struggle with the problem of creating a senior officer corps of professional competence and political neutrality. In this they were to be unsuccessful, primarily for lack of time. Likewise, they were unsuccessful in beating back the attempt of President Moncado to introject further politics into the GNN.

The year 1932 saw a serious incursion by Sandino's forces along the Corinto–Granada railroad. The Guardia was wracked with two serious mutinies and had suffered a disheartening number of causalties in ambushes. In over 150 contacts between 1 January 1932 and the November election, neither the GNN nor the Sandinistas enjoyed an advantage.[50] Had it not been for the continued dramatic success of Company M, the Sandinistas would have gained the moral ascendancy. The election saw the former Liberal Vice-President, Sacasa, elevated to the Presidency after a minimal amount of fraud, corruption and intimidation but a maximal amount of American supervision. As a result of Sacasa's victory, his slate of thirty-nine nominees was approved to take command of the GNN.[51]

His nominee for director of the National Guard was a certain Anastacio Somoza, the Vice-Minister of Foreign Affairs under Moncado. It should be noted that Somoza was neither a creature of the marines nor of the Guardia as has so often been alleged, but was a dyed-in-the-wool product of domestic politics.

On 15 December the marines serving in the bush with the GNN were withdrawn to Managua preparatory to a final departure from Nicaragua in early 1933. Sandino was still undefeated in the hills. The Guardia was semipoliticized. Forty-seven marines, seventy-five Guardia and a reported 1,115 guerrillas had been killed.[52] The marines left with appropriately mixed feelings about the success of their mission. There was much to be considered in the evaluations of the Nicaraguan operations over the course of the next five years.

A number of lessons were derived from the Banana Wars, particularly the Nicaraguan campaign. The marines perceived that in a counterinsurgency environment their capabilities could be employed best in two types of missions: providing the primary element for combating mainforce guerrillas, and furnishing the training and leadership cadre for the development of an incountry constabulary. This second role did not imply a status at all similar to that occupied by advisory personnel in the post World War II years. Rather, it meant that marines would exercise command, both tactical and administrative, until such time as indigenous officers were available.

The marines developed a proper appreciation for the virtues of combined units in which the superior firepower and discipline of the marine contingent would be complemented by the local knowledge and terrain familiarity of the indigenous personnel. It was also well established that such combined formations gave the best advanced individual training to the indigenous troops. Marine officers and NCOs were able to overcome cultural and linguistic barriers as well as racial prejudice to cooperate effectively with and lead local troops in prolonged, stressful patrols. This degree of institutionalized cross-cultural combat cooperation experience is unique in American military history. The marines also found that mixed patrols had the best effect on civilian morale, as they were a highly visible sign of what would later be termed "U.S. commitment."

Often the marines constituted the civil government, a role for which they were only marginally suited and even less well prepared. Nonetheless, their experience in such nonmilitary areas as public health, public works and public education developed an awareness of civic action as a military option far transcending any equivalent perception in other services. The marines were in the business of nation building over a quarter of a century before the term became common. An acute sensitivity to the tight interaction between civilian, social and economic concerns was developed.

On the more mundane level of tactics and operations, the marines came to a set of conclusions which were at variance with those derived by the army from postwar guerrilla conflicts. The marines favored small, mobile, independent patrols aggressively led and free of logistics constraints which could effectively hunt down and fix guerrilla units. In Nicaragua, the lack of a sufficient number of such patrols was specifically identified as a major reason for the failure to suppress Sandino. Even where small patrols did not fix and kill large numbers of guerrillas, they developed valuable intelligence which the marines properly assessed as the centrality of successful counterinsurgency. The marines eschewed large search and clear operations, noting that large operations invariably failed. The marines were psychologically prepared for protracted conflict, as such had been the nature of the Banana Wars.

Perhaps most importantly, the marines did not define guerrilla war as partisan war. There had been nothing in the Banana Wars which led them to look for external support or control of the conflict. Even in activities such as the Coco river patrol where the severing of lines of supply was a goal, it was clear that there was no expectation that the mere severing of these would end the war. In no other way is the difference between army and marine views made clearer.

NOTES

1. U.S. Senate Committee on Foreign Relations, "Use of the U.S. Navy in Nicaragua" 11–18 February 1928, 70th Congress 1st Session, Appendix "Summary of Operations in Nicaragua December 23, 1926–February 5, 1928" (Washington, D.C.: Committee Print 1928), p. 2.

2. Ibid.

3. Ibid., pp. 5–7.

4. Julian Smith et al., *A Review of the Organization and Operations of the Guardia Nacional de Nicaragua*, (Quantico, Va.: Marine Corps Schools 1937), p. 21.

5. Ibid.

6. "U.S. Navy in Nicaragua—Summary of Operations," p. 15.

7. Evans Carlson, "The Guardia Nacional de Nicaragua" *Marine Corps Gazette*, vol. 21 (June 1937), p. 9.

8. HQMC, Division of Operations and Training, "Combat Operations in Nicaragua #2" *MCG*, vol. 13 (March 1929), pp. 3–16.

9. Ibid., pp. 4–5.

10. Ibid., p. 16.

11. Ibid.

12. Smith, *A Review*, pp. 15–23 passim.

13. HQMC Division of Operations and Training, "Combat Operations in Nicaragua #3" *MCG*, vol. 14 (June 1929), pp. 81–84.

14. Ibid., p. 84.

15. Ibid., p. 85.

16. Smith, *A Review*, p. 306.

17. "Combat Operations in Nicaragua #3," pp. 87–88.

18. Ibid., p. 90.

19. Ibid.

20. Ibid., p. 93.

21. Major Rowell, "Report" quoted in ibid., p. 91.

22. Ibid., p. 92.

23. Ibid., pp. 92–93.

24. Smith, *A Review*, p. 27.

25. "U.S. Navy in Nicaragua—Summary of Operations," pp. 48–49.

26. Ibid., pp. 63–64.

27. John Gray, "The Second Nicaraguan Campaign" *MCG*, vol. 17 (February 1933), pp. 37–38.

28. HQMC Division of Operations and Training, "Combat Operations in Nicaragua #4" *MCG*, vol. 14 (June 1929), pp. 177–179.

29. Merrit Edson, "The Coco River Patrol" pt. 1 *MCG*, vol. 20 (August 1936), p. 38.

30. Ibid., pp. 21–22.

31. Merrit Edson, "The Coco River Patrol" pt. 2 *MCG*, vol. 20 (November 1926), pp. 41, 60.

32. Ibid., p. 69.

33. Merrit Edson, "The Coco River Patrol" pt. 3 *MCG*, vol. 21 (February 1937), p. 40.

34. Quoted in ibid., p. 43.

35. Ibid., pp. 62–63; Smith, *A Review*, pp. 305–6.

36. Smith, *A Review*, p. 18.

37. H. H. Hanneken, "A Discussion of the Voluntario Troops in Nicaragua" *MCG*, vol. 26 (November 1942) pp. 118–20, 247–66.

38. Ibid., p. 266.

39. Carlson, "The Guardia Nacional," p. 12; Smith, *A Review*, p. 310.

40. Smith, *A Review*, p. 25.

41. Carlson, "The Guardia Nacional," p. 12.

42. Smith, *A Review*, p. 27.

43. Ibid., p. 28; Carlson, "The Guardia Nacional," p. 11.

44. Smith, *A Review*, pp. 355–70 passim.

45. Ibid., p. 37.

46. Ibid.

47. Carlson, "The Guardia Nacional," p. 11. See the report of L. B. Puller quoted in Smith, *A Review*, pp. 273–75.

48. Smith, *A Review*, p. 38.

49. Burke Davis, *Marine!*, (Boston: Little, Brown 1962), p. 86.

50. Ibid., pp. 357–62 passim.

51. Carlson, "The Guardia Nacional," p. 18.

52. Smith, *A Review*, p. 408.

TOTEMS AND TRIBAL
MEMORIES

7.

Selecting and Erecting
the Pole

In many essential respects the creation of military doctrine is an exercise in highly selective historical interpretation. The way in which past conflicts are used as the basis for preparing the "theory of victory" hopefully appropriate to a future war is determined by such factors as overall view of the world and general understanding of the nature of war as seen in the totality of a nation's military experience.

The first factor is like the air, pervasive and invisible, and again, like the air is capable of exerting terrific force when moved. In the American view of guerrilla war, the conviction that no society could possibly engage in insurgency served both to mirror the American understanding of social change through political mechanisms and to force an understanding of guerrilla war which recognized only the partisan model with its emphasis upon external support.

The second consideration is also pervasive within the military. The general American understanding of warfare, as it emerged in the period between World Wars I and II, has been quite Clausewitzian. It has not only borrowed the formulations of the great nineteenth-century German military theorist, it has improved upon them. At bottom, the American view of war emphasizes combat, set-piece battles between organized units as the centrality of conflict. Americans also put a high priority upon the use of firepower and high mobility, both controlled by a sophisticated communications system, as the means of assuring that decisive combat is achieved in the field. The desirable aim of combat has been seen as the destruction of the enemy's army in the field, with the inevitable consequence being that the enemy must submit. An alternative which became

practical in World War II has been understood as the destroying of the
enemy's will and ability to continue in combat. These basic principles
have been considered to be equally appropriate to all types of war, from
nuclear to guerrilla. In the development of a theory of victory in guerrilla
war they helped assure that the partisan model would be the only one
seen and prepared for.

Consider the following statements of Clausewitz:

> The *military power* (of an enemy) must be destroyed, that is,
> reduced to such a state as not to be able to prosecute the war. This
> is the sense in which we wish to be understood hereafter, whenever
> we use the expression "destruction of the enemy's military power."[1]
> [emphasis in original]

or:

> In this manner we see that the destruction of the enemy's military
> forces, the overthrow of the enemy's power, is only to be done
> through the effect of the battle, whether it be that it actually takes
> place or that it is merely offered and not accepted.[2]

Now compare these with the following statement of purpose dating from
the eve of World War II:

> The *conduct of war* is the art of employing the Armed Forces of
> a nation . . . for the purpose of effecting a satisfactory peace. The
> ultimate objective of all military operations is the destruction of the
> enemy's armed forces in battle. Decisive defeat in battle breaks the
> enemy's will to war and forces him to sue for peace . . .[3] [emphasis
> in original]

It is quite obvious that the goal of effecting the destruction of the opponent's military power is considered as the necessary prerequisite for
achieving the ultimate goal of compelling the opponent to seek peace on
terms favorable to the United States. In 1944 the two goals were formulated in a manner even more in the mold of Clausewitz.[4]

The introduction of the concept of limited war, after the dawning of the
nuclear age, in no way altered this:

The nature of the political situation at any time may require the employment of armed forces in wars of limited objective. In such cases the objective ordinarily will be the destruction of the aggressor forces and the restoration of the political and territorial integrity of the friendly nation.[5]

In the last pre-Vietnam conflict edition of FM (Field Manual) 100-5, additional qualifiers were placed on the concept of limited war. A firebreak was blazed between nuclear and conventional munitions as well as between "cold war" and "limited war," but the end goal remained the destruction of the enemy forces in the field.[6] The defined constraints against allowing limited war to develop over time into "general (nuclear) war" did not reduce the Clausewitzian objective of destroying the opponent's field force and thus his capability to conduct war.[7]

The Clausewitzian approach was not confined to the rarified air of grand strategy. It applied to the conduct of ground combat operations as well, as the following statements of purpose show.

(A) The mission of the rifle company of the infantry battle group is to close with the enemy by means of fire and maneuver in order to destroy or capture him or to repel his assault by fire, close combat and counterattack.

(B) The mission of the rifle company of the airborne battle group is to move by air to close with the enemy and destroy or capture him.[8]

Whether dealing with grand strategy or minor tactics, considering the army as a whole or its smallest tactical element, the guiding principle was the destruction of the enemy's military power. Despite the oft-repeated assertion by military commanders that ". . .the deterrence of war is the primary objective of the armed forces," the focus of military operations was and has remained Clausewitzian in nature.[9]

Doctrine is not the pristine product of disinterested martial scholars working in a sandbag tower, concerned only with the optimal merging of past experience and present weapons systems to assure success on future battlefields. Rather, doctrine is heavily influenced, even dictated, by political and budgetary considerations. During the Eisenhower administration the emphasis was upon "massive retaliation" and the nuclear weapons of the air force had priority. The army was deprived of a role as protracted ground conflict was deprecated or ignored. The army's policy echelon bureaucratic warriors had to seize and defend a mission-oriented high ground. Not surprisingly, the army both embraced nuclear weapons and made immense efforts to show that ground combat forces were a viable, even an inevitable, component of the nuclear battlefield of future. To this end, the doctrinal efforts to restructure army organization and tactics for a nuclear age were urged by the high command. These efforts were collectively known as the "New Look" army.

Throughout the development of the New Look, as was noted by an experienced military commander and opponent of the all-nuclear policies of the Eisenhower years, Maxwell Taylor, the army was not and never had been satisfied with the allocation of missions among the services which had resulted in a severely limited role for ground forces.[10] This unhappiness not only propelled research into the development of low-yield tactical nuclear weapons; it had doctrinal implications as well.

The growing recognition of the possibility of a nuclear parity between the United States and the U.S.S.R., as well as a general perception that limited war along the world's periphery was not only possible but probable, doctrinal development became conditioned by a desire on the part of the army to demonstrate that its organization, tactics, and weapons were capable of meeting any contingency along a wide spectrum, without any costly or delay-producing reconfigurations. This concept was formally embedded into doctrine in 1962.[11] An excellent summary view of the army's doctrinal position was provided by a military commentator well respected by the Services, Hansen W. Baldwin, who wrote in 1956: "What we must do is prepare the Army to fight conventional wars, to stand guard in the Cold War and to fight in limited nuclear wars."[12]

The problem of adapting to nuclear munitions was seen as twofold. On the one hand, it was necessary to maximize the survivability and combat effectiveness of ground combat forces on the nuclear battlefield. On the other, it was necessary at least to demonstrate that the forces constructed for the nuclear mission could carry out other tasks since, "dropping atomic bombs on enemy cities may not always be the smart solution to block semidisguised aggression."[13]

At an early date it was recognized that survivability and combat effectiveness could be assured only by structuring the ground forces to emphasize mobility, flexibility, dispersion, small unit size, logistic independence and sophisticated command and control capabilities.[14] The first tests of these new concepts were held in Germany in 1954.[15] These were followed within two years by an official army study, "Atomic Field Army-1 (ATFA-1)," which concluded that major structural and doctrinal revisions were necessary as the battlefield of the future would be "cellular rather than linear."[16] The resulting "Pentomic" organization was first subjected to testing in September 1956 with the newly reorganized 101st Airborne Division. As a result of the effectiveness perceived in this test, the army urged the Secretary of Defense and the President to authorize the reorganization of all the army's divisions.[17]

The full plans for these new divisions, known variously as "Pentomic" and ROCID (Reorganization of the Current Infantry Division), were unveiled by Chief of Staff Maxwell Taylor with the explanation that the army could not maintain two sets of forces, one for conventional affrays and the other for nuclear wars. Rather, the army would now be able to "use atomic and nonatomic weapons in any combination."[18] It was described as a "lean, powerful, versatile organization."[19]

Smaller than its predecessor, the new infantry division contained five battle groups capable of operating independently under the control of a remote divisional headquarters. These maneuver units were supported by organic divisional artillery.[20] By coupling improvements in communication with new high mobility vehicles, including helicopters, it was believed that ROCID would inaugurate a new era in infantry operations for both nuclear and conventional warfare. It should be mentioned that the capabilities for dispersed and independent action were seen as guaranteeing an increased effectiveness in irregular and counterguerrilla operations. Pentomic reorganization of the infantry division was complemented by analagous treatment of armored and airborne units.

Contemporaneous with the formation of the first pentagonally configured airborne division, army aviation enthusiasts, led by James Gavin and John J. Tolson, were developing the operational and doctrinal concept of airmobility. Borrowing heavily from Marine Corps experiments in vertical envelopment, the Airmobility Division of the Airborne-Army Aviation Department published the first field manual detailing the organization, equipment and techniques for helicopter-supported tactical mobility.[21] Shortly thereafter requirements for a new generation of helicopters were drafted and placed into the procurement pipeline. Although the requirements, like the doctrine, were oriented toward the nuclear battlefield, the latent implications for counterguerrilla activities were enormous.

No sooner had the Pentomic concept been placed in operation than it was modified heavily in an attempt to promote operational flexibility, superior firepower, high tactical mobility and improved command and control. The net result was the creation of divisions into which infantry, armored or airborne battle groups could be plugged as required by operational tasks.[22] This plug-in or "building block" approach was strongly supported by the spectrum of conflict and flexible response notions of Maxwell Taylor. Taylor, in his widely read and influential criticism of the Eisenhower New Look concept, argued for changes which "would make the Army an integrated mobile force for ground combat . . . a hard, mobile striking force ready to move and fight anywhere on the ground."[23] The desired alterations were completed by Secretary of Defense Robert McNamara who recognized the necessity of improving the capabilities of the general purpose land forces.

The resulting ROAD (Reorganization Objective Army Division) concept divisions were expected to supply the type of versatility and power for which General Taylor argued and Secretary McNamara searched. The central characteristic of the ROAD division was the common divisional base of headquarters and support assets to which various combat arms maneuver battalions could be attached as required by mission, environment, threat and terrain. Although still slightly skewed toward the nuclear battlefield, the ROAD division embodied an apparent degree of flexibility and adaptability far transcending its Pentomic and triangular predecessors (three regiments each of three battalions). These characteristics seeemed to contemporary planners to make the new divisions particularly useful in counterinsurgency missions.

It was not until 1962 that the army conducted its first internal review of general counterguerrilla warfare capabilities. Although primarily concerned with matters of equipment, particularly aviation capabilities, the final report did comment sharply:

> The tactical doctrine for the employment of regular forces against insurgent guerrilla forces has not been adequately developed and

the Army does not have a clear concept of the proper scale and type of equipment necessary for these operations.[24]

At the time the governing doctrine for guerrilla operations derived from the *Field Service Regulations: Operations* which in its 1962 edition included for the first time a chapter on "Unconventional Warfare."[25] Unconventional warfare was defined as comprising guerrilla warfare, escape and evasion as well as subversion, with all three occurring "within the enemy's sphere of influence largely by local personnel and resources to further military, political or economic objectives."[26] The doctrinal focus was upon the offensive employment of these components in conjunction with friendly conventional forces and the local population of enemy-controlled areas. It was observed:

> The ideological nature of modern conflict gives an important role for all forms of war. Particularly in Cold War the struggle for influence over the minds of men makes unconventional warfare a key element. Successful conduct of unconventional warfare could be decisive in achieving national objectives. Counter unconventional warfare is equally important.[27]

Entirely in keeping with the emphasis upon the offensive which typified army doctrine, initial guidance in the area of "counter unconventional warfare" was limited to:

> Enemy unconventional warfare operations must be countered. Measures include the use of consolidation psychological operations in conjunction with civil affairs, and the use of combat troops or friendly guerrillas in an antiguerrilla role.[28]

All further statements of general doctrine and principles were clearly oriented toward situations in which commanders found themselves opposed by partisan adjuncts to conventional hostile forces. Although the word partisan was not actually employed, that certainly was the operational understanding.[29] It was stated that irregular forces usually develop in rural areas. Proper recognition of the existence of both active fighters and passive supporters was given as was the possibility of protracted conflict. In short, while it appears to provide a paradigm applying equally well to the experiences in Greece, Korea, the Philippines or Malaya, it is obvious that the thrust was definitely skewed in favor of the partisan model.[30]

The "school solution" to the threat presented by irregular forces of all kinds was based upon mobility and aggressiveness.

> Operations to suppress and eliminate irregular forces are primarily offensive in nature. Thus, the conventional force must plan for and seize the initiative at the outset and retain it throughout the conduct of the operation. These operations may be required in situations wherein the an irregular force either constitutes the only enemy or threatens rear areas of regular military forces which are conducting conventional operations. The operations are similar in either case.[31]

It is important to underscore that this doctrine drew no distinctions between indigenous insurgencies either with or without effective external support and sanctuaries and partisan activities in conjunction with regular forces. These distinctly different opponents were to be countered in identical fashion.[32] The cruciality of extensive and flexible communication systems and the essentiality of effective intelligence and counterintelligence were detailed. It was stressed that plans must "employ all available weapons."[33]

Several specific tactical employments were delineated, including the isolation of the irregular force through border closure, the creation of restricted zones, population resettlement, resource controls, population movement restrictions and, "extensive ground and air search for and destruction of irregular force supply caches and installations."[34] The establishment of strong points, helicopter patrolling, raids, ambushes and search and seizure operations were all recommended as well. The tactics of cordon and search, search and destroy and search and clear employed in Greece and Korea were presented as the proper tactical solutions to irregular forces.

In addition to the more customary military responses to guerrilla activities, references were made to the desirability of effective psychological warfare and civil affairs operations. In these areas the guidance provided to commanders compared quite unfavorably in both detail and incisiveness with that given in such areas as logistics, transportation and intelligence. Where these latter topics were treated in detail and with specificity, the approach to psychological operations and civil affairs was that of generality and homilies.[35]

It may be inferred that doctrine at the highest level, the level from which subordinate operationally-oriented techniques and tactics derived, was predicated upon the partisan model of Greece or Korea to a far greater extent than the insurgent-driven model of the Philippines or Malaya. Also, it should be emphasized that the doctrinal focus upon interchangeability, independent operation, mobility, small units and thus command span through enhanced communications capability and firepower dovetailed quite nicely with the perceived strengths of the ROAD formations. It is less clear that the doctrine took proper cognizance of previous experience. It is even less clear that the doctrine presented any indication of even the slightest appreciation of the differences between insurgent and partisan guerrilla war or even the probability of guerrilla war occurring outside of the framework of wider conventional conflict.

An example of the shortcomings is to be found in the area of intelligence. The presence or absence of a sound system for the collection of information and its reduction into a reliable, timely and exploitable intelligence product was critical in all the insurgent and partisan conflicts described. Nonetheless, in the field manual covering combat intelligence issued in 1960, the last edition prior to the Vietnam commitment, there is not even a single mention of counterguerrilla situations.[36] By 1962, FM 100-5 at least acknowledged that "accurate, detailed and timely intelligence is essential to successful operations against irregular forces."[37] The use of clandestine operations as a "primary source of information" and infiltration "of the irregular force itself" were suggested.[38] Unfortunately, these sound notions, based primarily upon the Philippines experience but also acknowledging British practice in Malaya, did not widely permeate the army as is obvious from the 1963 edition of the *Combat Intelligence* field manual. Here the recommended methods were:

(1) Search and seizure
(2) Establishment of checkpoints and roadblocks
(3) Documentation of civilians

(4) Censorship
(5) Physical and electronic surveillance of suspects
(6) Maintenance of extensive dossiers
(7) Intensive interrogation.[39]

The manual's recommendations did not realistically meet the needs of the tactical echelon intelligence personnel to whom it was directed. These critical individuals were left adrift. The intelligence officer or commander who actually attempted to utilize the techniques listed would locate the opponent only through the benign intervention of chance. Clearly the lessons apparent from Malaya and, to a lesser extent, the Philippines had not been learned.

Were the guerrillas to be found, the commander and his unit would be expected to act aggressively, as the subordinate manuals emulated the offensive mindedness of the *Field Service Regulations*. "A defensive attitude . . . permits the guerrilla to concentrate superior forces, inflict severe casualties and lower morale," asserts the 1961 field manual on irregular warfare.[40] Its 1963 successor, the official authority on counter-guerrilla operations on the eve of direct U.S. troop commitment to South Vietnam, stated:

> Purely defensive measures only allow the guerrilla force to grow and become strong. They are justified only when the strength of the friendly forces available does not permit offensive action. Even limited offensive operations are preferable to a purely passive attitude. Offensive action should be continuous and aggressive.[41]

This language closely followed that contained in a study of previous guerrilla conflicts, particularly focusing upon Greece, the Philippines and Malaya, prepared under the aegis of the Special Warfare Division of the army's Directorate of Strategic Plans and Policy.[42]

The doctrinally agreeable focus on aggressiveness and the importance of the offensive was predicated upon an accurate and well-assimilated appreciation of the Greek Civil War and the partisan adjuncts to the Korean War. Other lessons which were equally agreeable to the army's command echelon were those concerning the importance of mobility, firepower, continuity of pressure, surprise, communications security and the centrality of imaginative, aggressive leadership.

The failure of the Greek Army to maintain effective pressure on the guerrillas was identified as a major reason for the prolongation of hostilities.[43] The American tactical doctrine was designed to preclude this eventuality:

> Continuous pressure is maintained throughout a campaign against guerrilla forces. If contact with the guerrilla force is lost, aggressive efforts must be made to reestablish contact through the use of aerial surveillance, extended patrols, aerial "hunter-killer" teams and coordinated harassing actions.[44]

The same was reflected in the doctrine for tactical elements:

> Continuous pressure is maintained by vigorous combat patrolling. This keeps the guerrillas on the move, disrupts their security and organization, separates them from their base of supply, weakens them physically, destroys their morale and denies them the opportunity to conduct effective operations.[45]

In the bare bone words of a company standard operating procedure (SOP) established by the commander of Bravo Company, 1/35 Infantry, and subsequently given broad professional dissemination, the doctrine cited is given its ultimate institutional application:

> Once enemy contact is made it should not be lost. Be aggressive. Patrols (even recon) will be organized in such a manner to allow them to act immediately and decisively upon locating guerrilla units . . . continually keep pressure on guerrillas to keep them on the defensive.[46]

The lesson of continuity of pressure derived from Greece and Korea had obviously been well assimilated, transmitted and implemented at the maneuver unit level. It is also worth noting the recognition given by the counterguerrilla doctrine to the Malayan and Philippine use of long-range and independent aggressive patrols to turn the bush from friend of the guerrilla to his foe.

The same might be said of the importance of surprise and its concommitant the need for security during the planning and preparation of actions against guerrilla forces. In all the insurgent conflicts mentioned, the conventional forces had experienced a significant degradation of combat efficiency, as a result of their inability to strike with surprise or through having their plans and preparations compromised by hostile intelligence assets. As FM 31-16 observed:

> Surprise is sought in all operations. Against well-organized guerrilla forces it is difficult to achieve and requires that every echelon of command, to include platoon and squad leaders, employ the most ingenious and imaginative methods. Surprise may be gained by continually varying operations and by the use of unorthodox tactics and techniques.[47]

Unfortunately, the operational employment of this sound distillation of previous experience was rendered virtually impossible because to do so would have rendered all SOPs virtually impossible. Without these handy pieces of operational commonality, the span of control necessitated by the ROAD concept was impossible. A basic and unresolvable conundrum existed. As deviations from the routine, the SOP, were the basic input for hostile intelligence collection nets and the SOP itself was the *sine qua non* of effective routinization, the goals of surprise and orderly operations were not merely incompatible: they were frankly opposite. In an environment permeated with civilian supporters of the insurgent force, as one later observer noted, "the SOP, the commander's tactical signature" is all the guerrillas need.[48] It failed to recognize the competing realities; the regularity required of military units stood in opposition to the unpredictability and deception required to prevent compromise and effect surprise.

Deception is more practical in a controlled environment, such as exists between conventional opponents whose front line and airspace can be penetrated in a finite number of predictable and therefore controllable fashions. Spies can be caught and "played back"; photo reconnaissance can be deceived; signals can be fabricated, mimicked or avoided, but a host of hostile, unsympathetic or merely intimidated eyes searching, first to identify a pattern and subsequently, to mark the slightest deviation is not so amenable to neutralization or receptive to the feeding of misinformation.

Improvements in technology did much to assure that the conclusion regarding mobility and communication derived historically would not prove so visionary. The governing doctrine was specific: "A mobility differential over the irregular forces must be attained."[49]

> Superior mobility is essential in counterguerrilla operations to achieve surprise and to successfully counter the mobility of the enemy force. The extensive use of airmobile forces, if used with imagination will ensure the military commander superior mobility.[50]

This assertion served to enshrine doctrinally airmobility as the technological anodyne to the all too real experiences of guerrilla terrain familiarity, initiative and hit-and-run tactics. Airmobility was the lynchpin.

> The imaginative, extensive and sustained use of airmobile forces offers the most effective challenge available today to this mobility differential of the enemy guerrilla force. It is imperative that, whenever possible, the concept of counterguerrilla operations be based on the maximum employment of this type of force.[51]

Airmobility was not limited to any specific type or composition of unit but was presumptively available to any formation whose equipment fell within the lifting capability of army aviation aircraft. Further, the presence of armed helicopters provided the airmobile force immediately available firepower in addition to, or in lieu of, artillery or Tactical Air Force close air support. The experiences of Greece and Korea had convinced army planners that the presence or absence of close air support capable of effectively engaging important targets was every bit as important in guerrilla as in conventional war. Unity of command dictated that such aerial firepower would be most effective if under operational control of the ground commander. This would be impossible unless the army had armed helicopters as the interservice jurisdictional disputes precluded the army from having a private air force like the Marine Corps' air wings.

The integration of armed and troop carrying helicopters was an attractive concept as early as 1954 to such aerial enthusiasts as former Airborne

General James Gavin. Gavin and others argued that the helicopter boded well to fulfill the needs not only for the rapid tactical movement of troops but also as a way of supplying additional artillery support for troops staging a contested insertion.[52] Initially the helicopter was seen solely as a means of rapid dispersion and reconcentration on the nuclear battlefield and all thinking and training was done for that purpose.[53]

By the late 1950s it was realized that this concept was too narrow and that the helicopter as a troop carrier would serve as a type of superior truck in any type of combat. With this broadening of concept, the army became genuinely helicopter happy and proceeded to develop the proper organization and doctrine for the use of helicopters. It was also necessary to develop the proper kinds of machinery to provide airmobility. The latter task was partially addressed in 1959 with the maiden flight of the Bell XHU-40, later the famed HU-1 "Huey" and finished the following year with the recommendations of the Army Aircraft Requirements Review Board (Rogers Board). The second task, that of developing airmobile organization and doctrine was addressed by the Howze Board and the proof of concept testing performed by the 11th Air Assault Division. The concept which the 11th Air Assault tested was contained in a 1957 description: "The required forces, then, for the small (guerrilla) war would appear to be much the same as those for the atomic war against the Soviet Union."[54]

The 11th Air Assault Division (Test) was activated at Fort Benning to validate the Howze Board's organizational and doctrinal concepts in a guerrilla war environment. The results of this test were combined with the assessments of the Army Concept Team in Vietnam which was attempting to evaluate the effectiveness of armed helicopter tactics in combat.[55] The result was a body of doctrine for airmobile counterguerrilla operations.[56]

The beauty of airmobility operations was that they were so mundane that the troops needed neither arcane knowledge nor much specialized training to use helicopters effectively. At the same time airmobility was revolutionary: it provided a great increase of mobility for ground elements; it enhanced command and control; it improved reconnaissance and even placed the commander on a new high ground, better even than that enjoyed by Napoleon, Lee or Patton.[57] The doctrine was rapidly extended throughout the army to include the smallest tactical elements.[58] Although drawbacks such as a mandated "dependence (being) placed on a previously prepared SOP" in order to preclude "operations using fragmentary oral orders" existed, the advent of a practical airmobility concept appeared to obviate the frustration attendant upon slow-moving, road-bound counter-insurgency units such as had been experienced during the Greek Civil War.[59] In the words of one anonymous Infantry School commentator, "The extensive use of Army aircraft offers more possibilities for decisive success against irregular forces than any other innovation of modern war."[60] It was believed that the utility and, therefore, the possibility of success was limited only by the imagination, initiative and drive of the unit commander.

Observations from both Greece and the Philippines indicated that success in guerrilla war was, if anything, more dependent upon the actions and personal qualities of the unit commanders than was the case in conventional conflicts. It was concluded correctly that commanders must operate on independent missions where "much of their support, both moral and material, depends on their own skill, ingenuity, knowledge, courage and tenacity."[61] The answer to these and related problems was to be found in "strong and capable leadership" as well as good and continuing troop indoctrination and in "utilizing self-reliant and daring junior leaders."[62] This was an accurate observation, soundly rooted in both American and British experience. So was its companion statement:

> The scope and nature of a commander's mission may emphasize political, economic and social considerations to a greater extent than in conventional operations.[63]

The traditional American emphasis upon firepower was seen to have been validated. Since the outbreak of World War II the American propensity to expend materiel and munitions rather than hazard troops had been well known and commented upon. The reorganization efforts incorporated in the Pentomic and ROAD formations had facilitated the effective integration of improved conventional munitions and heavy self-propelled artillery into combined arms formations, while the development of larger and more powerful helicopters provided the capability for the rapid deployment and displacement of previously road-bound towed medium artillery. The net result of these developmental trajectories was to place a tremendous weight of firepower into the hands of junior commanders. It must be recalled that the Greek Civil War had underscored for the Americans that artillery was vital in the prosecution of antiguerrilla operations and, in tandem with air-delivered munitions, often had served to provide the tipweight necessary to achieve victory. The contradictory experience from Malaya and the Philippines was not apparently considered.

Despite a rather cautious approach in the *Field Service Regulations*, "heavy combat support units are frequently held in a state of constant readiness at central locations until situations develop which permit their effective use," the counterguerrilla doctrine for tactical echelons provided for a maximization of artillery fire.[64] This was elaborated for tactical echelons:

> In this technique [the "fire flush"], the blocking or ambush forces encircle an area approximately 1,000 meters square and await the enemy to exit the area as he is subjected to intense saturation type indirect fire and/or attack by tactical air support.[65]

The same field manual advised that "nuclear fires normally cannot be profitably employed in counterguerrilla operations" but hastens to add that "chemical and biological weapons may be used effectively."[66] As with so much else, the doctrine asserted that artillery can be used effectively in support of counterguerrilla operations, "if used with imagination and ingenuity."[67] The desirability of coordinating armed helicopters with artillery is referred to but much more attention is paid to the use of aviation assets in lieu of tube artillery. "Helicopters armed with antipersonnel, antimateriel, area and point fire weapons are capable of providing destructive and suppressive fires."[68]

The perceived importance of carefully controlled artillery fire in counterguerrilla actions was well assimilated and widely disseminated throughout the doctrine.[69] As both preplanned and forward observer-directed fire missions were advocated in guerrilla war as well as in conventional conflicts, the incorporation of artillery support of the smallest tactical elements was examined in detail. The resultant blurring of conventional and counterguerrilla operations was justifiable on the basis of the partisan model of guerrilla war growing from the Greek and Korean experiences and facilitated the training of junior officers and maneuver units alike. In short, the conventional war doctrine for artillery deployment was translated on a direct and unchanged basis into the guerrilla war environment which, while marginally justifiable in the setting of a partisan conflict, was completely unjustifiable and of a demonstrably high potential for being counterproductive in an insurgent setting.

It is all too obvious that the army either did not look closely at the Huk Insurrection or the Malayan Emergency. The lesson of these two conflicts was that artillery is more likely to be dangerous to those who employ it, for its effect on the civilian population is to make more insurgent fighters than it kills. Arguably, a closer scrutiny of the Greek Civil War might have caused some rethinking of the proposition that guerrillas are not able to tolerate artillery fire as well as veteran conventional force combatants. In any event, the doctrinal planners were quite sanguine concerning the efficacy of artillery fire:

> Terrain and the disposition and tactics usually limit the effectiveness of artillery. However, the demoralizing effect of artillery fire on guerrillas often justifies its use even though there is little possibility of inflicting material damage.[70]

It might be concluded that the ostensible lessons of the partisan wars had been better assimilated and implemented than either the substantial lessons of those conflicts or the messages of the insurgencies. True, fire kills, but without either the precision or automatic effect assumed by doctrine.

Command, control and communication systems had been proven necessary in the assorted guerrilla conflicts, not merely to direct fire that it might efficiently kill the appropriate parties, nor simply to marshall, move and supply men, but, most importantly, to attempt the coordination of dispersed detachments or units separated by rugged terrain. It was found that the command, control and communications requirements in guerrilla war were actually greater and more critical to success than had been the case in conventional wars. Doctrine placed an emphasis upon the need to overcome the disadvantages of dispersion through the implementation of proper communications procedures using the most sophisticated radio technology. Of course, this does not represent a radical departure from accustomed practice but rather a slight shift in emphasis, an underscoring of the conditions existing in conventional wars. The ROAD concept divisions were already radio heavy as this was necessary to maintain integrity and combat effectiveness on the nuclear battlefield. But the fear concerning loss of command and control channels in the guerrilla environment was so great that specific provisions were made to augment the communications capability already possessed by maneuver and headquarters elements.

> The extreme dispersion of the elements of the battalion will normally require an extensive substitution of radios and an augmentation of other signal equipment.[71]

The helicopter was seen as providing the means to ease command, control and communications problems while, theoretically at least, avoiding the possibility of compromise by hostile intelligence. It had been perceived in previous guerrilla wars that placing the senior tactical commander in visual contact with the battleground was quite desirable. Despite brief, ad hoc attempts, most notably in the Philippines, to employ light liaison aircraft in the role of airborne command posts, the effective use of aircraft for this purpose awaited the development of commodious helicopters and light weight radios. Doctrine for the "flying CP" was developed as early as 1957; its usage had to wait another five years.[72]

The elements of operation, such as mobility, firepower and command and control, having been established in doctrine and implemented in equipment, it is possible to examine the guiding doctrine of operations presumed to be necessary or desirable in the suppression of guerrillas. It is here that the appropriateness and accuracy of the experiential assessments become most clear.

U.S. Army analysts have traditionally divided the problem of combating guerrillas into two complementary parts: locating the hostile forces and effectively bringing them to battle with the desired end result being the destruction as opposed to the mere dispersement of the guerrilla unit. Subordinate or collateral goals have included isolation of the active combatants, the interdiction of supplies and the disruption of lines of communication from external sources of support. The elimination of the guerrilla force in the field would lead to consolidation efforts to fully establish friendly control over the former operational area.

Much ink has been spilled on the problems surrounding the gathering of intelligence upon hostile guerrillas. Typically, genuflections have been offered in the direction of unconventional acquisition methods and sources, the need for every soldier to be a part-time collector, the desirability of personality files and police dossiers, the need for native agents of reliability and initiative. Despite this, the army was fixated at an early date by the Greek Civil War on two specific targets for intelligence: the "supply and command channels between the guerrillas and the sponsoring power" and "the location of guerrilla base camps."[73] It had been found as early as the Greek Civil War that traditional intelligence gathering procedures such as photo reconnaissance, prisoner interrogation and double agents or line crossers were of only marginal utility due to the sporadic flow of men and supplies over lines of communication and the small number of guerrillas using a remote base camp in difficult terrain.[74] Effective location of the guerrilla concentrations, it was determined in the wake of the Chiri mountain campaigns, could be accomplished only through continuous pressure by small units, air strikes and artillery.[75] This approach came to be termed "harassment."

The doctrine for harassment, including the suggested use of chemical and biological munitions, was first published by the Infantry School in a service journal following several years of formulation.[76] This set of ideas, minus the chemical and biological munitions option, was expanded in FM 31-16:

> At the start of combat operations against a guerrilla force, the location and strength of the elements will seldom be known . . . normally, however, an extended program of harassment by the military force is necessary to:
> (1) Locate the guerrilla force
> (2) Inflict casualties
> (3) Gain detailed knowledge of the terrain
> (4) Restrict the freedom of action of the guerrillas
> (5) Force the guerrillas to consolidate or cease operations.[77]

Essentially, the notion was akin to poking about in the dirt until a nest of fire ants is discovered. When the guerrillas, like the fire ants, made their presence known by stinging the offensive foot, its possessor was expected to react immediately with overwhelming force. This gambit of perhaps prolonged provocation followed by guerrilla response, friendly reaction, pursuit and blockage was suitable for uninhabited terrain possessed of only modest cover and concealment and accessible to roadmobile or air-inserted reaction and blocking forces. In short, it was suitable for the situation that spawned it, the barren and sparsely populated hills of Korea.

Harassment was an attractive technique, as it relied on the strengths in the new American tactical elements. It was predicated upon the use of small, dispersed, artillery equipped bases capable of aerial resupply from which aggressive patrols could be mounted on a round-the-clock basis.[78] When these combat bases were coupled with air inserted hunter-killer teams, preplanned harassment and interdiction fire missions and aerial surveillance, it can be seen that counterguerrilla planners were making complete use of the characteristics built in to the new, airmobile divisions.

Once an area containing a significant concentration of guerrillas had been located, it was army doctrine to attempt a set-piece engagement. The general governing provision was that:

> Those irregular forces willing to fight in open battle are isolated to prevent escape and are immediately attacked; those which avoid open battle are forced by a series of police and military actions into areas which permit encirclement. Once surrounded such forces are destroyed by continuous determined attack.[79]

This was expanded for the benefit of tactical elements:

> Once a sizeable guerrilla force has been definitely located, priority of all available combat power is given to offensive operations to elim-inate the enemy. Offensive operations normally require a friendly force much larger than the located guerrilla force. The brigade, battalion, and company may conduct offensive operations or partic-ipate in the conduct of such operations by larger units . . . offensive operations are extremely difficult to execute and, consequently, should be planned in great detail. Troops must be well briefed and rehearsed.[80]

Despite the emphasis placed upon assembling superior forces, planning, briefing, and rehearsing, activities which are quite time-consuming by their very nature, the FM continued immediately to urge that time is of the essence and air-inserted forces a requirement.[81]

The favored combat deployment was encirclement. In selecting this modality, the American planners were drawing on German experiences in Russia, Yugoslavia and Greece, as well as the U.S. efforts in the Greek Civil War and Huk Insurrection. Disregarding totally the comparative absence of success obtaining in any of these venues, regardless of whether the encirclement attempts employed pronged or concentric attact configurations or maneuver elements operating in tandem with a static blocking force, the school solutions elaborated a number of elegant geometric models of approach march and attack. In all, the notion was to isolate and constrict the guerrilla force through a contracting line of encirclement until a "critical mass" was achieved and heavy fire brought to bear destroying, the presumptively, hopelessly trapped and compacted irregulars.[82] As an alternative, it was suggested that pursuing elements act as beaters and drive the guerrillas into a prepared ambush or air and artillery killing zone.[83]

Although it may have been recognized that tactics and techniques of the sort recommended had been less than spectacularly successful, or, certainly, less than decisive when employed by the Germans and by JUSMAPG, it was widely believed that their relative success in Korea, particularly in the Taebaek mountains, showed what dividends these approaches could be expected to pay when carried out by a high mobility, heavy firepower force such as that possessed by the United States. The potential of airmobility, coupled with enhanced command, control and communications capability, combined to convince the theoreticians that evolutions and modes of attack previously too complex to be performed in rough terrain would be possible now. With the command post in the sky and an array of frequency modulated batons, the commander would be able to conduct even the most complicated martial dance in the densest of bush without even the most lonely spear carrier missing a beat. Of course, it would help if the guerrillas were to read the same score.

Americans had a fixation on borders, the notion of an external sponsoring power. The Greek Civil War concern with Soviet bloc borders had constituted a bacillus which had deeply infected the U.S. Army, skewing its view of guerrilla war to emphasize external aid and assistance avenues nourishing and directing the incountry guerrilla forces. All guerrillas, whether of the partisan type or of the insurgent variety, were seen as being of the sponsored partisan stripe. What misappreciated experience teaches an individual or institution to see will be seen, whether the vision is accurate or not. From the earliest days the official view of guerrilla war exhibited this characteristic astigmatism:

> Because self-supporting, spontaneously created guerrilla groups are a rarity, intelligence concerning the supply and command channels between the guerrilla and the sponsoring power is an indispensable factor of sound antiguerrilla plans. [84]

With the Khrushchev pronouncement concerning Moscow's support for "wars of national liberation," the border fixation, already reinforced by the Korean experience, mushroomed, becoming a virtual cornerstone of policy as stated by W.W. Rostow, then Deputy Special Assistant for National Security Affairs, in a speech to the graduating class at the Special Warfare School.

> My view is, then, that we confront in guerrilla warfare in the underdeveloped areas a systematic attempt by the communists to impose a serious disease on those societies attempting the transition to modernization. [85]

The officially sanctioned army translation of this perception was: "The ideological basis of an irregular force frequently is inspired by out-of-country elements who create and sponsor irregular forces as a means of promoting their own cause." [86] After an impressive flurry of discussion in service schools and journals, some of which was edifying, the importance of denying putative outside support to guerrillas was raised from a rather tepid level in previous manuals to a veritable white heat in the 1962 version of *Counterguerrilla Operations.*

> Operations are initiated simultaneously with other counterguerrilla operations to deny guerrilla elements the benefit of "safe havens" across international boundaries and support by an external sponsoring power. These operations require effective measures to secure extensive land border or sea coast areas and to preclude communications and supply operations (to include aerial resupply) between a sponsoring power and the enemy guerrilla forces. [87]

The difficulties of, and requirements for, the effective control of a hostile border, including the use of electronic sensors, air and ground reconnaissance, static security posts and reaction forces, were cited in detail. Two operational concepts which had only minimal basis in experience were discussed: restricted zones and friendly population buffers. The restricted zone was a full precursor of the "electronic fence" concept put forward by Secretary McNamara for use in Vietnam some four years after adoption in army doctrine.

> Under this concept [restricted zone], an area of predetermined width contiguous to the border is declared a restricted area. Appropriate proclamations are issued to the civilian population so all personnel understand that any individual or group encountered in the area will be considered as an element of the enemy force if it cannot be readily identified as a member of a friendly military or paramilitary unit.
>
> In as far as practicable, the restricted zone is cleared of vegetation and other obstacles to good observation over the area. Defoliates and earthmoving equipment may be used for this purpose.
>
> . . .
>
> The restricted Zone is controlled by the use of ground and aerial observers, electronic listening posts and patrols.[88]

The friendly population buffer concept might be best understood as a specialized variant of the British resettlement scheme in Malaya.

> Utilizing this concept, the civilian population in the area of operations is redistributed as necessary to assure that all civilian personnel residing in the vicinity of the border are sympathetic to the friendly force.
>
> . . .
>
> This concept provides:
> (1) A good potential informant net along the border.
> (2) Friendly local civilians for employment as self-defense units to control the border area.
> (3) A lack of potential civilian contacts and "safe houses" for use by the enemy in border crossing activities.[89]

Although proper notice was taken of the enormous manpower requirements necessary for the interdiction of borders and the suggestion was
made that indigenous forces be used for the security detachments, no
assessment was made concerning the inherent porosity of borders regardless of either the aggressiveness of patrolling or the surveillance technology employed. Neither was any attempt made to contemplate flanking
options available to the enemy. More debilitating to the concept of border
control and interdiction was the simple reality, repeatedly ignored, that
in the Philippines, Malaya and to a large extent Korea and Greece,
friendly forces served as the guerrillas' quartermaster corps.

In summary, it can be seen that the major conceptual thrusts were
predicated upon incorrect understandings of historical experience. The
development of army counterguerrilla doctrine arose not from an accurate
appreciation of the nature of guerrilla war nor from the process by which
guerrillas were suppressed, but rather from the capabilities of the forces
developed for the purpose of fighting a mechanized opponent upon the
presumedly nuclear battlefields of Europe. As a result the emphasis of
the counterguerrilla, or less properly, counterinsurgency doctrine was
upon those aspects of heavy firepower, high mobility, particularly airmobility, sophisticated command, control and communications systems
which were contained within the newly developed American formations.
The doctrinal employment of these formations was made more palatable
by the assumption that the guerrilla could be fought with the same tactics
and methods which were used to fight a conventional opponent. Quite
without regard to the historical experience taken as a totality, the assumption was that guerrillas could be encountered and destroyed by using
conventional tactics and heavy firepower in a set-piece battle.

NOTES

1. Karl von Clausewitz, *On War.* Translated by J. J. Graham, 3 vols., (London: Routledge and Kegan Paul 1968), vol. I, Bk. I, Ch. II, p. 26.

2. Ibid., vol. I, Bk. III, Ch. I, p. 173.

3. Department of the Army FM 100-5, *Field Service Regulations: Operations,* (Washington, D.C.: DA 1939), p. 27.

4. FM 100-5, *Field Service Regulations: Operations,* (Washington, D.C.: DA 1944), p. 32.

5. FM 100-5, *Field Service Regulations: Operations,* (Washington, D.C.: DA 1954), p. 6.

6. FM 100-5, *Field Service Regulations: Operations,* (Washington, D.C.: DA 1962), pp. 4–5.

7. Ibid., p. 9.

8. FM 7-10, *Rifle Company, Infantry and Airborne Battle Groups,* (Washington, D.C.: DA 1962), pp. 3–4.

9. Maxwell D. Taylor, *The Uncertain Trumpet,* (New York: Harper 1960), p. 35.

10. Ibid., p. 23.

11. FM 100-5 (1962), p. 4.

12. Hanson W. Baldwin, "Land Forces as an Element of National Power," *Army Combat Forces Journal,* vol. 7 (January 1956), p. 21.

13. Ibid., p. 222.

14. Ibid., p. 207.

15. Gen. Bruce Clark, "The Designing of New Divisions for our Army," *Armor* (May–June 1955), pp. 22–25; Gen. James Gavin, *War and Peace in the Space Age,* (New York: Harper 1958), pp. 137–39.

16. William Murden and Lt. Col. John Yakshe, *Evaluation of Procedures Employed in Tests of the 1956 Field Army (ATFA-1),* (Fort Monroe, Va.: U.S. Army Operations Research Office 1956), p. 9.

17. "Smaller 'Pentomic' Divisions on the Way," *Army-Navy-Air Force Journal,* (29 December 1956), p. 3.

18. Maxwell Taylor, "Safety Lies Forward—Technologically and Tactically," *Army,* vol. 7 (December 1956), p. 21.

19. Marvin Worley, *A Digest of New Developments in Army Weapons, Tactics, Organization and Equipment,* (Harrisburg, Pa.: Military Service Publishing Company 1958), p. a58.

20. FM 7-40, *Infantry and Airborne Battle Groups,* (Washington, D.C.: DA 1960), pp. 4–10.

21. FM 57-35, *Army Transport Aviation-Combat Operations,* (Washington, D.C.: DA 1957).

22. Ibid., p. 68.

23. Taylor, *The Uncertain Trumpet, p. 171.*

24. Special Warfare Board (Lt. Gen. Hamilton Howze, Chair), *Final Report* (HQ USCONARC Fort Monroe, Va.: 28 January 1962), p. 12.

25. FM 100-5 (1962), pp. 127–35.

26. Ibid., p. 127.

27. Ibid.

28. Ibid., p. 130.

29. Ibid., p. 136.

30. Ibid., pp. 137–39.

31. Ibid., p. 139.

32. Ibid., p. 140.

33. Ibid., p. 141.

34. Ibid.

35. Ibid., p. 153.

36. FM 30-5, *Combat Intelligence,* (Washington, D.C.: DA 1960).

37. FM 100-5 (1962), p. 147.

38. Ibid.

39. FM 30-5, *Combat Intelligence,* (Washington, D.C.: DA 1963), p. 65.

40. FM 31-15 *Operations Against Irregular Forces,* (Washington, D.C.: DA 1961), p. 25.

41. FM 31-16 *Counterguerrilla Operations,* (Washington, D.C.: DA 1963), p. 20.

42. Deputy Chief of Staff for Operations and Plans, Office of the Director of Strategic Plans and Policy, Special Warfare Division, *Counterinsurgency Operations: A Handbook for the Suppression of Communist Guerrilla/Terrorist Operations,* (Washington, D.C.: 1962), p. 43.

43. Ibid., p. 39.

44. FM 31-16 (1963), p. 21.

45. FM 7-10, p. 179.

46. Burton Lesh, "Antiguerrilla SOP," *Infantry,* vol. 52 (July–Aug. 1962), p. 31.

47. FM 31-16 (1963), p. 21.

48. Samuel Grier, "Black Pyjama Intelligence," *MCG,* vol. 51 (April 1967), p. 40.

49. FM 100-5 (1962), p. 140.

50. FM 31-16 (1963), pp. 21–22.

51. Ibid., p. 31.

52. Gen. James Gavin, "Cavalry, and I Don't Mean Horses," *Harpers Magazine*, (April 1954), pp. 54–60.

53. Director of Combat Aviation, *1957 Estimate of the Situation*, (Fort Rucker, Ala.: U.S. Army Aviation School, Department of Combat Aviation, 1958).

54. Ibid., p. 11.

55. Army Concept Team in Vietnam, "Airmobile Company in Counterinsurgency Operations" (Saigon: ACTV 1963).

56. FM 31-16 (1963), pp. 31–32.

57. FM 57-35 (1962), passim.

58. FM 7-10 (1962), p. 213.

59. Ibid., p. 214.

60. "Military Operations Against Irregular Forces," *Infantry*, vol. 52 (July–Aug. 1962), p. 45.

61. FM 31-16 (1963), p. 22

62. Ibid.

63. Ibid.

64. FM 100-5 (1962), p. 140.

65. FM 31-16 (1963), p. 63.

66. Ibid., p. 89.

67. Ibid.

68. FM 31-16 (1962), p. 51.

69. FM 6-20-1, *Field Artillery Tactics*, (Washington, D.C.: DA 1962), passim; FM 6-20-2, *Field Artillery Techniques*, (Washington, D.C.: DA 1962), passim; FM 7-20, *Infantry, Airborne Infantry and Mechanized Infantry Battalions*, (Washington, D.C.: DA 1962).

70. FM 31-15 (1961), p. 28.

71. FM 31-16 (1962), p. 116.

72. *1957 Estimate of the Situation*, p. 15; FM 57-35 (1957), passim.

73. "Antiguerrilla Operations," *Officer's Call*, vol. 3 (March 1951), p. 11.

74. "Operations Evaluation: Intelligence," (Athens: JUSMAPG 1949), (mimeo) n.p.

75. *Counterinsurgency Operations*, p. 51.

76. "Considerations in Fighting Irregular Forces," *Infantry*, vol. 52 (July–August 1961), p. 40.

77. FM 31-16 (1963), p. 72.

78. FM 21-50, *Ranger Training and Ranger Operations*, (Washington, D.C.: DA 1962), p. 2.

79. FM 100-5 (1962), p. 142.

80. FM 31-16 (1963), p. 86.

81. Ibid.

82. FM 31-16 (1963), pp. 63–66.

83. Ibid., pp. 67–70.

84. "Antiguerrilla Operations," p. 11.

85. W. W. Rostow, "Guerrilla Warfare in the Underdeveloped Areas," *Department of State Bulletin,* vol. 45 (7 August 1961), p. 237.

86. FM 100-5 (1962), p. 137.

87. FM 31-16 (1962), p. 100.

88. Ibid., pp. 103–4.

89. Ibid., pp. 104–5.

8.

Carving Totems:
At the Top and at the Bottom

Beneath the technologies, techniques and tactics, the reality remains that guerrilla wars are fought by men. The central army shibboleth was that any good infantryman was by definition a good guerrilla fighter. It was recognized that the German practice of using second-class and police formations as the primary opponents of partisans was incorrect. This preliminary opinion had been reinforced effectively in both Greece and Korea, where it was obvious that only top-quality, well equipped and energetically led formations had any measurable success against the guerrillas. The army had also developed in the Greek venue an antipathy toward elite, specially trained commando-type units. Partially, this was a continuation of the historic prejudice against "private armies" widely held in the American Army. But, in large measure, the negative perception was based on demonstrable actuality: the commando units consumed a disproportionate share of logistic support compared to the results achieved; the presence of the commando units served to enervate the morale and will to combat of line units.

The army retained a somewhat ambivalent attitude toward special units in the context of counterinsurgency operations. This was obvious from the existence within the army of the Special Forces whose training for the mission of being unconventional warfare cadres and leaders of friendly guerrillas prepared them for a counterguerrilla role under the theory of setting a poacher to catch a poacher. But more substantially, the army had come to recognize the viability of special penetration and patrol units operating in the "pseudo-gang" role. In this recognition the army had not only come to the realization that the Special Forces had the capability to lead and train such teams of indigenous personnel, it had also properly appreciated the experiences of such units in both the Huk Insurrection and the Malayan Emergency. High-echelon guidance provided that:

> Small special units may be organized, equipped and trained to combat irregular forces using the tactics and techniques of the latter. Special units can be very effective in maintaining the initiative with a minimum number of troops, and often they are more effective than standard troop units.[1]

Not all echelons shared this enthusiasm for special units, as was indicated in the *Counterguerrilla Operations* manual, where there is no specific reference to such detachments operating in cooperation with or in support of conventional battalions and their subordinate tactical elements, save under the rubric "provisional long range reconnaissance patrols."[2] Even this mild note was deleted by the following year.

The Special Forces are of interest not simply because their use in the counterguerrilla war represented a critical option in the doctrine. More importantly, an examination of the doctrine developed for their use in the role of offensive guerrilla operations deep behind the enemy lines in Europe assists in demonstrating the mirror-imaging concerning guerrilla warfare which served to reinforce skewed perceptions of past experience.

The initial Special Forces Group, the 10th SFG, was activated at Fort Bragg in June 1952. The original intent was for the members of this unit to follow in the path of the Jedburgs and Operational Groups of the World War II Office of Strategic Services (OSS). That is, Special Forces personnel were to be highly trained as deep penetration specialists equally adept at reconnaissance, sabotage and the training of indigenous guerrilla bands. The graduates of the Special Forces' Special Warfare Training Center would be dispatched to wreak appropriate havoc behind enemy lines as small independent teams composed almost exclusively of senior noncommissioned officers.

The absence of either war or active implementation of the "roll-back" policy in Eastern Europe precluded the originally envisioned mission. However, a useful alternative, the training of indigenous forces faced by a guerrilla threat, did materialize. In response to the insurgent challenge perceived to be facing the South Vietnamese government of Ngo Dinh

Diem, a Special Forces training mission was authorized as a part of the ongoing U.S. Military Assistance Advisory Group. On 24 June 1957 the 1st SFG was activated on Okinawa and commenced its training assignment at Nha Trang, South Vietnam.

These trainers, like the Special Forces generally, had been developed first and foremost as offensively oriented guerrillas, with all the technical and leadership skills that such implies. The doctrine of guerrilla war and special operations to which they were extensively exposed represents the best official summary view of the subject. American doctrine drew its primary inspiration from the various wartime European resistance movements and their external sponsors, the British Special Operations Executive (SOE) and the American OSS. This was appropriate, as through the 1950s the only employment envisioned for U.S.-sponsored guerrillas was in Europe as partisan auxiliaries in a conventional conflict between NATO and the Warsaw Pact. The idea of guerrilla employment as part of an ostensibly or actually indigenous insurgent movement eluded military planners. This focus did not change, even as the potentialities for insurgency in underdeveloped former colonies became more evident in the closing years of the Eisenhower Administration, when guerrilla war was defined as:

> . . . that part of unconventional warfare which is conducted by relatively small groups employing offensive tactics to reduce enemy combat effectiveness, industrial capacity and morale. Guerrilla operations are normally conducted in enemy controlled territory by units organized on a military basis.[3]

One, if not the, major activity of guerrilla forces was seen as the destruction of,

> enemy lines of communication . . . However, the increasing dependence of modern war machines on industrial support makes industrial and economic targets increasingly profitable objectives for guerrilla forces.[4]

Enhancing the attractiveness of guerrilla forces as partisan adjuncts were a number of improvements in weapons and materiel:

Technical advances in signal communications, advanced techniques of supply by air and sea and the introduction of specially designed aircraft, such as helicopters . . . make support of guerrilla operations easier for modern armies. The introduction of new and powerful light weight weapons also increased guerrilla warfare potential.[5]

Three years later, with the increasing awareness of insurgencies and "wars of national liberation" as well as the developing perception that the strategic *Schwerpunkt* of East-West confrontations had shifted from the European heartland to the world's periphery, important changes in emphasis entered the army's view of guerrilla war. It was now understood as:

Unconventional warfare consists of interrelated fields, guerrilla warfare, evasion and escape, and subversion against hostile states (resistance). Unconventional warfare operations are conducted in enemy or enemy controlled territory by predominantly indigenous personnel usually supported and directed in varying degrees by an external source.[6]

This perspective, a point of view appropriate to the initiating rather than the responding actor, was echoed by the overall operational doctrinal view.

Unconventional warfare is conducted by field organizations trained, equipped and directed to operate against sources of enemy strength. It is closely integrated with economic, political and psychological warfare. It differs from other military operations because it involves close working relationships with the local population of enemy controlled areas.[7]

It was predictable that the doctrinal view for the respondent to guerrilla war would be a mirror image.[8] This was translated to the tactical level in an expanded but unchanged form:

A guerrilla force is the armed manifestation of a resistance move-

ment against the local government or an occupying power by a portion of the population of the area.

. . .

The factors which inspire a resistance movement may arise inter-
nally in an area or country, or they may be created or assisted by
"out-of-country" elements which desire to sponsor the movement for
their own cause. Often another country will lend support to a local
resistance movement and attempt to control the movement to further
its own aims.[9]

Whether viewed from the perspective of the initiator or the respondent,
the view of guerrilla war is identical and focuses upon the external sponsor.
The army did not believe that the organic and unsponsored insurgency
was a viable possibility.[10] Even if one started, it would either be crushed
in infancy by the security forces or be captured by an external sponsor.

The Special Forces were established and maintained to operate as
America's guerrillas on the offensive.

U.S. Army Special Forces are highly trained troops who conduct
military operations far behind enemy lines. They foster and organize
indigenous resistance potential in enemy territory in order to develop and exploit guerrilla forces.

The primary mission of Special Forces is to develop, organize,
equip, train, support and control guerrilla forces and to conduct
guerrilla warfare in support of conventional operations.[11]

With the advent of high-level concern over insurgent activities supported
by Moscow or Peking, the definition of the Special Forces, their mission
and operational concepts were altered to include activities other than partisan warfare.

The Airborne Special Forces Group is the United States Army's
organization trained to conduct guerrilla warfare and related unconventional warfare activities. Special Forces is a strategic force employed under the direction of a theater commander. Deployment of
Special Forces units allows the theater commander to conduct offensive operations deep in enemy territory.

Mission. The mission of Special Forces is to develop, organize, train, equip and direct indigenous forces in the conduct of guerrilla warfare. Special Forces may also advise, train and assist indigenous forces in counterinsurgency operations.[12]

The poacher was now the game warden. In appearance this was an extremely rapid evolution. In 1959, in the course of a lengthy article in a service journal, an author, himself an officer in the 10th SFG, made absolutely no reference to any present or projected counterinsurgency mission.[13] Even as late as June 1961, in an article obviously intended to further Special Forces recruiting, no mention was made of any counterinsurgency mission.[14] The actuality was that, while the evolution was rapid, it was not dramatic; neither was it unexpected.

The Nha Trang experiment had proven successful. The team from the 1st SFG had turned out reasonably competent Vietnamese commandos in remarkable quantity. Given that the Special Forces contained a large number of highly skilled, well-motivated and articulate individuals, it is not surprising that its leadership actively sought institutional employmnet on the basis of this training accomplishment. Given the strength of the argument that the best answer to a tank is another tank and the most effective riposte to incoming artillery is counterbattery fire, it is scarcely remarkable that this line of reasoning was expanded to include the contention that guerrillas were best neutralized by other guerrillas. Underutilized resources married an unaddressed threat, and guerrillas became counterguerrillas without even the ignominy of a hyphen.

But these tame guerrillas were Americans trained to fight in Europe with a very great dependence upon high-quality communications, logistics and weapons technologies. All rejoinders to the effect that the Special Forces were trained and indoctrinated to reduce this dependence in no way reduced the reality that their doctrine and training were bent toward an industrial war in an industrial theater. Simply because a unit was capable of effectively attacking a modern, Soviet bloc army and its supporting infrastructure by guerrilla means did not imply automatically that the same unit could furnish effective defense, either active or passive, against guerrillas operating under a different set of assumptions. The unwarranted drawing of this inference constituted a major and egregious misapprehension. Guerrillas who could not fathom the necessity of a forty-page "Catalogue Supply System" covering literally hundreds of prepackaged units incorporating thousands of individual items, let alone rely upon the sophisticated communications and supply capability necessary to deliver such items to men in the field, simply were not playing by the same rules as the Special Forces.[15]

Conditioned by their doctrine, which was predicated in the main upon World War II experience, American guerrillas expected to be interlopers, strangers in a strange land, unable to submerge in a population dominated by a hostile power. They would need to be inserted, supplied, communicated with, controlled and finally extracted by an external organization. An elaborate headquarters unit, the Joint Unconventional Warfare Task Force (JUWTF) under the theater commander was designed specifically for the task of operating in support of Special Forces field teams. JUWTF procured necessary materiel, maintained liaison and generally acted to facilitate Special Forces activities.[16] Outside of JUWTF lengthy and elaborate component service logistic apparatuses were established.[17] Likewise, specialized transportation, medical evacuation and supply delivery mechanisms were delineated; elaborate provisions for automatic and demand resupply were necessary and were planned.[18] Intelligence was processed and transmitted by JUWTF or the Special Forces Operations Base, with field responsibilities being limited to combat information collection.[19] This degree of centralization, impossible in traditional partisan or insurgent groups from the Balkans to the Philippines, required a comprehensive communications system located in friendly territory. It also required safe locations within the operational zone.[20] It is obvious that American guerrillas required secure bases within the denied area for purely military and operational needs, rather than political dictates as exemplified by Huklandia or "Liberated Greece" in the Vitsi. The American guerrilla was all too much like the astronaut, who, whether in his capsule or walking in his moon suit, was dependent completely upon a complicated life support system for viability and external command, control and intelligence for even limited operational effectiveness.

A synergy can be seen at work. The American guerrilla saw himself as prototypic. This self-perception and its inevitable mirror-imaging served improperly to validate aspects of counterinsurgent war which were either not particularly crucial or frankly absent in the various guerrilla wars, but which became American fixations: external support, lines of communication and supply and insurgent base areas. Magnifying this military misperception in a darkling mirror was the American political shibboleth that insurgency could not be organic. Again W. W. Rostow serves as spokesman:

> The truth is that guerrilla warfare mounted from external bases— with rights of sanctuary—is a terrible burden for any government to carry. . . .
>
> . . .
>
> A guerrilla war mounted from outside a transitional nation is a crude act of international vandalism.
>
> . . .
>
> The sending of men and arms across international boundaries and the direction of guerrilla war from outside a sovereign nation is aggression. . . .[21]

It is with a certain elegance of misplaced logic that American doctrinal fixations caused the United States to prepare, particularly in the employment of the Special Forces, poachers as gamekeepers, to fight itself rather than an actual opponent.

American doctrine did not simply see the guerrilla as an alienated stranger. At the command echelon, doctrine took notice of the political nature of guerrilla war, mentioning that it was inspired or assisted by the presence of social or economic dissatisfaction and exacerbated by such factors as low standards of living, crop failures and the like.[22] Along with military mechanisms of coercion the following was recommended:

> Irregular forces accompany their operations with extensive propaganda designed to gain support of the local population. As a countermeasure, the local government being supported by the U.S. as well as U.S. forces must present a concrete program which will win popular support. Such action includes a maximum exploitation of civil affairs and psychological warfare capabilities.[23]

To facilitate the development of such a program the doctrinal guidance continued:

> . . . political considerations will materially influence military operations. A political advisor is normally provided the military com-

mander and the campaign is planned and conducted in close coordination with the Department of State, Department of Defense and other U.S. or allied agencies.[24]

Command guidance with respect to the subject of civil affairs showed a less sure hand but apparently assumed that the requisite degree of detail would be forthcoming from those "other U.S. or allied agencies" mentioned.[25]

Doctrine for tactical elements was of greater specificity and, in the areas dealing with civil affairs, exhibited some tentative gropings after the EDCOR model, at least in terms of military capabilities being directly employed for nation building activities. The basic doctrine concerning propaganda was obviously derivative and quite unremarkable.[26] It is interesting that the attention paid to the importance of propaganda was much more pronounced in the final manuscript draft of FM 31-16 than in the final published version. The draft states:

> The vast majority of the population in any given target area is initially non-responsive and apathetic to either the aims of the indigenous government and what it stands for or the advocates of the revolution. The active advocates of revolutionary war constitute a very small but capable and active segment of the population. It is estimated that less than 10% of the total of the population has actively participated in or supported the initial efforts of the movement. Because of this, the effort to influence the balance of the population is important.[27]

In the published version this eminently sensible and experience-based observation was stricken to be replaced with vague generalities about how guerrilla forces depended upon propaganda comprised of vicious half-truths and lies to maintain a hold on the population. The helpful tip is given that a surrendered guerrilla is just as neutralized as a dead guerrilla and, therefore, psychological warfare operations have a useful role in the greater scheme of things.[28]

Such a brief treatment was not all that unusual, as psychological operations were not a primary or even a normal duty for tactical elements. Psychological warfare units were to be attached temporarily to maneuver battalions and their controlling brigades on an ad hoc basis.[29] Doctrine

for psychological warfare units was unusual in that it frankly stated that
the counterinsurgency mission had a potential for their employment lacking in conventional conflicts.[30]

The psychological warriors emphasized an approach which had the un-
wieldy sobriquet of "National Positive Action Program." Following the lead
of Linebarger and his associates, the thrust of this schemata was the
effective presentation to the target population of the beneficial results of
the government's security and infrastructure improvement programs.

> In an effort to eliminate the causes of insurgent activities, coun-
> terinsurgent operations seek to support a local, national positive
> action program which consists of military, political, social, economic
> and psychological actions undertaken by the local governments to
> modify the causes motivating the resistance movement. Counterin-
> surgency operations embracing military action (both local and for-
> eign), economic programs, political actions, etc., is the positive
> action program.[31]

The context in which this programmatic goal was to be achieved would
have been familiar to anyone having a nodding acquaintance with the Huk
Insurrection and the Philippine government's response of nation building
projects. A central theme was:

> No tactical counterinsurgency can be effective without concurrent
> major nation building programs. The causes for unrest must be in
> the process of reduction for the successful counterinsurgency oper-
> ation. This implies extensive political, economic and social re-
> form. . . . Counterinsurgency operations of the American military
> cannot be considered as separate from political aspects.[32]

The origin of this assertion is found in the service journal writings of the
psychological warriors with Philippine and Korean experience, such as
Colonel Beebe:

> Adequate incentives to support the government and oppose the
> guerrillas must be provided. Propaganda should be addressed to the
> local population and deal with local problems. The people must be
> reassured that it is in their interest to support the government.[33]

With this emphasis upon nation building as the necessary precondition for effective psychological operations on other than the narrowest tactical level, doctrine firmly tied propaganda to the least well understood of all military missions: civic affairs, or as it became known, civic action—a much more vigorous and dynamic term. As has been indicated, concepts of civic action were somewhat vague in command echelon doctrine. Fortunately Col. Robert Slover, Deputy Chief, Plans and Doctrine Division, Office of the Chief of Civil Affairs, had a much more definite notion of the nature of civic action as when he addressed a March 1962 symposium on the army's role in limited war: "I submit to you . . . that civic action is an important and valuable way of gaining the necessary control of the population."[34] He noted the following definition of civic action as approved by the National Security Council in its directives:

> By civic action we mean using indigenous forces on projects useful to the populace at all levels in such fields as training, public works, agriculture, transportation, health, sanitation and others helpful to economic development.[35]

While he asserted that civic action is both a preventive and cure for insurgency, in that it provided a viable means for remobilizing support to the government, he cautioned that "civic action must not be looked upon as a substitute for military power and combat capable forces."[36] However, he argued expansively that civic action comprises "any action which makes the soldier a brother of the people, as well as their protector."[37] It is not at all surprising, in light of Colonel Slover's attitude toward the ability of civic action to establish true bonds between citizen and soldier, that he specifically cited civic action in the Philippines as having been a "dramatic success."[38]

At this time the army was rather new at civic action activities, having been authorized only as recently as 1961 by Section 505 (b) of the Agency for International Development Act to employ its forces by request in underdeveloped countries for the purpose of constructing public works and similar infrastructure improvements oriented toward economic development. In September 1961 Secretary of Defense McNamara broadened the army's civic action bailiwick by making it the executive agent for all military services in the civic action sphere. Quickly the army moved to assist a number of governments, including Guatemala, South Vietnam, Laos, Iran and Ecuador, to establish indigenous civic action programs under military sponsorship.

There was, perforce, a lack of field experience which Colonel Slover acknowledged.[39] Despite this perceived lack of hands-on experience, doctrinal statements were speedily developed for tactical elements. Flowing from the positive, direct experiences of the Philippines, the doctrine incorporated several major goals: the improvement of the morale of indigenous forces, enhancing civil-military relationships within the country and encouraging the population to identify its self-interest with the national government. Traditionally, army civil affairs had been the provenance of assorted, specifically designated and organized support units, but with the advent of the new civic action orientation, all tactical elements to company level were to consider civic action as an adjunct mission.[40]

> Civic action is any action performed by military forces of a country, utilizing military manpower and skills and cooperation with civil authorities, agencies or groups and which is intended to better the economic or social status of the civilians of the area. Civic action is often a major contributing factor in the development of favorable public opinion and in the defeat of the guerrilla force. All commanders are encouraged to participate in local civic projects when such participation does not distract from the accomplishment of the primary mission. . . .[41]

The objectives for civic action programs to counter the revolutionary resistance movement were identified as:

(1) Stabilization of social and political institutions.
(2) Development of a balanced economy.
(3) Provision of individual and group legal equality.
(4) Establishment of an acceptable educational program.[42]

Unfortunately, these well thought-out considerations of civic action and the importance of the peaceful employment of military manpower and capabilities in the defeat of insurgents were deleted in a later version of the same manual.[43]

The backward step indicated by the more barechested approach taken in the final version of *Counterguerrilla Operations* was not universally applied as indicated by the specific recommendations contained in field manuals for tactical elements. Most common among the recommended actions were:

(1) Use of individuals with needed skills such as building trades, cooks and bakers or medics.
(2) Provision of troop labor in construction projects.
(3) Provision of safe water supplies.
(4) Construction of roads and public works.
(5) Furnishing medical assistance.
(6) Loaning military construction equipment.
(7) Escorting critical civilian convoys.
(8) Sponsoring youth and civic organizations.
(9) Provision of emergency relief and disaster relief.
(10) Participation in civil ceremonies.[44]

Unfortunately some realities were ignored. In the enthusiasm generated for civic action by reports such as that of the Presidential Task Force known as the Draper Committee, which noted in a discussion, or perhaps an extollment, of the U.S. civic action programs in Korea that, *inter alia*, U.S. forces had completed 3,780 projects for a direct cost of less than 21 million dollars by 1 January 1959 and that:

> The accomplishments of the program have done much to demonstrate to the world that while communism destroys and exploits, the United States reconstructs and assists those who need aid. . . .
>
> . . .
>
> It exemplified the possibilities of using military resources to assist in social-economic fields without detriment to the military mission. The same approach would seem to have application in all underdeveloped areas.[45]

In this rosy view, as in others of similar hue, the critical distinction between Korean civic action or dramatic activities such as flood relief in Germany or refugee resettlement in immediate postpartition Vietnam, and civic action as an integral part of an active counterinsurgent campaign, was completely overlooked. The Korean civic action programs alluded to occurred either in the more secure rear areas of a conventional war, or after the termination of active hostilities as a species of postwar relief; in Germany and Japan the civic action programs were either straight postwar relief or humanitarian aid in a peaceful environment; in Indochina these activities were simultaneously humanitarian, short-lived and divorced from support for the Bao Dai regime. None of these projects and programs, praiseworthy as any and all may have been, should have been considered properly as paradigmatic for counterinsurgency applications.

The very magnitude of the Filipino success, the impressive statistics of the American activities in posttruce Korea, and an understandable desire to seize the initiative in true American fashion insensibly conspired to assure that doctrine did not emphasize, as had the various external analyses of the civic action experiences, the unique nature of the Huk Insurrection. Consultants, such as Alfred Hausrath, underscored the indigenous nature of the EDCOR scheme as well as kindred, smaller projects, but policy makers and doctrine formulators in search of the new approach or the quick fix, the anodyne for unrest which could be expeditiously administered and not interfere with the main business of an army, did not.[46] The primary business of an army is to fight. Given that civic action at the tactical level was assigned as an added duty and time or manpower committed to it would be time and energy unavailable for the accomplishment of the major mission, it is not surprising that the commitment to civic action was more apparent than substantial. Confusion as to the nature of effective civic action assured that the superficially showy would prevail.

Army doctrine regarding counterguerrilla operations saw an identity between partisan war and insurgency and, projecting upon others the American guerrilla's need for massive external support upon other guerrillas, emphasized the importance of sealing borders and engaging hostile bases with large formations of highly mobile troops drawn from the firepower-heavy general purpose forces embodied in the ROAD concept. Not only were unconventional operations, psychological operations and civic affairs subordinated to traditional, aggressive military tactics, doctrine on civic actions was vague and contradictory. There was confusion as to the actual role of civic action: was it to be of a major, organized nature operated as a portion of the military responsibility for counterinsurgency or was it to be an ad hoc, extra duty assignment of tactical units? Also left unsettled was the nature of civic action: preemptive social reform or act of individual GI charity?

NOTES

1. FM 100-5, *Field Service Regulations: Operations,* (Washington, D.C.: DA 1962), p. 143.

2. FM 31-16, *Counterguerrilla Operations,* (Washington, D.C.: DA 1962), p. 133.

3. FM 31-21, *Guerrilla Warfare and Special Forces Operations,* (Washington, D.C.: DA 1958), pp. 3–4.

4. Ibid., p. 4.

5. Ibid.

6. FM 31-21, *Guerrilla Warfare and Special Forces Operations,* (Washington, D.C.: DA 1961), p. 3.

7. FM 100-5 (1962), p. 127.

8. Ibid., p. 137.

9. FM 31-16 (1963), p. 3.

10. Ibid.

11. FM 31-21 (1958), p. 16.

12. FM 31-21 (1961), p. 18.

13. Roger Pezzelle, "Special Forces," *Infantry,* vol. 45 (June 1959), pp. 13–19.

14. Charles Dodson, "Special Forces," *Army,* vol. 12 (June 1961), pp. 44–52.

15. FM 31-21 (1961), pp. 190–233.

16. Ibid., pp. 15–16.

17. Ibid., p. 46.

18. Ibid., pp. 51–52.

19. Ibid., pp. 54–57.

20. Ibid., pp. 58–62.

21. W. W. Rostow, "Guerrilla War in Underdeveloped Areas," *Department of State Bulletin,* vol. 45 (August 1961), p. 236.

22. FM 100-5 (1962), p. 137.

23. Ibid., p. 140.

24. Ibid., p. 144.

25. Ibid., p. 152.

26. Deputy Chief of Staff for Operations and Plans, Office of the Director of Strategic Plans and Policy, Special Warfare Division, *Counterinsurgency Oper-*

ations: A Handbook for the Suppression of Communist Guerrilla/Terrorist Operations, (Washington, D.C.: 1962), p. 64ff.

27. FM 31-16 (1962), p. 33.

28. FM 31-16 (1963), pp. 14, 61, 63.

29. See Table of Organization and Equipment (TOE), 33-500E, 33-600E and 41-500E in their 1961 editions.

30. FM 33-5, *Psychological Operations*, (Washington, D.C.: DA 1962), pp. 122–23.

31. Ibid., p. 123.

32. Ibid., p. 124.

33. John Beebe, "Beating the Guerrilla," *MR*, vol. 35 (December 1955), p. 18.

34. Robert H. Slover, "Civic Actions in Developing Nations" in *Proceedings of the Symposium: The US Army's Limited War Mission and Social Science Research*, 26–28 March 1962, (Washington, D.C.: American University [SORO] 1962), p. 71.

35. Ibid.

36. Ibid., p. 72.

37. Ibid.

38. Ibid., p. 73.

39. Ibid., p. 78.

40. FM 41-10, *Civil Affairs Operations*, (Washington, D.C.: DA 1962), p. 4.

41. FM 31-16 (1962), p. 34.

42. Ibid.

43. FM 31-16 (1963), p. 110.

44. FM 7-20, *Infantry, Airborne Infantry and Mechanized Infantry Battalions*, (Washington, D.C.: DA 1962), p. 46; FM 7-30, *Infantry, Airborne and Mechanized Division Brigades*, (Washington, D.C.: DA 1962), p. 31; FM 61-100, *The Division*, (Washington, D.C.: DA 1961), p. 64.

45. The President's Committee to Study the U.S. Military Assistance Program (Draper Committee), *Annexes*, supplement to *The Final Composite Report to the President's Committee*, vol. II, (Washington, D.C.: USGPO 1959), pp. 132–33.

46. Alfred Hausrath, *Civil Affairs in the Cold War*, (Bethesda, Md.: Johns Hopkins University, Operations Research Office 1961), pp. 50–51.

9.
Tribal Memories

During the decade following the end of the Korean conflict in 1953, the United States Marine Corps underwent numerous, far reaching changes in personnel structure, organizational patterns, equipment and aspects of doctrine. But in two important ways it did not change at all: the corps remained an expeditionary light infantry force; because of its small size, the tradition of informal transmission of past experiences, "passing the word" about how it was done "in the Old Corps" remained intact. Thus the marines weathered the storms of the New Look period modified but not transformed.

The marines were spared the worst effects of the budget reductions of the New Look period thanks to the abilities of General Lemuel Shepherd, the first Marine Commandant to meet with the Joint Chiefs of Staff. His relations with JCS Chairman Admiral Arthur Radford, as well as Chiefs of Naval Operations Robert Carney and Arleigh Burke, meshed well with the marines' formidable congressional liaison capability to assure that the corps would be fairly treated within the Administration and on the Hill in matters of interservice relations, missions and budget.

Despite some reductions in its budget, the corps proceeded with the development of an important new concept in amphibious operations, that of vertical envelopment. The doctrinal formulations in this area served to insulate the marines from the mania for nuclear combat which swept the army. The Advanced Research Group appointed by General Shepherd developed plans to reorganize the marine combat division so that it might be lifted ashore and supported in combat by helicopters.

Despite some opposition from marine fixed wing pilots who saw the concept as needless competition for funds and pilots, it was approved by

General Shepherd and CNO Burke in 1955, with the amendation that future navy-marine doctrine provide for the helicopter lift not only of the ground troops but the support structure of the Marine Air Wings as well.[1] Superficially, this drive to airmobility paralleled that occurring in the Pentomic reorganization and was often so interpreted by army observers. However, the marines were much less interested in the possibilities of fighting in a limited nuclear war than they were in achieving the goal of a heliborne assault capability without undue resistance from other services.

In part prompted by the ongoing personnel and organizational turmoil and in part by the reduction a drastic navy ordered in heavy lift helicopters, the corps undertook a thorough review of its doctrine and organization with the creation of a panel, called after its chairman, the Hogaboom Board. The Board's conclusions were at great variance with conventional wisdom as they frankly doubted that the Corps would ever fight the Warsaw Pact on the nuclear battlefields of Europe. Instead, the Board concluded that the most likely employment of the corps would be in the combat of Soviet proxies along the world's periphery, particularly in Southeast Asia.[2] Although finding the basic amphibious assault doctrine adequate, the Board concluded that marine divisions should be transportable over strategic distances by air and that the assault echelons should be completely capable of helicopter based tactical mobility.

Obviously, significant organizational changes would need to be effected if combat efficiency was to be maintained while meeting the weight and volume constraints imposed by the considerations of strategic and tactical airmobility. Infantry regiments and battalions lost their heavy weapons and organic supply and maintenance capabilities. Battalions received a fourth rifle company in lieu of the weapons company. Artillery regiments were altered so that individual batteries, separated from their parent battalions, were capable of acting independently in cooperation with an infantry battalion. Heavy artillery was shifted to a Force level artillery group which would be deployed only for protracted operations. Similarly tank battalions were relegated to Force level. A significant addition to the tactical echelons was the expansion of the reconnaissance company to battalion size in recognition of the greater difficulties confronted in intelligence collection and target acquisition in counterguerrilla operations in difficult terrain.[3] These recommendations were endorsed by the Commandant in 1957, becoming the foundation of the "M" series of tables of organization and equipment, which were the basis of Fleet Marine Force (FMF) organization and doctrine for a period of more than twenty years.

In the early 1960s the Corps, under the command of David Shoup and his Chief of Staff (and successor) Wallace Greene, implemented the Hogaboom reforms, facilitated by the emphasis placed upon the strategic doctrine of flexible response as well as the McNamara concept of budgeting which was predicated upon mission rather than service. The basic tactical unit by this time was the manpower-heavy but firepower-light Marine Expeditionary (later Amphibious) Unit (MEU/MAU). Grouped on the basis of mission requirements into Brigades and Forces, these reinforced Battalion Landing Teams (BLT) were augmented and supported by air, artillery and other Force level assets to provide a unique mixture of rapid response and capability for sustained action through seaborne support far surpassing that of army airborne units.

The capability of the corps to project power in support of diplomatic policy had been firmly impressed upon both the marines and their political masters by the landing in Lebanon. Here, although caught unaware by the order to land on 15 July 1958, the 6th Fleet marine units were able to put a MEU ashore immediately and have a total of 6,000 marines ashore within four days. Although no combat was necessary, the rapidity of the response and the capability to remain ashore for 102 days with only over the beach resupply impressed all observers and convinced the corps that the doctrine and reorganization alike were sound.[4]

With the exception of Major General Victor ("Brute") Krulak, who was the Special Assistant on Counterinsurgency to the JCS, the Marine Corps leadership was less than enthusiastic about incorporating antiguerrilla operations into the new body of doctrine. In part this was the result of a natural reluctance to direct energy away from further preparation for the marines' major mission of forcible entry on hostile shores; in part it was the consequence of a belief that the corps had been competent in counterinsurgency for years and had no need to join the army in embracing a New Frontier fad. Commandant Shoup observed:

> The Marine Corps has long recognized that fighting guerrillas is an inherent part of landing force operations. Counterguerrilla war-

fare is essentially one of small units and we have traditionally emphasized individual leadership and small unit operations.

. . .

I am convinced that [Marine Corps] training properly equips our tactical units to combat rabble, insurgents, guerrillas. . . .[5]

Despite this ringing example of the Marine Corps "can do" spirit, the marines did go through the motions and upgraded counterinsurgency instruction and training in the FMF. However, little attention was paid to the modern subtleties of counterinsurgency, such as population control, psychological warfare and civic action. The reason for this is not hard to find. The prevailing doctrine in 1962 was a strange pastiche of old experience, new technology and borrowings from army doctrine. This strange stew was a giant step down from the *Small Wars Manual* of 1940, which was an excellent distillation of the experience of the "Banana Wars" in all their contradictions and frustrations.[6]

It should not be inferred that the marines were totally unaware of the new developments in guerrilla war and insurgency which had occurred. They demonstrated familiarity with the modern interpretative fashion:

A condition resulting from a revolt or insurrection against a constituted government which falls short of civil war. In the current context, subversive insurgency is primarily communist inspired, supported or exploited.[7]

The residual influence of the *Small Wars Manual* continued to give the overall marine understanding of the nature of guerrilla and insurgent warfare a different coloration from that held by the army or the simple model of external sponsorship seen in the preceding passage.

Reinforcing the continuation of doctrine from Nicaragua to Vietnam was the tribal nature of the Corps. It is worth recalling that senior marines, such as Shoup and Wallace, had been commissioned in the early 1930s and thus had been aware of the exploits of their contemporaries in Haiti and Nicaragua. Others, such as Lewis Walt, who as Commander of III MAF (Marine Amphibious Force), was to be responsible for authorizing and facilitating such dramatic and effective programs as GOLDEN FLEECE, COUNTY FAIR, STINGRAY, and, above all else, the Combined Action Platoons, had been a young officer candidate under the dynamic and aggressive former captain of the renowned Company M, Lewis Puller, in 1936. There can be no doubt that the young cadet was affected by the personality and experiences of jungle fighter Puller.

> Puller was my company commander and to me was the epitome of what Marine Corps training should do. . . . He told us tales about fighting in Haiti and Nicaragua, of his patrols living off the land, and fighting natives—all his experiences, not just guff. Every tale had some point.[8]

The *Small Wars Manual* demonstrated an insight into the nature and character of insurgency which well justified the 1962 suggestion that it be reissued as the primary doctrinal guidance for the Corps.[9]

> The difficulty is sometimes of an economical, political, or social nature and not a military problem in origin. In one recent campaign the situation was an internal political problem . . . but had developed to such a degree . . . it had outgrown the local means of control.
>
> . . .
>
> The application of purely military measures may not by itself restore peace and orderly government because the fundamental causes of the condition are economical, political or social.[10]

Although a cynic might look askance at the marine model as being "white man's burden"-oriented, it remains an acute distillation of experience which was far in advance of the doctrine of other services. Fortunately, this set of descriptive insights was not removed from the 1962 manual, although it was attenuated. In the chapter concerned with troop indoctrination and training the manual stated:

> Furthermore, it must be understood that the basic causes of the situation may stem from a variety of political, social, economic or religious problems. The application of purely military measures alone may not be sufficient to achieve the purpose of the operation; however, the efficiency of military operations can be greatly increased when the troops understand the total problem.[11]

It is significant that the authors of the *Small Wars Manual* placed an emphasis upon understanding the psychological and morale components of the insurgent combatants and the counterinsurgent troops alike. It was an explicit marine belief that a sound knowledge of these factors would allow a more efficacious employment of traditional military elements. The authors insisted, for example:

> The aim [in small wars] is not to develop a belligerent spirit in our men but rather one of caution and steadiness. Instead of employing force, one strives to accomplish the purpose by diplomacy. A Force Commander who gains his objective in a small war without firing a shot has attained far greater success than one who has resorted to use of arms.
>
> . . .
>
> The motive in small wars is not material destruction. It is usually a project dealing with the social, economic and political development of a people. . . . That implies a serious study of the people, their racial, political, religious and mental development.[12]

In examining the origins and dynamics of insurgency, the marine theoreticians exhibited a pronounced proclivity toward economic determinism as an explanatory tool. They took note of the intrinsic conservatism of peasants and their ability to accept and absorb the ill-flavored fruits of misgovernment which served to place automatic limits on the size and rate of growth of the insurgent movement. They commented perceptively on the interaction between the alienated poor and charismatic revolutionary leaders with the result that a definite elan could and, typically did, develop within the guerrillas until they became "capable of heroism to the extent of giving their lives unhesitatingly in support of their beliefs."[13] Implicit in this discussion was the experience so common in the Banana Wars where leadership neutralization equaled neutralization of the entire insurgent group. By 1962 it was no longer considered good form to say favorable things about guerrillas, nor were discussions of economic determinism appropriate in field manuals.[14]

The marines in 1940 and again in 1962 underscored a point which was absent in army doctrine: relations between the field force and the U.S. State Department and other American governmental agencies as well as the host government. Considered in this category were questions of liaison, command and control, relations with host country law enforcement agencies, and the press; factors which go a long way either to assist or fatally hinder the conduct of the military mission. The *Small Wars Manual* carefully elucidated the necessity for "earnest" cooperation between marine units and the U.S. Embassy in the host country, noting that ". . . diplomacy does not relax its grip on the situation . . ." and the "underlying reason for this condition is to keep the war 'small,' to confine it within a strictly limited scope, and to deprive it . . . of the more outstanding aspects of 'war.'"[15] The original thrust of marine doctrine was the subordination of military to diplomatic concerns; by 1962, there had been a significant shift in this position to the view that the American diplomatic mission "does not command US military forces operating in the country."[16]

In its treatment of military relations with the host country's government and population the doctrine set forth in the *Small Wars Manual* was oriented toward the reduction of frictions which, if allowed to continue, would impair the effectiveness of the landing force, particularly in the collection of intelligence information. The same concern served to govern relations with the local police and underlie the recommendation that U.S. troops not be used in civil law enforcement.[17] While less explicit and detailed, the 1962 doctrine had the same concerns and motivations.[18] Where the original doctrine was modified, it was on the basis of marine perceptions of the Malayan Emergency. It is obvious that the corps warmed to the more muscular aspects of British policy, particularly population control and resource denial rather than to those less robust measures, such as methodical police approaches to intelligence collection.[19]

The overall marine awareness of the necessity of civilian cooperation in the successful accomplishment of counterinsurgency operations was summarized nicely:

> Every endeavor should be made to assure the civilian population of the friendliness of our forces. No effort should be spared to demonstrate the advantage of law and order and to secure their friendly cooperation.[20]

The same substance was continued in the 1962 doctrine:

> The success of operations against guerrillas is affected by the at-

titude of the civilian population of the area. It is important that the
local populace be favorably impressed by the standard of conduct of
all units. . . .[21]

The doctrinal guidance by 1962 concerning civic action and psychological operations was far more specific than had been the case in the preceding manual. After a discussion of criteria to be applied to civic action
projects, which emphasize local generation of projects and the necessity
that the results of the projects be observable and measurable, a listing of
twenty-three illustrative projects is provided.[22] There was no suggestion
that civic action be considered merely as extra duty, but neither was there
any implication that a priority should be afforded to civic action programs.

> A successful civic action program must be pursued as actively and
> deliberately as military operations if the counterinsurgency mission
> is to be accomplished. A vigorous military civic action program pro-
> vides the professional military man with an unusual opportunity to
> be a statesman.[23]

The doctrine recognized the importance of linking civic action and psychological operations. While recognizing that the newer approaches to
psychological operations required that propaganda and its means of delivery would be prepared and directed by the U.S. commander in the host
country, the 1962 doctrine charged tactical elements with the necessity
of being aware of psychological warfare needs in terms of intelligence; it
also insisted that the tactical echelons must properly request psychological
operations support as well as seeing their own actions as having an impact
upon matters of psychological warfare. More than that of the army, the
marine doctrine approached the Linebarger ideal of every soldier being a
conscious psychological warrior:

> The conduct and attitudes of the individual participant in opera-
> tions against guerrillas will have a decided psychological influence
> on the civil populace and indirectly upon the guerrilla force.[24]

Although quite brief and at times giving the impression of having been
drafted in some haste, marine doctrine concerning civic action and psy-

chological operations was less contradictory and more easily implemented than the army equivalent. It also showed a clearer understanding of experience both from before World War II and after. The major flaws were the sloughing off of responsibility to higher echelons and the almost impalpable, but still detectable, attitude of being less than serious in the commitment to the nonviolent employment of military forces and assets. If the payoff had been expressed in terms of intelligence and operational benefits or if the basic premises of the *Small Wars Manual* had been reified, then the marine doctrinal commitment to the less hairy-chested approaches to counterinsurgency would have been more credible.

In defining the force application aspects of military intervention, the earlier marine doctrine took proper account of several salient features of the corps' Central American experience. First, small wars were not Clausewitzian. That is, the destruction of the opposing force was rarely, if ever, the primary goal. Most often the primary military mission was the establishment and maintenance of law and order by supporting a civil government. It was necessary that the mission be accomplished with a minimum loss of life, a minimum destruction of property, and a minimum of postconflict resentment of the United States or bitterness on the part of the country's population. Finally, it was recognized that the chaotic nature of the host country's politics, the dispersed nature of guerrilla war, and the impracticality of assuring the availability of detailed orders covering all contingencies to all junior officers and other detachment commanders, placed a burden on all leaders to be flexible and demonstrate initiative as well as to draw inferences for operational guidance from the general policy of the United States or the stated intents of higher authority.

In sharp contrast with army doctrine which deprecated, at least implicitly, the weapons, equipment, organization, and combat efficiency of guerrilla forces, marine doctrine posited past efficiency on the part of the guerrillas as well as the likelihood of its continued improvement in the future.[25] The marines asserted that, at least initially, the guerrillas would possess pronounced superiority in intelligence capabilities and terrain familiarity. It was acknowledged that guerrillas enjoy mobility and the initiative. Usually the interventionary force would find itself confronted by guerrillas formed, not in small, isolated bands, but rather "organized into fairly large groups controlling certain definite areas."[26] By 1962 the marines were not so saturnine. A similar change in attitude might be noted with respect to the marine evaluations of guerrilla weapons. In 1940, it was observed:

In the past, these irregulars have been armed with old types of weapons, most of which have been considered obsolete, while the intervening forces have been equipped with superior, modern arms. Due to the ease with which modern arms can be obtained from outside sources, it can be expected that, in the future, irregulars will have weapons and equipment equally as effective as those of the intervening forces.[27]

It should be underscored that the marine doctrine initially lacked the focus on border closure and the interdiction of sponsoring power lines of communication which had become such a focus of concern by 1960. To the marines of 1940, "outside sources" meant the international arms market rather than any particular ideological bloc. Later doctrine did take into account the rise of ideologically predicated transnational mischief making but did not raise border interdiction to the level of importance which it had with army planners.

A constraint upon military operations which was recognized in 1940, but unfortunately not remembered in the 1962 manual, was that of domestic and world public opinion. The recognition of this constraint was not only remarkably advanced for 1940, it also continued to have a pronounced relevance for tactical operations in later decades and might have been restated with profit.[28]

In the final analysis, despite all the guidance as to the desirability of accomplishing the mission through diplomacy and without the firing of a shot, marine doctrine in 1940 and in 1962 was predicated upon the notion that success in counterinsurgency operations rested ultimately upon the effective application of force. Several lessons had emerged from the Central American bush to be incorporated in doctrine. Among these were that forces assigned to a small war mission must be tactically self-sustaining, highly mobile, and prepared to act independently—both tactically and administratively.[29] Infantry units were the centrality of counterguerrilla operations.[30] This did not change in later doctrine. Also unchanged was the perceived importance of physical conditioning, footmobility in difficult terrain under trying climatic conditions, high morale, light equipment and the absolute necessity of offensive activity.[31] The marines agreed completely with the army that offensive operations were the *sine qua non* of counterguerrilla operations.[32] Additionally, it was argued that the aggressive spirit as expressed in vigorous patrolling was essential to prevent the recombination of previously dispersed guerrillas, wear down guerrilla morale and will to continue the struggle as well as to insure the collection of combat information and operational intelligence by the security forces.[33] Later doctrine expressed the same orientation, particularly elimination and harassment operations.[34]

The marines agreed across the generations about the importance of continual, imaginative and persistent combat patrolling.[35] In 1940 patrolling was seen as being an "essentially offensive action. Accordingly, its use in small wars operations is universal even under conditions which require the strategic defensive."[36] As explicitly stated, this initial commitment to the gospel of the patrol was reinforced by the experiences of the Huk Insurrection and Malayan Emergency.[37] Patrols were highly recommended despite the fact that they were inherently frustrating and exhausting, because they were the only way in which the initiative could be wrested from the insurgents, and they were the most effective way of both collecting reliable intelligence and disturbing the guerrillas. Unlike the army doctrine, the marines emphasized the use of infantry rather than artillery in the harassment role. Despite the fact that the corps had a private air force of no little ability, the marines were still willing to utilize people on the ground to acquire information and inflict casualties. Although the 1962 doctrine carefully treats the use of organic airpower, there is no implication that the intent was to use it as the primary force projection or reconnaissance instrument rather than in its initial role, the support of ground elements.

The marines refer to such offensive maneuvers as the cordon and search, but without the elaboration provided by army doctrine. A technique unique to the early marine doctrine was that of the "zone of refuge." This was defined as a system of protected zones in the vicinity of garrison points established so as to provide secure refuge for the displaced rural population.

Peaceful inhabitants are drawn into this protected area with their effects, livestock and movable belongings. Unauthorized persons

found outside of these areas are liable to arrest and property that
could be used by insurgent forces is liable to confiscation.[38]

This approach recognized the existence of refugees fleeing either the effects of counterguerrilla operations or the impositions of the guerrillas
and, at least tacitly, encourages activities aimed at refugee generation as
a method of population control through resettlement. The marines recognized at an early date the necessity of separating the guerrillas from
the potential of civilian support and cover. This recognition was reinforced
by later appreciations of Soviet partisan and Chinese insurgent tactics as
well as security force responses.[39] Even before the British in Malaya, the
marines had come to understand that the population must be separated
psychologically or physically from the guerrillas. They developed the tactics of offensive patrols, continual pressure and the openhanded treatment
of civilians necessary to encourage the desired separation. The additional
experiences of Malaya, the Philippines and Korea caused a further refinement of the doctrine until by 1962, the marines, unlike the army,
recognized not only the establishment of restricted zones but population
resettlement as well.[40] It was obvious too that the marines had understood
the mechanisms employed by the British in the resettlement scheme in
Malaya, if not the underlying ethnic situation which made resettlement
successful.[41]

The original marine view of the best method to counter insurgent warfare might be characterized as being that of a human rolling barrage
driving or destroying the guerrillas as it advanced; behind this civilians
could be protected and indigenous civil and military institutions restored
or created. While marine or mixed formations of marine and indigenous
personnel constituted the components of the aggressive barrage, indigenous forces were required to complete the pacification of the formerly
guerrilla-controlled areas as well as maintain social order and insure governmental authority after the marine forces were withdrawn.

Marine doctrine carefully examined the motivations and dynamics of
guerrillas and, as a result of this, came to the understanding that it was
not appropriate for Americans to become guerrillas in order to fight guerrillas. Because U.S. forces would of necessity be quite distinct from the
population of any host country, their personnel would not be able to employ the traditional strengths of guerrillas and would not enjoy the mass

support base of insurgents. It was asserted that counterinsurgent forces must be composed of "the best regulars, able to exploit all the technological and administrative advantages of modern military organization and to employ them in unconventional fashion as well."[42] Consequently, the corps had never embodied an organization equivalent of the U.S. Army's Special Forces. Nonetheless, it was envisaged that marine personnel could not only effectively assault guerrillas directly but also could raise, equip, train and advise civilian militias for local defense purposes. This combination of tactical elements in the field and marine-guided civilian auxiliaries in rear areas represented an efficient and politically suitable way of modernizing the constabulary concept of the Banana Wars.

If the corps made a major mistake in the development and implementation of counterinsurgency doctrine in the period 1958–1962, it was in essence too complacent about its capabilities and experience. In its particular hubris the corps both rested on its laurels and too readily invoked the "can do" spirit. It is glib to the point of flippancy to assert that counterguerrilla operations constituted a normal part of landing operations or to maintain that since counterguerrilla operations are the provenance of junior commanders and as marine training produced exceptional squad leaders and company commanders, the situation would be well in hand.

The marines committed a major and egregious sin of omission. The Marine Corps, which had demonstrated such prescience and determination in the Advanced Research Group and the Hogaboom Board, was remarkably passive and reticent in formulating counterinsurgency doctrine on both the operational and tactical element level and following through by adequately exposing all hands to it. A doctrine which brought the muscular elements of tactics, weapons and techniques into better balance with the nonmaterial elements of counterinsurgency would have better tapped the unique reservoir of marine experience. Where the doctrine of 1962 was true to its predecessor, allowing modifications to account for changes in technology and political realities, it constituted an excellent effort. But, where the doctrine of 1962 unthinkingly copied its army counterpart, as it did in places too numerous to cite, the result was to weaken the proper emphasis upon the doctrine of minimum force and the diminution of firepower. The marines gratuitously weakened their understanding of guerrilla war and how to fight it. The corps did not take good but elderly doctrine and improve it through the measured consideration and assimilation of more recent experience. The marine planners instead hurriedly threw together a pastiche which had the opposite effect, the mutation of good but elderly doctrine into a species of pernicious hybrid.

Why the corps did such an ill-considered thing, particularly since it was aware of the developing situation in South Vietnam and the likelihood that marines would be sent there, is difficult to fathom. Perhaps the requisite staff energy or talent was simply not available, given the massive reorganization then taking place. That is a possible and charitable interpretation. Perhaps the corps was simply so certain that the same elan and courage which had carried it through the bloody coral and sand to victory in the Pacific would serve in the Asian bush; that also is a possible but much less charitable interpretation. In any event, concerning counterinsurgency, the corps acted either as the wastrel who dissipated his inheritance or the miser who left his fortune to molder in a disregarded shoe box.

NOTES

1. *USMC Landing Force Bulletin* #12, "Concept of Future Amphibious Operations," HQMC, 15 December 1955. (USMC Archives).

2. Fleet Marine Force Organization and Composition Board (Hogaboom Board), *Report*, HQMC, 7 January 1957. (USMC Archives). See also summaries of the Report in the *Marine Corps Gazette*, vol. 41 (April 1957), pp. 26–30; (May 1957), pp. 10–12; (June 1957), pp. 8–12; (July 1957), pp. 20–24.

3. Ibid.

4. Sidney Wade, "Operation Bluebat," *MCG*, vol. 43 (July 1959), pp. 10–23; Harry Hadd, "Orders Firm But Flexible," *USNIP*, vol. 88 (October 1962), pp. 81–89; Robert McClintock (US Ambassador to Lebanon in 1958), "The American Landing in Lebanon," *USNIP*, vol. 88 (October 1962), pp. 65–72, 74–77, 79.

5. Testimony of General David Shoup, House Armed Services Committee Hearings, "Department of Defense Appropriations FY 1964," 88th Congress 1st Session 1963, p. 909.

6. FMFM 8-2, *Operations Against Guerrilla Forces*, (Washington, D.C.: HQMC 1962); USMC, *Small Wars Manual* (*SWM*), (Washington, D.C.: HQMC 1940).

7. FMFM 8-2, pp. 1–2.

8. Lewis Walt quoted in Burke Davis, *Marine: The Life of General Lewis Puller* (Boston: Little, Brown 1962), p. 87.

9. Michael Sparks, "Guerrillas, Small Wars and Marines" *MCG*, vol. 46 (January 1962), p. 53.

10. *SWM*, p. I-9-15.

11. FMFM 8-2, pp. 75–76.

12. *SWM*, p. I-10-18.

13. Ibid., p. I-13-22.

14. FMFM 8-2, pp. 2–13 passim.

15. *SWM*, p. I-18-35.

16. FMFM 8-2, p. 13.

17. *SWM*, p. II-15.

18. FMFM 8-2, pp. 17–24.

19. Ibid., pp. 32, 71–72, 109–15.

20. *SWM*, p. II-19.

21. FMFM 8-2, p. 75.

22. Ibid., pp. 74–74a.

23. Ibid., pp. 74a–74b.

24. Ibid., p. 40a.

25. FM 31-16, *Counterguerrilla Operations*, (Washington, D.C.: DA 1962), pp. 5–15 passim; *SWM*, Section I passim; FMFM 8-2, p. 76.

26. *SWM*, p. II-3-5.

27. Ibid.

28. *SWM*, p. II-3-3.

29. Ibid., p. II-2 passim.

30. Ibid., p. II-2-40.

31. FMFM 8-2, pp. 26, 78 inter alia.

32. *SWM*, p. II-3-5; ibid. passim.

33. Ibid., pp. II-15-25-28.

34. FMFM 8-2, pp. 34–37.

35. Ibid., pp. 82–98; *SWM*, pp. V-20ff.

36. *SWM*, p. V-20-15.

37. FMFM 8-2, pp. 81–82.

38. *SWM*, p. V-21-9.

39. For example: Ernst Von Dohnanyi, "Combatting Soviet Guerrillas," *MCG*, vol. 39 (February 1955), pp. 56–70; L. E. Haffner, "Guerrilla War and Common Sense," *MCG*, vol. 46 (June 1962), pp. 21–22; A. H. Sollom, "Nowhere But Everywhere," *MCG*, vol. 42 (June 1958), pp. 38–44.

40. FMFM 8-2, pp. 110–111.

41. Ibid., p. 110.

42. Peter Paret and John Shy, "Guerrilla War and US Military Policy: A Study," *MCG*, vol. 46 (January 1962), p. 31.

10.

Intrusions and Conclusions

Up to this point, the analysis of doctrine has been limited to the two ground forces. While the doctrines of the navy and air force, as such pertained to the perceptions of guerrilla war, were not unimportant or completely irrelevant to the decision-making process, they were neither central nor determinative, except insofar as the efficacy of air power was overestimated. It is important to remember that the navy saw its role in very traditional terms: projection of force, maintenance of forces ashore, air and naval gunfire support, reconnaissance, and sea control. The air force had no such clear-cut view.

The essential air force posture was based on the use of nuclear weapons in strategic and decisive theater roles. As General Thomas White, then Air Force Chief of Staff, commented to the USAF Scientific Advisory Board in a 1958 speech concerning the utility of nuclear munitions in limited war:

> From that fact it is deduced that nuclear strength did not prevent aggression in Korea, Greece and Vietnam. The implication is that nuclear strength cannot deter aggression.
>
> . . .
>
> But I would turn the implication around and ask whether they would have occurred had the US established belief in our determination to use nuclear weapons? Would these wars have run their painful course had nuclear strength been involved?[1]

He continued, in a context of demonstrating the necessity of ending local conflicts rapidly and resolutely, to suggest that nuclear munitions be employed when and where needed, "in a manner best suited to the objectives at the time."[2] In that connection, he asserted that "Air Force doctrine is in accord with the national policy, in fact is in anticipation of that policy. . . ."[3] In short, in 1958 the air force perceived itself as having the men, machines, special munitions and doctrine necessary to achieve the rapid delivery of nuclear support to remote battlefields. Such support would be appropriate to an entire spectrum of low-intensity conflicts including counterguerrilla operations.

The Tactical Air Command (TAC) formed a special organization, the Composite Air Strike Force (CASF) to facilitate the rapid injection of airpower into any limited war environment. The first employment of the CASF concept was in support of the Lebanon landings. As the commander of the TAC stated, roughly one hundred aircraft, including fighters, tactical bombers, reconnaissance, transport and tanker types, were deployed to Adena, Turkey within forty-eight hours of the executive order.[4] It was believed that this rapid response capability would operate as a significant deterrent to externally sponsored guerrilla war as well as more conventional border-crossing aggression or, should deterrence fail, the flexible firepower embodied in the TAC CASF would allow the projection of punishing force to be accomplished in an effective, low cost and manpower efficient fashion. The commander to the headquarters element of TAC CASF, the Nineteenth Air Force, averred that the existence of this capability obviated the need to station U.S. troops in strategically important countries where, "governments were generally shaky and . . . a strong communist underground movement was present."[5] In a cynical sense CASF might be seen, as also might the justification for the utilization of first line air assets including nuclear weapons in guerrilla conflicts, as having been an attempt by TAC to maintain parity with Strategic Air Command (SAC) during a budgetary period pregnant with strategic missiles and a space race. TAC bought in on a threat that SAC could not touch.

With the 1961 change in political priorities presented by the Kennedy Administration, the air force was not slow in buying in on the counterguerrilla program. In a stroke of public relations genius, the air force established in April 1962 the romantically named 1st Air Commando Group and the Special Air Warfare Center at Eglin Air Force Base, Florida. For the preceding year the Air Commando Group had been laboring under a pedestrian appellation, the 4400 Combat Crew Training Squadron. The alteration of designation left its mission unchanged: the training of foreign personnel in the tactics and techniques of close air support, aerial resupply, harassment and interdiction, and reconnaissance with an emphasis upon counterguerrilla operations.

By late 1961, it had become obvious to the air force that a more high profile commitment was necessary, or the U.S. Air Force (USAF) would be a definite nonstarter under the new priorities. Thus, the heavy airborne artillery was rolled out and launched in support of the air force commitment to counterinsurgency. An example of the inhouse propaganda campaign was an article by Curtis LeMay directed at the enlisted and NCO personnel of the air force, in which he attempted to outline the nature and quality of communist insurgent activities in South Vietnam, and indicate how the USAF had the capability and intent to assist the Saigon government forces through training, advice and equipment to successfully resist the threat. He analyzed the Special Air Warfare Center, noting that in the development of techniques for counterinsurgency the air force would "build capabilities on the basis of our experience with this kind of operation over the past twenty years in Korea, the Philippines, World War II and South Vietnam."[6] It would be hard to imagine a less warranted or accurate invocation of history.

By 1962 the air force had evolved a posture and a doctrine which, while quite irrelevant to the needs of counterinsurgent operations and totally divorced from any historical experience in that area, seemed to provide a quick, efficient and clean, in terms of American lives, method to project power in support of friendly governments confronted with an insurgent threat. The generally accepted model of guerrilla war being synonymous with externally sponsored partisan war served to reinforce the attractiveness of the air force's capabilities as contained in TAC CASF. Here was the means to interdict lines of communications and inhibit cross-border reinforcement and resupply operations. Here also was the technically efficient means to provide answers to the most significant tactical problems of guerrilla war, finding the guerrilla and concentrating the friendly forces and firepower to destroy him. Aerial reconnaissance, aerial insertion of troops and, above all, aerial firepower boded well in the minds of many to serve as the perfect counters to subversion and guerrilla conflicts. Misreading the Greek experience and an overfixation on French airpower deficiencies at Dien Bien Phu also enhanced the attractiveness of the air force approach to dealing with guerrillas. And, as the air force never tired of reminding decision makers, the air force was the perfect instrument for ending wars of whatsoever level of intensity by that curious addendum to Clausewitz' *Vernichtungsstrategie*, the complete destruction of the opponent's will and capability for combat.

The army, like the air force, had developed a doctrine for counterguerrilla warfare not from an accurate reading of history but from the dictates of the service's major mission and the equipment, force configurations and doctrines developed for the execution of the major mission. In the case of the army, that major mission was mechanized combat in Europe against the Soviet bloc, a war in which nuclear weapons would be used. It is not surprising that the army view of its capabilities in fighting guerrillas would be skewed.

This skewing was made all the easier by the basic nature of the army's general theory of victory. As in the specific doctrine developed for guerrilla war, the focus was on the finding, fixing and destruction through standup combat, of the enemy's force in the field. If that was impossible, then the alternative, according to the American reading of Clausewitz, was the destruction of the enemy's will and ability to fight. This could be done by the destruction of the material and institutional bases of support for the guerrillas.

The Clausewitzian view of war, coupled with the belief that general purpose conventional forces of the American pattern could defeat all kinds of opponents, assured that the army planners would view history from a particular perspective. The general belief that revolution was not an activity which people embarked upon without the stimulation of an external sponsoring power, such as monolithic communism, assured that the guerrilla would always be seen as a partisan and never as an insurgent. The experiences of Greece and Korea served to reinforce that perspective as well as to provide support for the notions that the use of conventional forces employing conventional tactics assured victory. Both cases also validated the fixation upon the interdiction of lines of supply, communication and command between the guerrillas and the external sponsor. The Korean War convinced all observers that guerrillas were the early warning of cross-border conventional attack, a much graver danger. From these basic concepts, all the more specific doctrine flowed.

What the eye and mind are led to expect, they will find: guerrillas had to be supported by an external power including conventional forces in the wings, if not on the stage; guerrillas had to have base camps, concentrations and lines of communication; guerrillas had to form units of sufficient size and cohesion to accept set-piece battles. The onus was on tactical commanders to find these things, as, by definition, they had to be there. If the expected was not uncovered, it was simply because insufficient patrols had been mounted, sorties flown or 155mm rounds fired. The generation of body counts and refugees was acceptable and expectable; the generation of additional insurgent support or the invitation of increased levels of external support was not considered.

The existence of army doctrine concerning psychological warfare and civic action should not be taken as indicative of either an understanding of insurgency per se or the lessons of the Huk Insurrection or Malayan Emergency in particular. Despite the doctrinal attention paid to the subject, civic action was seen as a low order help in counterinsurgency. Significant civic action of the order of that employed in the Philippines, which sought to ameliorate in a highly visible fashion, if not correct altogether, the social and economic conditions which brought about the insurgency and thus demobilize popular support for the guerrillas, was simply not within the power of the United States, let alone its army, to effect directly.

Unless the United States was prepared to take over the government of the host country and implement systemic reforms, the best it could do would be to advise and urge the execution of the necessary programs. The army was in no position to undertake even the latter, except insofar as its personnel operating as advisors might be able to persuade their counterparts to halt conduct which unnecessarily exacerbated civil-military tensions and so aided the insurgents. The building of roads and schools, the provision of health and sanitation services, might serve to induce a spirit of gratitude or even friendship within local population groups, but this was likely to prove ephemeral. Thankfulness for a new school tends to be enervated dramatically as a result of being caught in a misaimed fire mission or eroded in a less dramatic fashion by the constant return of insurgent cadres. The alleviation of pervasive frustration and inequalities which give rise to insurgency cannot be "A Gift From the American People."

At least the marines understood the difference between partisan and insurgent warfare. They had evolved a reasonably successful set of tactics and techniques involving the use of military force implemented by aggressive small unit activity to disrupt, drive back, and disperse, if not destroy, the insurgents' guerrilla forces, while a native constabulary was formed under marine sponsorship in the rear areas to secure the territory and insure a continuation of internal tranquility. They saw their mission as being time limited and involving the creation of institutions as well as the destruction of hostile entities. Corps doctrine did recognize the lower lethality of the insurgent conflict and did attempt to restrict operations to the use of light infantry as much as possible. The marines better assimilated the lessons of Malaya and the Philippines as compared with the army. The structure of the marines as well as the doctrine assembled so obviously in a hasty fashion were nonetheless configured and written so as to make the corps well suited to the counterinsurgency role with an apposite emphasis upon a constabulary approach. It would have been better if the corps had not excised a significant portion of its own institutional memory. In the early 1960s the corps opted out of, or was forced out of, the counterinsurgency game at a critical juncture in the decision making process concerning the nature and degree of U.S. involvement in counterinsurgency campaigns.

It is not surprising that the army sought to create a simulacrum of itself in South Vietnam during the 1950s, since the Americans were convinced that this type of mobile and firepower-heavy force would not only be the best one to deter or repel a cross-border invasion, like that which had befallen Korea, but that it would be appropriate to meet and defeat any internal, insurgent threat. Any attempts to reconfigure the South Vietnamese Army to one more suitable to an internal security role would be stillborn, not because of obstructionism or paranoia on the part of military leaders who consciously misled the Washington decision makers, but because such notions fell outside the doctrinal universe of discourse. This is neither a justification nor an excuse, but a reason.

If the insurgents were capable of fighting as conventional units, then they must be fought by conventional forces in set-piece battles. If the insurgents were still in a developmental stage, reliant upon externally furnished supplies, command and control, training and leadership, then the lines of communication must be interdicted and the borders sealed by conventional forces using proven tactics and techniques including airpower. Army doctrine knew only one answer to the bifurcate conundrum.

If the situation was out of control, it was not due to any deficiency of doctrine or goal but rather a deficiency in the application of the doctrine. If an army receiving American assistance was not able to meet the challenge of combat, as was the case with the Vietnamese Army in 1961, it was not the fault of materiel or advisory manpower but rather managerial shortcomings in the host country. As General James Van Fleet found in Greece, an army can be put in the field fully equipped and reasonably well trained incomparably faster than an able high command can be developed.

Thus such managerial changes as the upgrading of the Military Assistance Advisory Group (MAAG) in Saigon to an Asiatic equivalent of JUSMAPG and its decision to respond to any communist reactive escalation by the introduction of necessary air and ground forces was not outside U.S. military experience or doctrine. Escalation like this was not an insensible drift deeper into the morass of war: it was the logical concomitant of the basic Clausewitzian thesis of destroying the enemy forces in the field. Joined with the desire, indeed the necessity, of keeping the cost in American lives low, airborne firepower not manpower was indicated in pursuit of the strategy of destruction. This was not the result of sheer institutional perversity. Neither was it due to the meeting of Colonel Blimp and Doctor Strangelove. Rather it was the ineluctable consequence of improper doctrine. Doctrine and incorrectly comprehended experience combined to assure that the very nature of the war in Vietnam would not be recognized.

NOTES

1. Thomas B. White, "USAF Doctrine and Limited War," *Air Force*, vol. 41 (January 1958), pp. 50–51.

2. Ibid., p. 51.

3. Ibid.

4. Otto Weyland, "Airpower in Limited War," *Ordnance*, vol. 44, no. 235 (July–August 1959), p. 42.

5. Henry Vicellio, "Composite Air Strike Force, *Air University Quarterly Review*, vol. 9 (Winter 1956–1957), p. 28.

6. Curtis LeMay, "Counterinsurgency and the Challenge Imposed," *The Airman*, vol. 6 (July 1962), p. 8.

FETISHES THAT FAILED

11.

The COIN of Camelot

During its thousand years Vietnamese society had developed a unique character: that of an armed peasantry slowly occupying the shoreline and coastal farm areas of the Indochinese peninsula. The Vietnamese experience had not only developed a view of the world which was dark and paranoid, but had resulted in a social structure which was severely localistic and particularistic in its attachments. The Vietnamese was an individual strongly attached to his family, his village, his secret society, and little else. Often Vietnam had lived through the yin of more or less forced unification, only to see that followed by the yang of partition. In 1954, after the agreement which ended the French Indochinese War, the wheel had again brought partition.

The American involvement with postpartition South Vietnam, after the ending of the uneasy de facto co-dominion with the French, concentrated on two major activities: building the Army of the Republic of Vietnam (ARVN), and providing assistance and advice to the man trumpeted as being the Magsaysay of the new nation, Ngo Dinh Diem. This last function was exercised primarily through Edward Lansdale, who was a close friend of Diem's as he had been one of Magsaysay's.

Unfortunately, Lansdale and the Americans did not prevent their new protégé from committing a massive and egregious error in 1956, when he prohibited the traditional and deeply cherished village elections and instead appointed as village chiefs fellow Catholic refugees from the North. This was a blunder which even the French and the Japanese had not committed during their terms as occupiers of Vietnam. It was a cause of massive discontent among the rural population of South Vietnam.

Diem rapidly moved to worsen the situation with a land reform program initiated in 1957, in which the failure to distribute land was matched only by the corruption and inefficiency of the officials charged with administering it. When the first rumblings of rural discontent were met by repressive moves from the security police under the direction of President Diem's brother, Nhu, it was scarcely remarkable that insurrection reared its head. While this incipient insurgency was certainly a more welcome development than the Marxist regime of Ho Chi Minh in the Democratic Republic of Vietnam (DRV), as North Vietnam was more properly known, the insurgent movement neither started in Hanoi nor was controlled from there. As was noted by the U.S. Defense Department, DRV organizing attempts in the South were severely curtailed in the years from 1955–1959, following a sharp initial rebuff.[1] While the details of Northern involvement in the late 1950s were obscure given the absence of "an effective and extensive intelligence apparatus functioning in Vietnam," there were many reasons to believe that the developing guerrilla conflict was of a primarily, if not purely, indigenous nature.[2]

The American perspective on the matter was quite simple: the guerrilla movement was not only controlled by the North as a partisan auxiliary to the large, well organized Peoples' Army of North Vietnam (PAVN), its actions were preparatory to a cross-border invasion. The conventional invasion of the South by the North had long been the primary concern of the American military in its training of ARVN and in the drafting of contingency plans for the region. Indeed, all the operational plans for Southeast Asia through 1965 were based on the assumption that the conflict would be a mixture of guerrilla and conventional war. The Pentagon feared a repetition of the Korean War despite the repeated CIA evaluation that the North was not preparing for that possibility but was contemplating guerrilla action.[3] In short, the U.S. Army had been preparing ARVN for an eventuality considered quite remote by U.S. intelligence. The army, as represented in South Vietnam by the Military Assistance Advisory Group (MAAG), had not been preparing ARVN for the threat considered most likely, the threat which was emerging more and more by 1960, the threat of insurgent guerrilla war. Even the formation of the National Liberation Front (NLF) in that year did nothing to make MAAG or its superiors in the Pentagon reevaluate the American training and advisory program. Rather, the NLF was taken merely as another indication, not simply of Northern involvement, but of the impending invasion. Be the threat invasion or guerrilla conflct, U.S. doctrine held that a conventional military, using conventional American methods, could successfully cope with either.

The Kennedy Administration took office with a realization that the situation in Vietnam was deteriorating and would continue to do so without some major changes in the policies of the South Vietnamese government and improvement in the proficiency of the South Vietnamese Army. Although the conflict in Laos absorbed the attention of the media as well as the new administration, it was, and would remain, a peripheral action. The strategic center of balance of Southeast Asia existed in Vietnam and the emerging struggle there.

In its last days, the Eisenhower Administration was presented with an evaluation of the situation by Ambassador Walter Durbrow which was far from optimistic, primarily because Diem was showing even more than the usual resistance to the adoption of reforms, while showing an ever greater commitment to the notion of solving the problem by the application of force, being quite insistent that the United States authorize the increase of his Civil Guard force by 10,000.[4] In taking this position, Diem was not simply responding to the increase in insurgent activities in an idiosyncratic fashion. The Americans had already shown an appetite for the use of increased military force to improve the "deteriorating situation in South Vietnam."[5] A primary suggestion to the Defense Department was that:

> The emphasis of the MAAG function should be shifted from purely training and organizational advice in preparation for defense against external aggression to include on-the-spot advice and assistance in the conduct of tactical operations against the Viet Cong.[6]

In addition to this somewhat muscular notion, other suggestions included the importance of assuring that the Cambodian government recognize the Vietnamese right of hot pursuit across the international border, the need to increase equipment in ARVN and the possible employment of U.S ships and aircraft to deter seaborne reinforcement of the southern insurgents.[7]

The impression of impending crisis was conveyed clearly by mission personnel, such as General Edward Lansdale, who reported to the Secretary of Defense on the situation in South Vietnam. His recommendations were robust as was his conviction that Diem was indispensable.[8]

General Lansdale not only viewed the threat of communism and the presumed ambitions of the North with the utmost of alarm, he also introduced a theme which would dominate American planning for years to come, because it fit so well with the mutually reinforcing notions that an insurgency could not exist without external inspiration and the doctrinal model of guerrilla war as partisan war. General Lansdale underscored that South Vietnam was open to infiltration.[9]

There can be little doubt that General Lansdale, as well as President Diem, were quite pleased by the reactions of the Kennedy Administration to the apparently worsening situation through the spring of 1961. The interagency task group headed by Undersecretary of Defense Roswell Gilpatrick reported that "South Vietnam is nearing the decisive phase in its battle for survival" and that the situation is "critical but not hopeless."[10] It was recommended that the United States demonstrate to "our friends, the Vietnamese and our foes, the Viet Cong, that come what may, the US intends to *win* this battle."[11] The Joint Chiefs of Staff saw the situation as a problem amenable to military solution and recommended a dramatic increase in U.S. support, including the Military Assistance Program (MAP), underwriting the entire expense of a 68,000 man Civil Guard and an increase of ARVN from 150,000 to 170,000 men.[12]

By the end of the month President Kennedy had approved these actions and was considering a lengthy draft, "Program of Action to Prevent Communist Domination of South Vietnam."[13]

A close study of this document, including its seven Annexes, indicates persuasively that it contained all the features, tensions and misunderstandings of the nature of insurgency in general and the conflict in Vietnam in particular, that were going to typify American policy throughout the balance of the Kennedy Administration. The major thrust of the military Annex was on the problem of sealing the border and precluding infiltration. It was assumed that if the infiltration problem were to be lessened, it would be legitimate to assume that a bolstered ARVN, with some new area denial weapons, could cope with the guerrillas.[14] After considering the need for greater training commitments and an increase in personnel attached to MAAG, the question of U.S. combat troops being sent to South Vietnam was addressed.

Should the situation in South Vietnam deteriorate to the point where the measures outlined above are not adequate to prevent the Communist domination of the country, it may be necessary to introduce US flag forces either as a part of a bi-lateral US-GVN defense agreement or as a fulfillment of US-SEATO obligations. In this event it is considered desirable to deploy to Tourane or Nha Trang a tailored, composite joint task force specially designed for carrying out a counterguerrilla-civic action-limited war mission in South Vietnam.[15]

This was an attractive idea save for the practical problem that the United States possessed no such utopian force.

While President Kennedy was able to resist the pressures for the immediate commitment of American troops to South Vietnam, he did authorize further study of that subject, including the size and composition of the necessary expeditionary force.[16] The U.S. funded increases in the ARVN and Civil Guard were likewise authorized as were the task force recommendations concerning psychological operations.[17]

Considering that U.S. support for South Vietnam was to have its initial focus on the military matter of internal security, it was proper that the subject of American military capability in counterinsurgency was raised.[18] While the official call was for an inventory and evaluation of existing resources, the practical effect was to stimulate the further development of such special purpose troops as the army's Special Forces.

There was an emerging consensus that whatever capabilities the United States possessed in the area of unconventional warfare would soon be put to use one way or another in Southeast Asia. Vice President Lyndon Johnson, sent on a handholding mission to Diem and others in Asia during May 1961, reported back to President Kennedy that:

The country [South Vietnam] can be saved—if we move quickly and wisely. We must decide whether to support Diem—or let Vietnam fall. We must have coordination of purpose in our country team, diplomatic and military. . . . The most important thing is imaginative, creative, American management of our military aid program.[19]

While alarmist reports purporting to justify the need for a massive increase of ARVN and the American MAAG were not surprising when coming from Diem, they took on an additional weight when paralleled by

MAAG studies which reached the same conclusions. By the late summer of 1961, it had been concluded by all hands that increased border surveillance was required as was the reorganization of the South Vietnamese armed forces, particularly in terms of its command structure. Further, the Vietnamese armed forces would have to be increased substantially, with the result that the troops would have first claim on the U.S. financial support. Finally, it was concluded by MAAG Chief Lionel McGarr that U.S. advisors should be authorized to accompany Vietnamese units into combat, as had been the case with American advisors during the Greek Civil War. Even Secretary of State Rusk, notable neither for his assertiveness nor for his hawkish proclivities, agreed that summer that the military should have first claim on resources, as when he commented upon a report of the GVN-US Special Finance Group which had recommended approval of the requested increase of the South Vietnamese armed forces to 200,000 men:

> The report recognized that military-internal security requirements must have first call on the available resources, and that success of the military-security program will be increased if accompanied by emergency economic and social measures and by the expansion of longer range development programs.[20]

Secretary Rusk's position was buttressed by that of the JCS, which agreed on 3 August 1961 that a 200,000 man Vietnamese Armed Forces should be able to handle the insurgency. In addition, the Joint Chiefs commented that a plan of population control existed and had been approved by MAAG, suggesting that the effective implementation of this plan would operate as a force multiplier.[21]

As Douglas Blaufarb, a close and careful observer, noted, this critical period in the deepening American involvement was marked by a serious lack of a "common approach and direction between American civilian and military organizations in Vietnam."[22] Insofar as there was a commonality it was by way of an attempt to utilize the resettlement and relocation program of the Malayan Emergency. The military demand for efficient use of manpower and the civilian programmatic need for preemptive reform seemed to coincide in the idea of the Strategic Hamlet Program formalized by National Security Council Action Memorandum (NSAM)

No. 65.[23] A nearly contemporaneous National Intelligence Estimate (NIE) underscored the cruciality of rural population control to the success of the counterinsurgency campaign.[24] The model of Vietnam as Malaya writ large was emerging.

The Malayan, or Filipino, analogy received a greater impetus when the CIA reported in the fall of 1961 that the overwhelming percentage of insurgent fighters were indigenous to South Vietnam, although some were stay-behind forces left from the 1954 partition.[25] The analysis also pointed out that the mainforce guerrillas were supported by a substantial number of part-time guerrillas, as well as a sizable mass support base which handled the traditional tasks of logistics and intelligence. Quite obviously, the latter categories of insurgents were neither ethnic Northerners nor stay-behind parties. The CIA stated that the guerrillas were primarily of a domestic nature and that, despite the usual American fixation on the closing of borders and the interdiction of supposed lines of communication, the answer to the Viet Cong was to be sought in the control of the South Vietnamese population and the severing of connections between the mass support base and the mainforce guerrillas. The CIA did not press this point vigorously and concluded with the specious contention that the capability of the Viet Cong to maintain their accelerated pace would "depend upon improved logistical support from the outside."[26]

The JCS was far from happy with the shift toward the Malaya-inspired Strategic Hamlet system. The Chiefs had not embraced the notion joyously, but had accepted it as a necessary expedient. The fear was that the Hamlet approach was not only essentially one of a defensive nature, but one more suitable for a police than a military force. In the estimate of many, the situation in Vietnam had degenerated to a level which police mechanisms could not deal with effectively. An excellent example of this position was the Chairman of The Joint Chiefs of Staff, Lymann L. Lemnitzer, who expressed the essence of the argument against the Malayan Emergency as a model and extolled the further "militarizing" of the conflict in a letter to Maxwell Taylor in mid-October 1961.[27] The Chief of the Joint Chiefs did not see that the conflict in South Vietnam should be treated as something other than a purely conventional war. This was not a minority view.

With respect to training the Vietnamese Army for the "wrong

war," it seems clear that in recent months the insurgency in South Vietnam has developed far beyond the capacity of police control. All of the Vietnamese Army successes this past summer have met Viet Cong opposition in organized battalion strength. Even larger Communist units were involved in the recent Viet Cong successes north of Kontum. This change in the situation has not been fully understood by many US officials.[28]

The tension continued between the more conventional military approach and the notion of employing methods of population control coupled with psychological operations directed against the rural population. Maxwell Taylor, after a fact finding mission, recommended to President Kennedy in an "eyes only" telegram on 1 November 1961 that the United States use the cover of emergency flood relief to inject a degree of effort far surpassing that which had gone before. Although much of this new aid and advice would be in purely civilian and infrastructure matters directed at improving the governmental efficiency and the economic base of South Vietnam, the primary thrust would be in the military sphere.[29] Taylor made a proposal which was clearly rooted within the American experience in Greece and was totally consistent with the doctrinal appreciation of the nature of guerrilla war. Further exhibiting the American way of guerrilla war, Taylor suggested the deployment of U.S. forces, specifically "a military Task Force to operate under US control" to conduct logistic and support activities as well as to demonstrate resolve, and thereby enhance the civilian and governmental morale within South Vietnam while presumably discomfiting the opposition.[30] In addition, the Task Force would "provide an emergency reserve to back up the Armed Forces of GVN in the case of a heightened military crisis."[31]

In a follow-up "eyes only" telegram to the President, Taylor reinforced his argument in favor of troop deployment, even though there are some immediate and obvious disadvantages to the idea. In this message, he suggested that the troops be primarily combat support specialists who would not engage in combat except in self-defense. Taylor believed that only through the introduction of American logistics, transportation and specialist communications and intelligence units could the ARVN forces be endowed with the capabilities to wage antiguerrilla war such as the doctrine proscribed. He concluded: "I do not believe that our program to save SVN will succeed without it."[32] Secretary of Defense McNamara advised President Kennedy a week later that he, the Joint Chiefs and Roswell Gilpatrick were in essential agreement with Taylor's position.[33] Predicating his evaluation upon the requirements of CINCPAC (Commander-in-Chief, Pacific) Plan 32-59, Phase IV for operations on the ground in Southeast Asia in a combination conventional and partisan war, Secretary McNamara cautioned that an American force of six division equivalents might be required.[34] The implication obvious throughout the memo was that the Joint Chiefs and the Secretary believed that the putative controllers of the insurgency, whether they be in Hanoi, Peking or Moscow, would not get the message of U.S. resolve and determination to prevail without a presence of great magnitude. The Secretary stated quite explicitly that the consensus was that an 8,000 man contingent, such as that proposed by General Taylor, would not transmit a message to the sponsoring power unless the United States relayed it through diplomatic back channels.[35]

Planning continued for the probability of U.S. combat troop introduction. This planning included a broad spectrum of contingencies from the overhaul of the ARVN command structure and the provision of personnel and equipment to improve the South Vietnamese intelligence system to the introduction of substantial U.S. forces.[36] Two alternatives were presented for the introduction of U.S. troops: a 3,500 Brigade Task Force of three battle groups or one and one-half division equivalents as required under the counterinsurgency-oriented Phase II of CINCPAC's Operation Plan 32-59.[37] The first force would be of the size necessary to act as a signal of resolve and to form the mobile reserve necessary to act against large Viet Cong concentrations. The second, larger force was of a size deemed sufficient to undertake significant spoiling offensives against insurgent base areas, as well as stiffen the local armed forces and act as a nucleus for a multinational task force.

The options considered beyond committing U.S. forces were designed to increase the mobility and firepower of ARVN divisions. U.S. Army helicopter units would be provided to equip at least some ARVN contingents with the degree of operational and tactical mobility necessary under army doctrine to meet the initiative of the insurgents, if not regain it. In a similar manner, provision of additional light and medium transport aviation, including both aircraft and personnel, would increase the operational flexibility of ARVN units and act as a force multiplier for certain elite formations such as the Rangers who, emulating the previous experiences with similar elite units in Greece and the Philippines, were bearing the brunt of offensive combat.

Of particular importance in increasing the combat efficiency of ARVN was the improvement of the Vietnamese Air Force in the area of close air support. U.S. doctrine, drawing heavily upon the Greek Civil War and the Korean conflict as well as the conventional war experiences in World War II, had a particularly high regard for the efficacy of close air support in counterguerrilla operations, a notion which lost nothing in the retelling of the 1st Air Commando. The military put a high priority on developing a high quality close air support capability in South Vietnam, including not just pilot training but the establishment of the elaborate infrastructure of Operations and Reporting Centers and other support facilities necessary for the provision of a systematic air support capability. The Joint Staff recognized full well that this type of system could not be created quickly or easily. Explicit in the plan was the introduction of U.S. personnel to handle all the support and control tasks as well as the forward air control responsibilities. In addition, at least some USAF tactical fighter squadrons would be deployed to Vietnam.

Major efforts would be made in the development of a maritime surveillance and interdiction capability so as to attenuate effectively or eliminate seaborne infiltration of personnel and materiel to South Vietnam from the North or the People's Republic of China, even though the presence or significance of such presumed maritime infiltration had not yet been demonstrated to exist. More realistically, it was proposed that major improvements be made in the training and equipping of the local defense forces, particularly those entrusted with the warding off of Viet Cong attacks, terror or political operations from villages in critical areas. This was a long-term project with the estimated completion time being two years.

No time estimate could be made concerning the program to improve the military intelligence capability of the South Vietnamese Armed Forces. The situation was so chaotic that specific recommendations had not yet been derived, although it was obvious to all that the secret police of Nhu had enervated all military intelligence operations and the system which existed did not address any of the true intelligence needs of a counterinsurgency effort.

The Joint Staff recommended to the JCS that the American advisory personnel emulate their predecessors in Greece and assume operational control of tactical units as well as the higher command. Supporting this suggestion, the Staff commented upon the superior American technical competence as well as the superior American vigor in carrying out field operations.[38] It was calculated that the full implementation of this proposal would require 2,500 more personnel being assigned to MAAG, but that this level would allow the provision of American advisors to every battalion and selected companies in ARVN, the Civil Guard and the Self-Defense Corps.[39]

The military continued to see and report a deterioration in the situation obtaining in South Vietnam. In a talking paper employed by the Chairman of the Joint Chiefs for a meeting with President Kennedy early in January 1962, points of emphasis included the heavy infiltration of Viet Cong personnel and the preparation of extensive base camp facilities in areas controlled by the insurgents.[40] It was admitted that the insurgents' primary source of weapons was the captured stocks of the security forces and that the majority of the Viet Cong guerrillas, both mainforce and part-time, were locally recruited and trained. Nonetheless, the major concern expressed was the problem of infiltration of cadre and specialist forces. JCS saw the course of action as being:

1. The building up of the armed forces with U.S. aid and assistance.
2. Defeat of the Viet Cong Forces.
3. The implementation of a series of reforms and measures to correct imbalances in the power hierarchy.[41]

The Chairman concluded by warning the President that the accomplishment of these points might yet require the commitment of U.S. combat forces.

In opposition to the pattern perceived by the military as indicative of continual deterioration, a pattern which continued beyond General Lemnitzer's January meeting with President Kennedy, there came a relatively encouraging assessment of the situation from the Department of State's

Bureau of Intelligence and Research. In this report the Bureau's Director, Roger Hilsman, noted quite favorably the progress of the "Delta Pacification Plan" implemented by the British with the support of Diem. He stated that by mid-May three Strategic Hamlets with 2,700 relocated inhabitants had been built, with two more under construction, and that the civic action program was well in place and delivering services to the residents of these new villages.[42] He described a number of other civic action and pacification programs, many of which to him seemed to be having an impact upon the dynamics of the insurgency.

It is obvious that Hilsman was particularly struck by the demonstrated and potential promise of the Delta project. He noted some potentially crippling problems with the implementation of the "Delta Pacification Plan," but these had nothing to do with the British concept, rather the difficulties involved Diem's delays in approving the project as well as a certain tendency to subordinate the British plan to the Strategic Hamlet plan of Diem and secret police chief Nhu.[43]

Hilsman was also bullish on the improved performance of the army and the paramilitary force. While he commented upon the lack of aggressive border patrolling by the ARVN Rangers, his overall impression of the combat efficiency of the Vietnamese armed forces was quite favorable. His comment on the use of air support was quite telling, as it hit upon a problem that blighted far more than the limited subject of discourse to which Hilsman tied it.

> The principal deficiency in the utilization of air support is not tactical but rather is related to the availability and reliability of intelligence upon the Viet Cong.[44]

Hilsman concluded that matters were improving.[45]

Six months later Hilsman prepared another appreciation of the situation which was not so completely optimistic. He took the flat position that the "Viet Cong insurgent-subversive movement in South Vietnam is directed, inspired and organized by the DRV."[46] He did, however, state that the physical and manpower support received from the North was minimal and that intelligence on the matter was spotty. Much more important to Hilsman was the gradual embodiment within the Strategic Hamlet Program of the recommendations of the British, the efficacy of which had been demonstrated in the highly successful "Delta Pacification Plan." While he stated, "it is still too early for accurate evaluation of the strategic hamlet program," it is obvious that Hilsman saw the matter quite favorably.[47] When the favorable reaction to the Delta project is combined with his deprecation of the infiltration threat, it is clear that Hilsman favored a pacification-oriented program with reduced emphasis on the traditional military concerns. His guiding lights were the Philippines and, more than anything else, Malaya.

Hilsman, who was a veteran of Ray Peer's swashbuckling OSS detachment at Fort Hertz on the Burma–China border during the palmy days of World War II, fancied himself something of an expert on guerrilla war and the methods of successful counterinsurgency. He had been quite favorably impressed by the British program in the delta as well as by its director, Sir Robert Thompson, personally. To Hilsman, Thompson's notion offered not simply a tool with which one fought insurgents, but a "strategic concept based upon a true understanding of the nature of internal war."[48] Here lay a grail, a powerful fetish with which to banish the discouraging prospect of prolonged and potentially fruitless conventional military operations against the Viet Cong.

Thompsons's view of the efficacy of the regroupment and resettlement approach to countering insurgency rapidly gained converts and supporters other than Hilsman and his associate Michael Forrestal, including W. W. Rostow, who later commented that Maxwell Taylor had agreed with the British ideas as early as late 1961.[49] Other important early converts included the MAAG commander, General Lionel McGarr as well as the first commander of the Military Assistance Command, Vietnam (MACV), General Paul Harkins, Ambassador Nolting and Diem himself. Despite General Lemnitzer's initial reservations concerning the British "police coordination" notions, it is quite easy to understand why some American military officials readily received the idea of the strategic hamlet with its emphasis upon a military framework in which the hamlets were placed like bits of fruit in a Swedish pancake, or why Diem warmed to a program which would legitimately place the rural pacification administration within the baliwick of his brother Nhu.

The muscular stance of the Joint Chiefs for the possibilities offered by increased training in counterinsurgency and police reactions to the guerrilla challenge was not shared by the State Department.[50] With this continued orientation toward the attempt to cope with the insurgent challenge by relatively less violent means, it is scarcely surprising that the strategic hamlets represented to Roger Hilsman and others outside the Pentagon the preferred alternative. For the moment, also, the staff at MACV and in the Defense Department were willing to see an emphasis placed upon the effective implementation of the hamlet program, for it did rely upon a significant military component in its design. Also, it was probably realized that the strategic hamlet program represented the last, best hope for a constabulary or civic action-oriented solution; if it failed, the decks would have been cleared for the implementation of the military approach.

The optimistic view of Hilsman's December 1962 report was echoed in April of 1963 by the CIA in its new National Intelligence Estimate.[51] In large measure this was the result of the perceived success of the Strategic Hamlet Program, which had been a major thrust of American effort in the preceding months. This perception was outdated by events virtually as soon as it had been promulgated.

By mid-1963 the United States had about as much effective control over Diem's version of the Delta plan, the nationwide Strategic Hamlet Program, as a heroin addict has over his habit. The Malayan seed had not only failed to develop into a beautiful plant, it had mutated in the harsh Vietnamese environment into a monstrous and evil weed. Widely differing interpretations of the Strategic Hamlet Program emerged, further complicating the task of measuring the effectiveness of the program. After the fact, various commentators pointed at programmatic overexpansion in 1962 and early 1963, but at the time no warning flags were raised.[52] Quite the contrary, the Agency for International Development (AID) and the Department of Defense fretted continuously over expediting the delivery of radios and "Strategic Hamlet Kits" in sufficient quantity and in a timely way to maintain the forced draft pace of hamlet expansion.[53] In April 1963 a CIA estimate provided no negative assessment of the Strategic Hamlet Program, although it was acknowledged that "further progress can be made in expanding the area of government control."[54]

Officially, the Strategic Hamlet Program failed because the Ngo family was unable to reform, coupled with the inability of the U.S. to induce them to mend their ways, with the situation made worse by poor programmatic implementation.[55] This assessment left out such important considerations as the American ability to detect incipient or even active program failures in a timely manner; or the U.S. ability either to induce better performance in implementation or to terminate the program before the potential loss became catastrophic; or the ability of the American planners to see the detail differences between Vietnam and other venues in which insurgent movements had been successfully suppressed.

In late September 1963 Secretary of Defense McNamara and General Taylor again visited South Vietnam at the express direction of President Kennedy. Their report was remarkably upbeat, commenting on the military campaign having made great progress and continuing to make progress, while acknowledging the existence of "serious political tensions in Saigon (and perhaps elsewhere in South Vietnam) where the Diem-Nhu government is becoming increasingly unpopular."[56] On the downbeat side, the report observed that the repressive actions of Diem and Nhu "could change the present favorable military trends."[57] Also pessimistic was the conclusion that any pressures exerted by the United States were unlikely to induce any modification of unacceptable behavior by the Ngo family.[58]

Despite this pessimistic assessment, the report discussed at length the pressures available to the United States and the probable effects if they were to be used. In terms of the actual operations, it was concluded that the military training program was succeeding to such an extent that the withdrawal of some advisory and support personnel would be possible in 1963 with "the bulk" of American military personnel to be removed by 1965.[59] With respect to the Strategic Hamlet Program, a period of consolidation was recommended and with steps being taken to assure that future hamlets not be built "until they can be protected and until civic action programs can be introduced."[60]

The political tensions were severely eroding the combat efficiency of the military as well as the paramilitary and pacification operations. The United States had many potential levers to employ in order to induce more constructive behavior on the part of Diem and Nhu, but the prospects of any achieving the necessary results in a timely fashion were low to nonexistent. The intransigence of government leadership was a problem which had not been encountered to the same degree in any previous counterinsurgency campaign, and the inability of the U.S. policy makers to deal with the problem efficiently was understandable. Less understandable was the prolonged period during which the counterproductive behavior of Diem had been quite visible but apparently unnoticed by the Americans or willingly ignored by them under the misapprehension that Diem was more valuable to U.S. national goals in Vietnam than they were to him. Once policy had elevated Diem to the rank of the indispensable man, the die of difficulties had been cast. The Philippine, and to lesser extent, the Korean and Greek models, had convinced the Americans that a single, strong leader was essential in an insurgency. Even the Malayan Emergency served to reinforce that perception. Once the United States committed itself to Diem as the Vietnamese equivalent of Ramon Magsaysay, it had mounted a tiger; by the fall of 1963 it had neither a way of dismounting nor controlling the tiger's mad career.

The disheartening view of the insurgency received reinforcement from the Bureau of Intelligence and Research, which focused upon a statistical appreciation of several key indicators, all of which pointed at a severely unfavorable set of trends. The conclusions were that a shift in the military balance, unfavorable to the Government of South Vietnam, had occurred since July 1963, while there had been a sharp and simultaneous deterioration in the political situation.[61] In all classes of measurement the balance was so definitely tilted against the Saigon government that no statistical excuse could be offered. The conclusion was that even without the political turmoil, "it is possible that the Diem government would have been unable to maintain the favorable trends of preceding periods in the face of accelerated Viet Cong effort since July 1963."[62]

The situation having deteriorated, it was necessary to account for the reasons and evaluate the possible remedial actions. At first all attention was directed at the internal political tensions mentioned by Secretary McNamara and General Taylor. There can be no doubt from the intelligence reports of the time that U.S. energies were focused quite narrowly on the interlocking questions of the role of the Ngo family in the developing internal factionalism and ways of inducing Diem and Nhu in particular to change their completely counterproductive behavior.[63] Attention was paid to the question of alternative leadership, but no plans were put in train to initiate or to actively encourage a coup through early and mid-October.

The effects of actions such as the constriction of monetary aid announced on 22 October 1963, encouraged those in the Vietnamese military who were contemplating a coup. As the coup plotting and social dislocation progressed, the conduct of the war deteriorated. The coup of 1/2 November against Diem introduced a period of chaos in which no efforts were directed to the problems of conducting field operations or pacification. The assets of American intelligence and the energies of American policy makers alike were devoted to the problem of attempting to sort out what viable actions the Americans could take in the new political arena; or, was now the time to cut the losses? This problem had not been settled when JFK was assassinated three weeks later.

NOTES

1. *Pentagon Papers, Senator Mike Gravel Edition,* 4 vols. (Boston: Beacon Press 1971), I:243.

2. Ibid., I:265.

3. See the following Special National Intelligence Estimates (SNIE) and National Intelligence Estimates (NIE) all reprinted in Department of Defense, Office of the Secretary of Defense, *United States-Vietnam Relations 1945–1967,* (Washington, D.C.: House Committee on Armed Services Committee Print 1971), hereafter *USVR.*

SNIE 63.1-2/1-55 dated 2 May 1955, X:955–959

SNIE 63.1-55 dated 19 July 1955, X:993–996

SNIE 63.1-4-55 dated 13 Sept. 1955, X:998

NIE 63-56 dated 17 July 1956, X:1067–1080

SNIE 63.1-60 dated 23 August 1960, X:1298.

4. Telegram from Durbrow to the Secretary of State dated 24 December 1960, reprinted in *USVR,* X:1348–1351.

5. Title cited in Memorandum from Edward Lansdale to Admiral E. J. O'Donnell entitled "Possible Courses of Action in Vietnam" dated 13 September 1960, reprinted in *USVR,* X:1307.

6. Ibid.

7. Ibid., pp. 1308–1309.

8. Memorandum from Edward Lansdale to the Secretary of Defense entitled "Vietnam" dated 17 January 1961, reprinted in *USVR,* XI:2.

9. Ibid., pp. 5–6.

10. Report of the Gilpatrick Task Force dated 27 April 1961, reprinted in *USVR,* II:25.

11. Ibid., p. 27.

12. Memorandum from the JCS to the Secretary of Defense dated 11 April 1961, reprinted in *USVR,* XI:19–20.

13. Reprinted in *USVR,* XI:69–130.

14. Ibid., p. 96.

15. Ibid., pp. 99–100.

16. National Security Action Memorandum (NSAM) 52 dated 11 May 1961, reprinted in *USVR*, XI:136.

17. Ibid., pp. 136–37.

18. NSAM 56, "Evaluation of Paramilitary Requirements" dated 28 June 1961, reprinted in *USVR*, XI:174.

19. LBJ/NSF/52,53/S.E.A. Memos I/21a, Memorandum from the Vice President to the President dated 23 May 1961 (declassified 14 March 1984).

20. Memorandum from the Secretary of State to the President, JFK Library/NSF/VN, dated 28 July 1961.

21. Joint Chiefs of Staff "Memorandum for the Secretary of Defense" JCSM 518-61, JFK Library/NSF/VN, dated 3 August 1961.

22. Douglas Blaufarb, *The Counterinsurgency Era*, (New York: The Free Press 1977), p. 118.

23. NSAM 65 dated 11 August 1961, reprinted in Gareth Porter, *Vietnam: The Definitive Documentation of Human Decisions*, 2 vols. (Stansfordville, N.Y.: Coleman 1979) II:114–15.

24. NIE 14.3/53-61, "Prospects for North and South Vietnam" dated 16 August 1961, reprinted in Porter, *Vietnam*, II:117.

25. SNIE 53-2-61, "Bloc Support of the Communist Effort Against the Government of Vietnam" dated 5 October 1961, reprinted in *USVR*, XI:293.

26. Ibid., p. 294.

27. Memorandum to General Taylor (CM-390-61), "Counterinsurgency Operations in South Vietnam" dated 18 October 1961.

28. Ibid.

29. Telegram from Maxwell Taylor to the President dated 1 November 1961, reprinted in *USVR*, XI:334–35.

30. Ibid., p. 335.

31. Ibid., pp. 335–36.

32. Telegram from Maxwell Taylor to the President dated 1 November 1961 (#2 of that date), reprinted in *USVR*, XI:341.

33. Memorandum from the Secretary of Defense to the President dated 8 November 1961, reprinted in *USVR*, XI:343.

34. Ibid., p. 344.

35. Ibid., p. 343.

36. Memorandum from Earle Wheeler, Director, Joint Staff, to the Joint Chiefs of Staff dated 14 November 1961, reprinted in *USVR*, XI:368–99.

37. Ibid., pp. 371–72.

38. Ibid., p. 397.

39. Ibid., p. 398.

40. Talking Paper prepared for the Chairman, Joint Chiefs of Staff for a meeting with the President of the United States 9 January 1962, reprinted in *USVR*, XII:428–39.

41. Ibid., p. 439.

42. Research Memorandum RFE-27, "Progress Report on South Vietnam" dated 18 June 1962, reprinted in *USVR*, XII:470.

43. Ibid., p. 473.

44. Ibid., p. 476.

45. Ibid., p. 479.

46. Research Memorandum RFE-59, "The Situation and Short Term Prospects in South Vietnam" dated 3 December 1963, reprinted in *USVR*, XII:496.

47. Ibid., p. 503.

48. Roger Hilsman, *To Move A Nation* (New York: Doubleday 1964), p. 429.

49. W. W. Rostow, *The Diffusion of Power* (New York: Macmillan 1972), p. 280.

50. See NSAM 131, "Training Objectives in Counter-Insurgency" dated 13 March 1962 and NSAM 132, "Support of Local Police Forces for Internal Security and Counter-Insurgency Purposes" dated 19 February 1961. (Dates and serials are confirmed).

51. NIE 53-63, "Prospects in South Vietnam" dated 17 April 1963.

52. Milton Osborne, *Strategic Hamlets in South Vietnam* (Ithaca, N.Y.: Cornell University Department of Asian Studies [mimeo] 1965), pp. 32–36, 38; for Thompson's concerns see David Warner, *The Last Confucian* (New York: Praeger 1963), pp. 17–18; *Pentagon Papers*, II:158.

53. *Pentagon Papers*, II:152.

54. NIE 53-63, p. 4.

55. *Pentagon Papers*, II:158–59.

56. Memorandum for the President entitled "Report of the McNamara-Taylor Mission to South Vietnam" dated 2 October 1963, reprinted in *USVR*, XII:554.

57. Ibid.

58. Ibid., p. 555.

59. Ibid.

60. Ibid.

61. Research Memorandum RFE-90, "Statistics on the War Effort in South Vietnam Show Unfavorable Trends" dated 22 October 1963, p. 1.

62. Ibid., p. 4.

63. LBJ/NSF/CF/VN/1/M1/2, "Memorandum to the Secretary of State" from Roger Hilsman in regard to Vietnam dated 16 September 1963, (declassified January 1985), presents a fine example of the problem and alternative solutions.

12.

Fetishes and Failures

Within a month of assuming office President Johnson was faced with a situation which was quite alarming from the American perspective. After a visit to South Vietnam in December 1963, Secretary McNamara presented a report to the President which detailed a marked deterioration compared to the views which he had sent President Kennedy only three months earlier.[1] Among the reasons for his gloom were the turmoil in the Saigon government and in the South Vietnamese Armed Forces, perceived deficiencies within the American Embassy, the United States Operations Mission (USOM) and MACV, and weaknesses in operational and intelligence reporting. McNamara was bothered by the appearance of significant infiltration of men and supplies across the border from Laos and Cambodia, as well as by sea, but he concluded in this area that "the infiltration problem, while serious and annoying, is a lower priority than the key problems. . . ."[2] At this juncture, infiltration ranked lower than the problems of government stability in Saigon, restoring combat efficiency to ARVN and developing realistic pacification plans to replace the defunct Strategic Hamlet Program. Also ranking higher than border security were institutional matters such as improving the efficiency of the Country Team consisting of the chief American officials in South Vietnam and the reporting procedures of MACV and the CIA station. The style of micromanagement, which was to characterize the Vietnam War during the Johnson Administration, was implicitly resident in the requirement for improved reporting.

The tendency toward micromanagement, which had been seen in the Kennedy Administration, was reinforced by the coup against Diem, which was perceived by U.S. officials to have occurred without sufficient warning to the United States.[3] There was a pervasive perception within Washington that information of insufficient quality and quantity was arriving in a less than timely fashion, thus impairing the decision-making process. This perception was justified, but it was quite irrelevant, as in a confusing situation without familiar cultural and institutional points of reference, decisions will be based upon an imposed sense, upon referents provided by institutionally sanctioned expectations. This was the case in Vietnam as order was sought in a disorderly and confusing situation by the deceptively comforting truths of doctrinally validated experience.

Over the next three months the situation did not improve. The rumored coups culminated in an actual coup bringing General Nguyen Khanh into control at the end of January 1964. This event did nothing to assist the development of a consistent U.S. policy focus. In this winter of extreme dismay, if not discontent, the Americans attempted to formulate a programmatic mix that would arrest the continued downward spiral of events. Gradually, a consensus emerged that placed four major elements on the priority list: inducing government stability, creating a viable pacification effort, defeating the Viet Cong in the field and sealing the borders to interdict infiltration. A problem existed: no one could agree on the relative importance of these items or which might prove to be the key to success.

Another element arose in January 1964 from the notion that the insurgency was sponsored by an external, hostile power: North Vietnam. It was thought necessary to take direct action against the North to convince it to cease its support for the Southern guerrillas and to call them to heel. Maxwell Taylor pointed in this direction in a lengthy dispatch sent from Saigon in early January:

> What I am suggesting is undertaking a conditional commitment that if, in the US judgement, the GVN reaches a certain level of performance, the USG will join in an escalating campaign against the DRV. Hopefully by such action we could improve the government, unify the armed forces to some degree . . . without which we see little chance of breaking out of present downward spiral.[4]

While plans had already been made for covert action against North Vietnam by South Vietnamese personnel, the proposals of General Taylor were of an entirely different order of magnitude, implying overt actions by U.S.

aircraft or ships against the territory and facilities of North Vietnam, and thus hardly under the umbrella of "plausible deniability" which covered covert and clandestine actions.

The debate over alternative courses of action did not come to an end until National Security Council Meeting number 524 on 17 March 1964.[5] The centerpiece of the meeting was a report by Secretary McNamara. This report was in some part based upon the Secretary's recent flying visit to South Vietnam from 8 to 12 March and had gone through several draft revisions. Importantly, drafts and discussion of basic policy goals and implementation methods and options had commenced at least as early as 1 March when William Bundy wrote the first discussion draft of basic policy and program options; it was circulated among such important second-echelon staff advisors as William Sullivan, the Special Assistant to the Secretary of State for Vietnam, and John McNaughton, the Assistant Secretary of Defense for International Security Affairs.[6]

An important and persistent feature of the report was the emphasis upon the increase of infiltrated assistance and manpower from North Vietnam. In the second draft, dated 5 March, specific reference was made, not just to infiltration and its growth, but to captured equipment which was presumed to illustrate the scope of the problem although the evidence was scarcely impressive.[7] Present in the drafts, but deleted in the final version, were ideas such as the takeover of the military effort by the United States through de facto assumption of the command function at all tactical and operational levels and the introduction of a U.S. combat unit to provide security in the region of Saigon as well as to demonstrate to the Vietnamese that the U.S. commitment was credible.[8]

The final discussion draft version of the McNamara report, dated 13 March, has a particular interest because it contained a robust demurrer entered by the Director of Central Intelligence (DCI), John McCone, from some of the Secretary's conclusions and recommendations, which the Director believed to be in the category of "too little, too late."[9] McCone vigorously argued that the reports he was receiving portrayed a picture of total dissolution of the armed defense efforts of the South Vietnamese government.[10] McCone concluded with a number of recommendations, including the following:

(1) . . . implement immediately "border control" item (d) . . . i.e., "hot pursuit" into Cambodian territory.

(2) Implement immediately "border control" item (b) i.e., Vietnamese patrols with appropriate US aerial resupply into Laotian territory.

(3) Have Khanh negotiate with Chiang Kai-Shek immediately for the movement of two or possibly three divisions into the southern tip of the delta in order to give impetus and support to the hard pressed ARVN effort in that area.

(4) Implement immediately "retaliatory" item (a) . . . i.e., overt US air reconnaissance over North Vietnam. He recommends that the overflights be over populous areas for psychological in addition to intelligence purposes.[11]

All of these views and muscular proposals were deleted from the version presented to the President. Not that McCone had been rejected, rather, the DCI was simply ahead of his time. Eventually, all of his proposals would be implemented, with the sole exception being the use of Chiang's troops.

The report presented to the President on 16 March defined the objectives of U.S. policy as being the achievement of "an independent non-Communist South Vietnam" and the prevention of further regional instability which would serve to facilitate the fall to communist domination of several Southeast Asian nations, as well as the erosion of pro-Western sentiments in other countries on the Pacific Ocean rim.[12] American policy at the present moment was described as assisting the South Vietnamese to defeat the Viet Cong by "means short of the unqualified use of US combat forces."[13] The report's assessment of the present situation in Vietnam asserted that "the military tools and concepts of the U.S./GVN effort are generally sound and adequate," although "substantially more can be done in the effective employment of military forces in the economic and civic action areas."[14] It was noted that "the situation has unquestionably been growing worse, at least since September."[15]

Three basic alternative option packages were presented: negotiation on the basis of neutralization; the initiation of GVN and U.S. military actions against North Vietnam, including border control actions, retaliatory actions and graduated overt military pressure against North Vietnam by South Vietnamese and U.S. forces; and, the initiation of measures designed to improve the current situation within South Vietnam. Quite obviously, these option packages represented the classic "Goldilocks" technique so well beloved of staff personnel in which the appearance of presenting a spectrum of choices actually dictates a single preferred choice.

The third option, the preferred option here was plainly that of doing more of what had been done to date—but doing it better. To this end McNamara presented a lengthy and tolerably well-reasoned analysis of areas which needed immediate improvement and measures which might be profitably taken to assure the necessary degree of improvement. Among these were the general mobilization of South Vietnamese society, putting the "whole nation on a war footing" so as to provide the necessary manpower and unity of support for the war effort.[16] This was seen as being essential for the increases required in ARVN and paramilitary manpower. Increases in combat efficiency were to be obtained by the provision of additional U.S. training and equipment, particularly close air support aircraft.

Quite obviously, if the preferred option package did not prove effective, there would be reason and opportunity to employ the more robust alternative of applying military pressure directly upon North Vietnam. In fact, the McNamara report suggested that this course might be desirable even if the progress proved to be satisfactory and stated that the United States should be prepared to undertake the "Border Control" and "Retaliatory Actions" with a seventy-two hour notice and the "Graduated Overt Military Pressure" program with a thirty day lead time.[17] Essentially the Secretary was suggesting that the United States prepare for actions, such as hot pursuit of Viet Cong forces into Cambodia and Vietnamese cross-border penetrations into Laos, with American aerial resupply and the presence of U.S. advisors, as well as tit-for-tat reprisal "bombing strikes and commando raids" by South Vietnamese forces against targets in the North.[18] Also covered by this recommendation, under the heading of graduated overt military pressure, was the bombing of North Vietnamese "military and possibly industrial targets" by U.S. aircraft marked as such.[19] The reason given for this military option program had two unspoken bases: the need to reinforce Southern morale and the need to coerce the North, without whose external assistance the insurgency could not exist, into both withdrawing its support and facilities and actively pressuring the guerrillas into quitting.

To implement the recommended option package and initiate the supplementary proposals concerning preparations for substantial escalation of the conflict, the Secretary proposed twelve specific programmatic points, ranging from making it clear that the United States supported the new Khanh government, to authorizing the increase in the size of ARVN and the paramilitary forces, to supporting a Program for National Mobilization, to providing increased funds and mobility and air support-oriented equipment to the Vietnamese military, as well as the preparatory stage for the various escalation options. The twelve points were approved by President Johnson, after some discussion that consisted primarily of General Taylor commenting upon the military options. General Taylor, who was at this time Chairman of the Joint Chiefs, stated that "the Chiefs support the McNamara report."[20] He stated that the Chiefs wanted "to examine the possibility of reducing from 72 to 24 hours the prior notice required to undertake operations against North Vietnam."[21]

The volume of cable traffic reporting the decision of the President concerning the twelve recommendations of the McNamara report and following up upon the implementation indicates persuasively that the program was receiving the wholehearted support of the upper-level officials, and that it represented a good faith attempt to deal rapidly and constructively with the situation obtaining in South Vietnam. The program could not really prove successful, even with the best will and most effective implementation efforts, because it attempted to do too much, resulting in the diffusion of effort.

As in the case of conventional war, an attempt to defend everything meant that nothing was adequately defended. The Americans lacked a clear focus as to what the operational center of gravity should be in South Vietnam. Should the primary target of efforts be the enemy's forces in the field as the military argued, or the causes of the insurgent movement and its support among the population as the civilian consultants recommended, or the separation of the population from the guerrillas as the British argued? Even military doctrine was divided between focusing on the defeat of the guerrilla force in the field, the interdiction of cross-border supply lines and coercive actions directed against the external sponsoring power.

From this point forward, the debate over the American management of the conflict revolved around which of three operational thrusts would prove the most effective. These three might be characterized as the field victory, the social pacification and the external support interruption methods. The question was never one of an either–or sort; rather, it was one of which should receive an emphasis. Not surprisingly, the first and third alternatives found their champions at MACV, CINCPAC and the Pentagon, while the second found its primary exponents within the State Department.

A quite articulate and able presentation of the pacification alternative was the swan song of Roger Hilsman who, as he left his job as Assistant Secretary of State for Far Eastern Affairs, wrote a thoughtful memorandum on Vietnam to Secretary of State Rusk which ultimately was passed on to the President's National Security Advisor, McGeorge Bundy. Hilsman argued for an approach based on the type of civic action which typified the Philippine response to the Huks and the British efforts in the Emergency. He argued forcefully against the heavy conventional forces, with their artillery and airpower being employed in a guerrilla war, and against the use of overt operations against North Vietnam.[22] He was worried over the possibility of over-militarizing the war. He was also concerned about the absence of a central controlling figure, an equivalent of Gerald Templar. Implicitly at least, he feared that the impossibility of creating the second would insure the first.[23] He was right.

Despite strong and well-reasoned efforts for an emphasis upon pacification, the emerging consensus was directed toward the application of pressure upon North Vietnam. In a series of memos, Michael Forrestal indicated to his chief, Presidential National Security Assistant McGeorge Bundy, the status of planning concerning the increase of pressure on North Vietnam as well as the political constraints operating on these actions.[24] His reaction to the initial planning was favorable.[25] The format of the plan was a three stage escalation going from covert to overt South Vietnamese actions and finally to overt joint South Vietnamese-American actions. These included warning actions such as overflights and preparatory ones such as visible build-up of U.S. forces to "destructive activities," including naval blockade, naval bombardment and air attacks on selected North Vietnamese targets.[26] In the detailed discussions of the international and domestic political steps which would need to be taken in order to support any of these escalatory actions, weight was placed upon the notion of sending a message to Hanoi to stop support of the Southern insurgents, as in this description of overt South Vietnamese attacks on the North:

"Tit-for-tat" and other overt SVN actions against the North continue accompanied by a series of SVN announcements and a call by Khanh for meeting and cessation of VC attacks.[27]

Considering overt U.S. actions against North Vietnam, the third draft of the scenario observed that:

The move from the previous categories of action to this one can be made either suddenly or slowly, depending upon the array of military actions from which we choose. In other words, we can proceed slowly and logically [from covert] to overt support of SVN sponsored actions or we might decide to move quickly and dramatically if international pressures had reached a dangerous point. . . .[28]

In connection with the overt American actions it was argued that the demands upon the North must be stated clearly:

Public speech by President setting forth US policy and explaining the necessity for direct action against the North. US direct action takes place in accordance with JCS plan and simultaneous deployment of US forces to offset possible escalation.

. . .

Convey to North our demands which need to be satisfied in order to stop our action, expanding on points in Presidential speech. Make clear limited intentions and determination. State actions we want taken by the North and fact that compliance will have to be visible to us.[29]

The political scenario was then sent to Ambassador Henry Cabot Lodge by McGeorge Bundy on 4 April.

Two weeks later it served as the focus for discussion at a high level meeting chaired by Secretary of State Rusk and attended by Lodge, MACV Chief Paul Harkins, General Earle Wheeler of the Joint Chiefs, both of the Bundys and the CIA station chief in Saigon.[30] Central to the discussion were points made by Ambassador Lodge and the Secretary. Lodge had one strong recommendation:

that we make fullest use of a diplomatic intermediary as we begin

an ascending scale of actions and that such an intermediary be used
to *tell* (not negotiate with) the DRV at the highest possible level that
the US would be forced to take military actions. . . .[31]

Secretary Rusk was concerned that the United States realize "the importance of the strongest possible evidence of DRV infiltration, preferably on
an ascending scale."[32] Rusk's point was well taken. It was not to prove at
all easy to determine the scale or type of infiltration, let alone its value
or cruciality to the Viet Cong.

Despite the energetic pursuit of the McNamara recommendations and
the equally energetic development of plans to send messages to Hanoi,
the situation in South Vietnam during the spring of 1964 showed no sign
of improvement. A close scrutiny of the CIA weekly and monthly reports
entitled "The Situation in South Vietnam" demonstrates a continued deterioration in all important categories of indicator.[33] In these reports some
common threads may be identified: ARVN was occasionally active but
always inept. Its big battalion sweeps were either falling on empty air or
being bested by even bigger insurgent battalions. In small actions of platoon or company size, ARVN was consistently bested except when one of
the few elite units was employed. Pacification was proceeding in reverse,
with the Viet Cong dispatching small subunits to reinforce the local self-
defense guerrillas, thus expanding the area of effective Viet Cong government. The Saigon regime was anything but confident vis à vis the insurgents, but had made some limited and, quite possibly, ephemeral
improvements in its treatment of noncommunist domestic dissident
groups. Progress toward the national mobilization scheme was proceeding
with the haste of a paralytic snail. Another common thread was the absence of any discussion of infiltration or the boosting of Viet Cong numbers
by individuals from outside of South Vietnam.

Some evidence of infiltration might be found in the cable traffic from
MACV and the Embassy. However, this is contradictory and often tanta-
lizingly vague. There can be little doubt that Viet Cong units were using
areas of Laos, and to a greater extent Cambodia, for base camps and
transportation routes. Intelligence reports as well as dispatches from the
Embassy made it quite clear that the insurgents were successfully employing Cambodian and Laotian territory for various hostile activities.[34]
While this did not provide substantiation of the belief that the insurgency

was dependent upon the North for materiel support as well as direction, it did provide a focus for American policy concerns. The existence of these cross-border sanctuaries provided a doctrinally compatible venue for the effective employment of American assets prohibited within Vietnam by the continued lack of stability in Saigon.[35]

Pressure to take action against the sanctuaries, if not the North, developed through April and May with an emphasis upon cross-border operations into Laos. Operations into Cambodia by clandestine or covert American assets was disapproved of by the State Department due to the continued delicate diplomatic situation between Cambodia and South Vietnam. Additionally, it was believed on the basis of aerial imagery that significant infiltration might be occurring through the Laotian panhandle.[36] Before any final decisions could be made on the best methods of interdicting the presumed lines of communication in Laos, a further problem developed when the Vietnamese strongman Khanh indicated a desire to issue a decree putting South Vietnam on a war footing.

At first, this seemed to be in line with the national mobilization recommendation in the McNamara report, but as Khanh explained his thinking to Ambassador Lodge on 4 May, it was obvious that the Vietnamese were contemplating something considerably greater in magnitude than the McNamara scheme.[37] Khanh's plan included a specific warning of possible invasion to Hanoi.[38] Lodge endorsed Khanh's desire to declare a state of war and his spirit of "get on with the job and not sit here indefinitely taking casualties."[39] In response to a Flash category interrogatory (immediate response required) based upon his initial report, Lodge evaluated Khanh's motives and conclusions:

> I don't think he has reached the conclusion that he cannot win the war in the South without military action in the North. And, you are, of course, right that there is an inconsistency between his statements about "making the agony endure" and his claim that he has regained control over two million people, which he repeated to me last night. This last is a very interesting point for many reasons, including public relations. I understand MACV J-2 will try to plot these two million on the map.[40]

This exchange gave the American decision makers cause for pause, as it provided additional impetus to the McNamara notion that the use of U.S. air or naval force against the North might be necessary for reasons of morale in Saigon.

By the middle of May 1964, it had again become necessary for Mc-Namara and Taylor to go to Saigon in an attempt to get some measure of understanding of a situation grown increasingly tenuous and nebulous. In a lengthy meeting with South Vietnamese President Khanh, McNamara and Taylor developed a number of significant points. Khanh saw himself in an unstable political situation which could only be stabilized by the mobilization of the South Vietnamese populace. That would necessitate the taking of action by sea and by air against the North, if the North, after warning, refused to stop the insurgents in the South.[41] In an attempt to gain greater American military presence in the war, Khanh shrewdly manipulated his listeners' preconceptions by asserting that control of the Viet Cong was to be found in Hanoi "and maybe further north."[42]

Faced with this attitude in Saigon, the United States decided to provide a back channel warning to Hanoi, using a Canadian diplomat as the intermediary. That the intent was to provide the North with a warning before embarking upon a program of sanctions, including bombing, was obvious in the wording of a Lodge telegram concerning the upcoming mission. After reminding the Department of his long-standing views, Lodge stated that the Canadian must tell Hanoi that "the Americans are utterly determined to win the struggle in South Vietnam and will do whatever is necessary to win it."[43] He continued, advising that the Canadian tell the North Vietnamese, "if they persist in their present gross and murderous intrusion into South Vietnam, they will unquestionably be punished."[44] Warming to the challenge of dissuading a hostile, external sponsoring power he added:

> If prior to the Canadian's trip to Hanoi there has been a terroristic act of the proper magnitude, then I suggest that a specific target in North Vietnam be considered as a prelude to his arrival. The Vietnamese air force must be made capable of doing this and they should undertake this type of action.
>
> . . .
>
> What is complicated, but really effective, is to bring our power to bear in a precise way so as to get specific results.

Another advantage of this procedure is that when, as and if the time ever came that our military activities against the North became overt, we would be in a strong moral position with regard to US public opinion, the US Congress and the UN. . . .[45]

Although Lodge's position was too robust for the Washington decision makers at that time, he foreshadowed the ultimate decisions in all major respects. Lodge also mirrored the decision-making process in another fashion. He assumed that the government of North Vietnam and its subordinates, including the Viet Cong insurgents, shared the Western process of evaluating costs and benefits so as to minimize the cost, even if benefits are not maximized.

The concept of "minimax," or the game of the "Prisoner's Dilemma," bedeviled not only Lodge but the American policy level generally. Originally a creation of the brilliant mathematician specializing in game theory, Johnny Von Neumann, the Prisoner's Dilemma represented a basic model of strategy in which each player would choose rationally his "least worst" alternative, the alternative that would provide the least negative or destructive payoff. This academic game had entered the venue of defense analysis through the Rand Corporation in the 1950s, with the rise of the systems analysis approach to the problems of nuclear targeting and the selection between alternative nuclear weapons systems and employment strategies. Subsequently, it had become a form of touchstone for the evaluation of all strategic options. While it might have been a useful tool in some strategic modeling, its utility existed only so long as both antagonistic players shared the same basic assumptions and values. As Von Neumann himself had commented, the game lost all value if one of the prisoners faced with the choice of talking or risking the possibility of a long jail term was absolutely indifferent to the difference between a long and short term of confinement. In short, the North Vietnamese were like that prisoner; they were indifferent to the seemingly rational choice of persist and be bombed or desist and receive economic assistance. The inability of the Americans to recognize that the basic rules of the game were not applicable to the putative opponent meant that they persisted in an ever more vain attempt to make the player accept those rules.

While the conversations and planning were continuing in Saigon, the war was continuing in the provinces with consequences that were ever more bleak, as a CIA Memorandum reported in mid-May.[46] At the same time, Saigon was reporting that the manpower and cost of patrolling the Cambodian border would be prohibitively high with results not guaranteed.[47] Shortly thereafter, the Embassy reports of prisoner interrogations provided more evidence of continued Cambodian complicity in the maintenance of the Viet Cong sanctuaries.[48] There were problems which required resolution at the highest levels.

On 25 May the recommendation was made to President Johnson by McGeorge Bundy that:

the US will use selected and carefully graduated military force against North Vietnam, under the following conditions: (1) after appropriate diplomatic and political warning and preparation, (2) and unless such warning and preparation—in combination with other efforts—should produce a sufficient improvement of non-Communist prospects in South Vietnam and Laos to make military action against North Vietnam unnecessary.[49]

No hasty decision was made on this proposal. Instead, a list of alternative demonstrative actions aimed at North Vietnam was made as were similar listings directed at the strengthening of South Vietnam. These were considered at a meeting held on 5 June.

At this meeting several actions were discussed with the intent of bolstering the Saigon government, particularly in terms of the so-called "Eight Critical Provinces." The net effect of the options available was assessed as being little or nil within the next three to six months. It was concluded that the taking of all feasible measures in the critical provinces would result, at best as follows: ". . . the situation will jog along about as it is (assuming Khanh is not assassinated)—it may continue to deteriorate slowly."[50]

Because there was no immediate joy to be sought within South Vietnam, actions in the North were seen as necessary; but before any bellicose alternatives might be planned, certain preparatory steps must be accomplished. In the area of public information and propaganda, a "peace offensive" was recommended to be aimed at Congress, the press, the public and foreign diplomats.[51] It was also recommended: "About mid-July consider requesting a Congressional Resolution supporting US policy in

Southeast Asia."[52] While this pacifistic effort was continuing, so also would the planning for more truculent activities.[53]

Helpfully, a list of military options illustrative of the moves designed to convincingly convey to the North the intentions of the United States to resist or prevent any further communist advances in Laos or South Vietnam was presented. In addition to the continuation and expansion of covert operations currently in place, the moves contemplated included the commencement of U.S. low level flights over North Vietnam, the use of ARVN reconnaissance teams in Laos and the introduction of low level armed reconnaissance flights along the supply lines believed to exist in the Laotian panhandle. Other actions discussed were the use of "harassment" teams in Laos and the concomitant expansion of U.S. military advisors in the "counterinsurgency program" by 500.[54] A broad spectrum of air operation options was presented as was a list of highly visible U.S. troop movements, which would result in the posturing of American forces to respond quickly to a South Vietnam deployment order.

The 5 June meeting was followed just five days later with another at which the centerpiece was the discussion of the political scenario necessary to achieve the desired Congressional Resolution endorsing U.S. policy and programs in Southeast Asia.[55] The primary goal was obtaining bipartisan support and removing Southeast Asia from the forthcoming presidential election. While the Congressional Resolution was not the only means by which this might be attained, it was the most preferred. The early adoption of the Resolution would not only provide the Administration with the desired degree of freedom; it would signal the world community clearly that the Administration had that freedom.[56] It was plain, although unstated at the time, that the Congressional Resolution would effectively clear the decks for any aerial interdiction efforts or the type of tit-for-tat and coercive bombardment of North Vietnam already discussed.

The Joint Chiefs had been proceeding with the planning of military operations, specifically CINCPAC OPLAN 37-64, 98-64 and 98A-64, following the directives of NSAM 288 and the instructions of the Assistant Secretary of Defense for International Security Affairs, John McNaughton. Of the three plans, OPLAN 37-64 was the main focus with the other two being in support roles. NASM 288 had been issued as a result of the decision taken at the March 15th McNamara report meeting, authorizing the Department of Defense:

To prepare to be in a position on 72 hours notice to initiate the full range of Laotian and Cambodian "Border Control Actions" . . . and the "Retaliatory Actions" against North Vietnam and to be in a position on 30 days' notice to initiate the program of "Graduated Overt Military Pressure" against North Vietnam.[57]

Working from this policy guidance as well as the governing doctrine, the planning staff of the Joint Chiefs as well as the planners of CINCPAC developed the necessary operational plans (OPLAN). These supplemented and refined the earlier 59 series of OPLANs which dealt with mixed conventional and partisan war contingencies.

The center of the new plans, OPLAN 37-64, stated the mission of the U.S. forces of Pacific Command (PACOM) as being support of, or participation with, "RVN forces in the conduct of graduated operations to eliminate or reduce to negligible proportions DRV support of VC insurgency in the Republic of Vietnam. . . ."[58] Three categories of action were envisaged: curtailment of VC activity across the borders of Laos or Cambodia; selective retaliatory actions by the South Vietnamese against North Vietnam; and expanded military pressures against North Vietnam by both South Vietnam and the United States.

This would result in the insurgents being deprived of sanctuaries, vital supplies and manpower. In addition, the North Vietnamese support of the insurgency would be halted because of the disruption of "selected portions of the military, logistic and economic structures of North Vietnam."[59] Recognizing the risks of operating close to the sphere of interest of the People's Republic of China as had been proven so dramatically in the Korean War, a concern of the planners was to posture U.S. forces appropriately for either offensive or defensive actions in the event of a Chinese response.[60]

The immediate tactical operations were divided into the three components of border control, retaliatory actions and graduated escalation. While provision was made in the first for the use of South Vietnamese ground teams, the primary instrument of implementation was American and South Vietnamese air power. The South Vietnamese Air Force (SVNAF) would act against lightly defended areas, but would be backed by the unmarked U.S. aircraft of the FARMGATE as well as other armed reconnaissance programs. In the tit-for-tat retaliatory option, marked U.S.

aircraft would engage in high and low level reconnaissance flights and in airstrikes as directed. SVNAF aircraft would engage in the majority of the bombing and would undertake operations such as the mining of major North Vietnamese ports.[61] The graduated overt military pressure option consisted almost entirely of airstrikes carried out by SVNAF, FARMGATE and, finally, U.S. B-57 bombers from Clark AFB (Air Force Base) in the Philippines.[62] Targets were given by categories and the number in each category. In the graduated escalation category, there were fifty-nine targets counted in addition to thirty-nine previously listed in the retaliatory action category.[63] A roster of the forces to be employed under OPLAN 37-64 was attached and indicated a very impressive chunk of U.S. assets in the Pacific.[64] The subsidiary plans were for the covert (98-64) and overt (98A-64) cross-border operations into Laos. Both constituted only modest increases in the war effort and, a success commensurate with the investment was confidently anticipated.

Although the two subsidiary plans were modest and relatively low risk, the major plan was not at all modest and not at all low in risk. While the planners foresaw the possibility of reaction from China or North Vietnam, they thought strictly in terms of conventional actions including airstrikes against American airbases in South Vietnam and conventional raids or invasions by ground forces as well as the strengthening of North Vietnamese air defenses by Chinese "volunteers." No thought was given to the possibility of a response by the guerrillas in the South, including sapper attacks against the American bases or other U.S. facilities and personnel—in a sense retaliation for retaliation.

These new plans were developed against a background of continuing covert operations under a number of programs directed against North Vietnam and the supposed supply routes in Laos. The generic term 34A covered the clandestine actions taken against North Vietnam by air-inserted ground teams, while various seaborne raids and seabased harassment actions were called MAROPS 34A. While most of the inserted or infiltrated ground teams were rapidly captured or killed by the North Vietnamese security forces, some were successful as were most of the MAROPS.[65] Thus it was intended that they continue as the only, even marginally successful, operational alternative to date. The semiclandestine use of unmarked aircraft in reconnaissance and interdiction roles into the Laotian panhandle under the rubric of FARMGATE would continue.

Even the marginal successes of the various clandestine and covert activities looked good in the summer of 1964 when compared with the performance of the South Vietnamese Armed Forces on the battlefield or the progress being made in the resuscitation of the pacification program. Reports reaching the White House through July painted an alarming picture of collapse on the battlefield.[66] No matter how these reports were examined, the conclusion was clear: ARVN was being consistently outfought on the battlefield and had lost the initiative to the Viet Cong in a clear and decisive way. Pacification plans remained just that, plans. The basic government ideas were described by the Embassy as a "systematic response to real challenge of communist subversion by aiming at destruction of Viet Cong covert politico-military organization of rural areas. . . ."[67] Nonetheless, they remained only in the talking and paper stage by late July, in large measure because of the continuing political turmoil in Saigon.[68]

Given the continued severe decline in ARVN and GVN morale, the pressure was on the United States not simply to continue the covert actions and activities such as the intelligence-oriented DESOTO patrols of the Gulf of Tonkin made by elderly destroyers, but to seek ways of legitimately instituting the air attack plans so long under consideration. The only additional actions potentially open to the Americans, which boded well to have any favorable effect, were those outlined the previous March aimed at the borders and the North. If these actions were undertaken, they might not only improve morale within the Government and Armed Forces of South Vietnam, they might serve as well to reduce some of the pressure building on the fragile Vietnamese government.

But first it was necessary to determine the probable responses of the adversary to these new gambits. Kremlin watching was a difficult art; Peking watching an arcane exercise in augury, but Hanoi watching in the 1960s was virtually nothing but the projection of preconceptions. DCI John McCone did his best, compiling the finest product of the CIA's stable of analysts and academic hired guns into a memorandum for the President in late July.[69] Looking at each of the three options under active planning and preparation, he assessed the probable responses of the North Vietnamese and their Chinese and Soviet sponsors. With the exception of airstrikes on North Vietnam itself, the determination was that the response would be of a low order and severely limited to the actual vicinity of the attacks.[70]

The predictions were not so optimistic regarding airstrikes on North

Vietnam. Although hopeful that the fear of further escalation would inhibit the level of riposte, McCone believed that the North might attempt isolated air raids on South Vietnamese cities, including Saigon, in the hopes of destroying morale.[71] Other projected reactions of a "local military or semi-military" character included the strengthening of North Vietnamese air defenses, rated "very likely," as was the increase in general Viet Cong ambushes and attacks; rated "likely" was the intensification of Viet Cong sabotage on airfields in South Vietnam.[72] Rated less than even in chances was the notion that the Viet Cong might initiate a "widespread campaign of terrorism against Americans, including civilians and dependents in South Vietnam."[73] Conspicuously and surprisingly absent from the analysis, considering the concern over the Viet Cong's increasing use of weapons such as rockets and large caliber mortars, was the idea that the insurgents might undertake the long-range bombardment of airfields, particularly those with U.S. aircraft, rather than make attempts at sabotage. Obviously, the precautions against the latter were quite different from those against sabotage.

In any event, the risks seemed to be quite acceptable, even very slight. What about the potential benefits? Other than perhaps improving the morale of the South Vietnamese government, which in and of itself would guarantee neither stability nor improved resolve and efficiency in carrying out the necessary programs of field operations and pacification, just what might be legitimately expected in the way of results, particularly from the border control option which was not only the least risky, but also did not involve the need for an unpleasantly high-profile event initiated by the insurgents or a high-volume debate in the United States prior to the election? The obvious answer lay in the control or interdiction of infiltration.

The problem of infiltration eludes easy definition and facile explanation. It was a focus of concern and debate from the very beginning of the war, particularly following the obvious escalation in insurgent activities in 1963. The Americans' military doctrine credited infiltration as the basic engine of guerrilla success and its absence as the basic cause of guerrilla failure. Given this official view, it was scarcely surprising that infiltration and how to curtail it occupied a high priority on the military's list.

The basic position on infiltration was established quite early in the Johnson Administration as the following CINCPAC situation report demonstrates:

Except for the communists, no one knows how many men have been infiltrated into SVN during 1963. COMUSMACV intelligence holds rather concrete evidence that some 784 persons infiltrated this year. However, the overland infiltration routes have not been effectively or militarily blocked.[74]

The problem of accurately determining the amount and type of infiltration was recognized at an early date as well, as COMUSMACV had stated in early December 1963.[75] While the military had a strong willingness to insist on the growth of infiltration, this tendency was not paralleled by the CIA whose weekly reports mentioned it only tangentially, if at all.

By mid-1964, MACV believed itself to be in possession of high-quality proof of continued and massive infiltration of personnel. COMUSMACV reported in July that recent interrogations of captured Viet Cong indicated that, while regular units of the People's Army of North Vietnam (PAVN) had not yet infiltrated the South, organized formations of draftees from the South were exfiltrated to the North and then reinfiltrated to the South after training.[76] The Embassy agreed with the MACV stance regarding the importance of sealing the borders as indicated by the number of reports regarding suspected infiltration from Laos and Cambodia. It is important to note that the Embassy was no more able than MACV either to quantify the infiltration pattern or to assess its importance to the increase in Viet Cong strength and combat efficiency. Further complicating the evaluation of the nature, extent and effect of the presumed infiltration was the simple reality that some, perhaps much or even most of the significant infiltration of materiel came by sea, making use of the complex of waterways in the Delta region. This was an initial concern of Secretary McNamara's as expressed in December of 1963.[77] The problem was of such magnitude that even with the assistance of several teams of naval experts and engineering consultants, the only response, even months later, to this aspect of the problem had been the repeated suggestion that the Government of South Vietnam tighten controls on international shipping using the Mekong river bound for Cambodia.[78]

Despite the later studies which sought to maximize the effectiveness of infiltration or its results in the increase in the Viet Cong's capabilities, it is quite difficult to assert with any degree of certainty that the infiltration occurring through the summer of 1964 was of very great importance in the development of the Viet Cong. As evidence of this it is only necessary to consult the MACV analysis of Viet Cong strength as it was perceived in July 1964, after improvements in the intelligence process allowed the identification of guerrilla units previously not located in South Vietnam. The U.S. command had identified 46 battalions, 132 separate companies, 29 separate platoons and five regimental headquarters comprising approximately 31,000 guerrillas.[79] In the same telegram MACV reported that the ARVN high command estimate was 34,000 guerrillas organized into 48 battalions, 150 independent companies, 126 independent platoons and seven regimental headquarters.[80]

No one suggested that all or even most of these guerrillas infiltrated from the North or had received their training in the North, Laos or Cambodia. Even a highly influential and misleading Rand report circulated to the JCS and to the White House on the urgings of Air Force Chief of Staff Curtis LeMay refrained from arguing the numerical importance of infiltrators, preferring to sound a theme to be echoed often: that the infiltrated personnel were the "quality" people: cadre, technicians and experienced field commanders.[81] The same argument was employed by the Department of State in the classified study which served as the basis for the later "white paper" on the growing American involvement in Vietnam:

> To some the level of infiltration from the North may seem modest in comparison with the total size of the armed forces of the Republic of Vietnam. But any one-for-one calculations are totally misleading in the kind of warfare going on in Viet Nam. It has long been realized by experts who have studied past experience in guerrilla combat that the burdens of defense are vastly heavier than those of attack. In Malaya, the Philippines and elsewhere it has been demonstrated that a ratio of 15-to-1 in favor of the forces of order is required for success in meeting the threat of the guerrilla hit-and-run tactics.[82]

The analysis of the effect of infiltration was of the same calibre as the history lesson concerning "tie-down ratios."

The amount of personnel and materiel being infiltrated across the land borders of South Vietnam was at best an insubstantial percentage of the insurgent strength and combat capabilities in the summer and fall of 1964. While there was without a doubt some infiltration and some of the weapons brought into the country were of a heavy nature, the main source of weapons for the Viet Cong was the armed forces of South Vietnam.[83] At this stage, foreign-manufactured weapons were few and far between as was indicated by the difficulty experienced by MACV in obtaining even a handful to substantiate the claims of external support.

Only later, after the fall of 1964, did externally supplied materiel become significant. Only later, after the fall of 1964, did infiltrators from the North constitute a significant fraction of the Viet Cong combat strength. This increase in infiltration, this enhancement of the combat effectiveness of the Viet Cong after September 1964 can be clearly traced. In a very real sense the American attempt to interdict infiltration and, failing that, to halt it at its source by means of aerial bombardment, actually served to create the increased and more effective supply of trained manpower and materiel from the North. One of the greatest ironies of the Vietnam War was that the Americans, in an attempt to solve a problem that did not exist, created a problem that could not be solved.

The plans to interdict infiltration or to coerce the North Vietnamese into ceasing their sponsorship of the Southern insurgents were not the dark and wicked plots of small-minded and evil men. They were the necessary result of an incorrect understanding of the nature of insurgent war in general and the situation in South Vietnam in particular. They were the consequence of a doctrine which emphasized the necessity of destroying the guerrilla in the field or his means and ability to wage war, to the exclusion of other means of countering the insurgent threat such as making the physical and social environment in which he operated a hostile place without refuge.

Neither was there a black conspiracy to provoke a direct North Vietnamese attack upon American aircraft or ships. The incidents in the Gulf of Tonkin on 2 and 4 August were not the results of deliberate and planned provocation. Neither were they fabrications invented by sailors fearful of radar ghosts in the dark, nor acts of conspiratorial tergiversation at the highest echelons desperate to cloak their aggressive designs in some semblance of legality.

The patrols in the Gulf of Tonkin, codenamed DESOTO, had been occurring on a regular basis for some time. As their primary purpose was the collection of electronic intelligence upon North Vietnamese radar and radio communications, the patrols took advantage of the MAROPS 34A activities. When the small craft of the MAROPS units closed upon their North Vietnamese shore targets to engage them at close range with small calibre artillery such as 57mm and 76mm recoilless rifles, the defenders would turn on their surveillance and fire control radars as well as their air defense radar system, and the command and control radio links. The DESOTO ships would catch all these valuable emissions in their wide open electronic nets. While the DESOTO patrols and the MAROPS 34A units would work in close proximity, the U.S. warships were not protective cover for the SVN small craft; nor were the U.S. destroyers acting as the provocateur of the piece.

It is not now known and probably never will be known whether the attacks on the American destroyers *Maddox* and *Turner Joy* were the result of local initiative on the part of the North Vietnamese patrol boat flotilla commander or the result of Hanoi's miscalculation or misappreciation of the situation or, contrarily, the result of careful calculation with the intent of warning the Americans and the South to cease the increasingly annoying MAROPS.

Quite possibly it was the reaction of a Hanoi regime made more sensitive to the dangers of aggression from the South because of the shrill "March to the North" campaign which had dominated South Vietnamese propaganda in preceding weeks. If the Americans were of the belief that this campaign was designed to "associate US with policy of increased military pressure on North Vietnam" it would be silly to have assumed that the North did not see the same potential in an obvious attempt to stir war hysteria in the South to a very high level.[84] In any event the North Vietnamese attack was not unpredictable; it was not unexpected, but it was not specifically sought.

The Congressional Joint Resolution proposed by President Johnson and passed with only two dissenting votes on 7 August was the Joint Resolution noted in the political scenarios for some months. Its passage was not sufficient reason to place the destroyers in hazard as the White House firmly believed that they would be able to acquire the desired bipartisan support in any event. Rather the President merely took advantage of an opportunity too good to miss to gain the desired Congressional endorsement of past and present policy as well as involvement and authorization for future policy and programs. The fact that the media attention on the Gulf of Tonkin incident had been both well focused and well handled served to assure passage of the desired Resolution with a whoop and a holler. It also had the effect of providing the incident with a degree of importance both politically and militarily which was, and is, totally undeserved. The two results of the incident, the Joint Resolution and the first of the tit-for-tat retaliatory responses, would have occurred in the fall of 1964 at the latest, even if the DESOTO patrols had continued to steam unhindered in the Gulf, trailing their electromagnetic nets behind them.

Before continuing, it should be noted that the careful distinction drawn in all sincerity by Secretary McNamara and other planners between "retaliatory actions" and "overt graduated military pressure" was patently absurd. It relied upon a degree of tacit agreement on the relative value of targets which, while well within the realm of the plausible to the defense theologians at such think tanks of great notoriety, as the Rand and the Hudson Institute, was quite impossible to achieve in the real world. However, the distinction was well suited to the micromanagerial style of the McNamara Defense Department and the desire, indeed need, for personal involvement of the President. That it was a sincere belief and not a cynical pose of the decision makers is obvious from the seriousness with which it was contained in the entire planning procedure as well as in the process by which individual targets and actions were approved at the highest echelons.

After a transient period of optimism concerning the return of political stability to Saigon and the possibility of regenerating the pacification program at last, during which the Embassy in Saigon apparently saw the strategy of the insurgents and their Hanoi patrons as being that of political destabilization rather than military victory, it became obvious that neither stability nor immediate improvements in the pacification portions of the counterinsurgency program were possible.[85] Again the GVN had dissolved in a whirling gavotte of coups, attempted coups and resignations which prompted the CIA to conclude in early September, "at present the odds are against the emergence of a stable government capable of prosecuting the war in South Vietnam."[86] Although somewhat more optimistic, the reports of the Embassy on the political situation were not sufficient to turn the scale against the increasingly truculent policy evolving in Washington.[87] William Bundy became frankly truculent as his draft scenarios succeeded one another. By the first week of September he had resolved

all previously held ambiguities in favor of the most hawkish interpretation.[88] Among the recommendations for improving the situation within
South Vietnam was the radical and previously rejected notion that the
United States take command of the ARVN effort, as well as more conventional steps such as enlarging the American advisory effort above the
currently authorized level of 23,000 and enlarging the combat role of U.S.
aircraft already in South Vietnam.[89] It was also suggested that American
military units be used in the pacification program but in a security rather
than civic action role.[90] Bundy also noted "general Washington" approval
for the idea of inserting a U.S. division onto the southern edge of the
Demilitarized Zone (DMZ) to relieve pressure on the overstressed ARVN
1st Division.[91] Looking beyond the tactical situation in South Vietnam,
he discussed a broad spectrum of options implementing the three interdiction and coercion categories first proposed by McNamara the preceding
March. His refinement of the objectives of such action included an emphasis upon the increase of the actual and "portended" cost of the war to
the DRV, "thus improving our bargaining position in the event of negotiations," as well as increasing the "actual and apparent contribution in
risk and effort by the US," thus improving local and regional images of
the United States as "a trustworthy ally."[92]

There was nothing new presented by the Bundy memorandum regarding interdiction efforts. Much of his argument and detailed planning was
taken from a July JCS memo outlining the air actions which might be
taken against the "Viet Cong supply lines in southern Laos" as well as
"Ground Operations into Southern Laos," including lists of targets, forces
or sorties needed and munitions to be employed.[93] Bundy listed the options perceived to be open to the North and the Viet Cong in response
to the attacks, particularly overt U.S. or U.S./GVN attacks on North
Vietnam. Apparently having been briefed on General William Westmoreland's previously expressed concerns, he included the possibility, which
he rated as "likely," of Viet Cong mortar attacks on U.S. aircraft in South
Vietnamese airfields.[94] Bundy took an interesting position on the graduated military pressure option, bemoaning the real possibility that the
communist response to new air and cross-border actions might not "give
us the occasion for clear and sharp retaliation. However, such opportunities may unfold and should certainly be taken."[95]

Bundy had the idea that graduated pressure on the North constituted a concept which in essence was provocative.[96] In discussing the actions included in the orchestration of an American-South Vietnamese "crescendo" against the North, Bundy again followed the JCS plan, particularly with regard to the mining of Haiphong. The Joint Chiefs had recommended, however, that such actions be clandestine.[97] Bundy commented that "general Washington reaction is that we should not consider very strong pressures of the character described, at least for the present."[98]

Strong pressures were not initiated. Rather the plans for the cross-border attacks on the supposed Viet Cong infiltration routes in Laos were implemented both by air and by land, employing plans which had been in the works for some while with the final refinements occurring during the previous month.[99] From the first, aerial interdiction was preferred to any ground efforts to achieve the same goal. The air strikes were planned in the greatest possible detail and integrated overt flights from both the Vietnamese Air Force and the Royal Laotian Air Force (RLAF) as well as covert aircraft from the United States under the FARMGATE and WHITE STAR reconnaissance and interdiction programs.[100] Authorization was provided for the overt U.S. jet aircraft of YANKEE TEAM to engage hostile aircraft encountered over northern Laos.[101] To facilitate carrying out the actions over and against Laotian territory, a special coordinating committee of the Embassies in Saigon, Vientiane and Bangkok was formed in order to deal with the interesting diplomatic problems arising from this combined clandestine effort.[102] After another three weeks of study and discussion between the respective governments, a list of acceptable and valuable targets was drawn up, specifying thirteen sites which would be engaged by the RLAF and another four which would be struck by YANKEE TEAM jets.[103] After months of intense military planning and weeks of diplomatic effort, it finally appeared as though the weight of U.S. ordnance would make itself felt.

During the same period, the U.S. Navy was attempting to secure the reauthorization of the DESOTO patrols, arguing that the reinstitution of the patrols would assist in getting the message to "Hanoi and Peiping that continuation of their present course in SEA will cost them heavily."[104] In addition to whatever message-sending capability existed in an elderly destroyer or two, CINCPAC stated that real military advantages would accrue from a continuation of the patrols both in terms of intelligence collection and in positioning U.S. ships to help deter or interdict seaborne infiltration. The argument for the resumption continued through the balance of September with the navy providing routes and other data to the Joint Chiefs to counter any potential political disapproval. Most importantly, CINCPAC had to generate and transmit to its component operational elements a series of fragmentary orders providing for the U.S. air units to conduct retaliatory strikes on North Vietnam as "punitive reprisal actions" for attacks by the North upon the revived DESOTO patrols.[105] Within the nineteen pages of these "frag orders" were the complete mission profiles for a wide assortment of targets, including the number of sorties, munitions and ancillaries. The prior issuance of these orders would later facilitate the employment of any type of airstrike against the North Vietnamese.

The air war was escalating within South Vietnam where U.S. aircraft had been allowed to operate in combat support roles for some time. The rules of engagement had been revised from time to time but the basic restrictions upon weaponry had remained unchanged. Finally, permission was given to employ the newer types of cluster bomb munitions such as napalm and white phosphorus bombs, which had been employed previously, and which were considerably more effective in antipersonnel roles than the World War II ordnance had been.[106] The combination of increased use of American and South Vietnamese aircraft in all the various venues, including Laos, South Vietnam and, at least on occasion, North Vietnam, with the increased effectiveness of newer air delivered ordnance, must have proven a serious annoyance to those on the receiving end. The result was an attempt to send a message of resolve to the Americans.

The message was sent on the night of 31 October when Viet Cong mortars attacked the Bien Hoa airfield. Although never achieving the notoriety of the Gulf of Tonkin incident, the Viet Cong attack on the Bien Hoa airfield marked an important point in the military conduct and the decision-making dynamics of the war. In a sense, the attack constituted the Pearl Harbor of the Vietnam conflict, for the reaction to it arose more from a sense of outrage at the temerity of the Viet Cong than from the actual effects of the attack. The enemy had done the unexpected. Despite the mention made of the possibility of a guerrilla attack by mortars or rockets by General Westmoreland and William Bundy, it was not really believed that the insurgents would have the barefaced affrontery to engage an American base directly. In the back of everyone's mind was the unspoken assumption that the North Vietnamese would react in a comfortingly conventional fashion. Assumptions and reality did not match and the Americans were upset.

NOTES

1. LBJ/NSF/CF/VN/1/M2/130, Memorandum for the President entitled "Vietnam Situation" dated 21 December 1963.

2. Ibid., p. 3.

3. An instructive view is that held by DCI John McCone in LBJ/NSF/CF/VN/1/M2/141, memorandum of conversation dated 21 December 1963, p. 2.

4. LBJ/NSF/IMT/3/12–16, Telegram from Taylor to Secretary of State dated 6 January 1961, serial 2052, sec. IV, p. 2.

5. LBJ/NSF/NSC/1/5/2, "Summary Record of the NSC Meeting No. 524 March 17, 1964 12:00 Noon—Report of Secretary McNamara's trip to Vietnam."

6. LBJ/NSF/CF/VN/2/M4/94.

7. LBJ/NSF/CF/VN/2/C5/69b, Draft Memorandum for the President entitled "South Vietnam and Southeast Asia" dated 5 March 1964, p. 6.

8. Ibid., pp. 13–14.

9. LBJ/NSF/CF/VN/2/M5/73a, Memorandum for the President, entitled "South Vietnam" dated 13 March 1964, p. 11.

10. Ibid.

11. Ibid.

12. LBJ/NSF/NSC/1/5/9, Memorandum for the President entitled "South Vietnam" dated 16 March 1964, (declassified 22 November 1982), p. 1.

13. Ibid., p. 2.

14. Ibid.

15. Ibid., p. 3.

16. Ibid., p. 10.

17. Ibid., p. 15.

18. Ibid., p. 7.

19. Ibid., p. 7.

20. "Summary Record March 17, 1964," p. 1.

21. Ibid.

22. LBJ/NSF/CF/VN/52,53/S.E.A. Cables I/2a, Memorandum to the Secretary entitled "South Vietnam" dated 14 March 1964, (declassified 14 March 1984), p. 3.

23. Ibid., p.4.

24. LBJ/NSF/CF/VN/2/C5/57,57A,59E,61,63, (declassified 14 August 1984).

25. Ibid., document 60.

26. Ibid., document 57a, p. 1.

27. Ibid., document 57a, p. 6.

28. Ibid., document 59e, p. 8.

29. Ibid., p. 9.

30. LBJ/NSF/CF/VN/3/M7/182, Memorandum for the Record entitled "Discussion of Possible Extended Action in Relation to Vietnam" dated 27 April 1964, (declassified 14 July 1983), p. 1.

31. Ibid.

32. Ibid., p. 4.

33. LBJ/NSF/CF/VN/2/C5/67; 3/M6/50; 3/M7/152; 3/M7/153; 3/M7/154; 3/M7/155; 4/M8/135; 4/M8/47; 4/M8/48; 4/M9/13 cover the period from mid-March to mid-May 1964. See also the USOM weekly reports such as 4/C8/41; 3/C6/118.

34. See as one example of many LBJ/NSF/CF/VN/3/C7/17.

35. As an example of the frustration of programs by the internal disarray see LBJ/NSF/CF/VN/3/C7/95, sec. II, p. 1.

36. LBJ/NSF/CF/VN/3/C7/11, (declassified 14 July 1983); 3/C7/119.

37. LBJ/NSF/CF/VN/4/C8/50, Telegram to Rusk, McNamara, Bundy and Harriman from Lodge, serial 2108, dated 4 May 1964.

38. Ibid.

39. Ibid., sec. 2, p. 2.

40. LBJ/NSF/198,199,200/LBJ-Rusk-Lodge/v1/63, Telegram from Lodge to Rusk dated 6 May 1964, (declassified 25 January 1984).

41. LBJ/NSF/195/AID Meeting/23, Telegram from Lodge to Rusk reporting Khanh-McNamara Conversation, dated 14 May 1964, (declassified 12 May 1983), sec. 1, pp. 1–2; sec. 2, p. 1.

42. Ibid., sec. 2, p. 2.

43. LBJ/NSF/198,199,200/LBJ-Rusk-Lodge/vol. 1/60, Telegram from Lodge to the President dated 15 May 1964, (declassified 25 January 1984).

44. Ibid.

45. Ibid., pp. 2–3.

46. LBJ/NSF/CF/VN/4/M8/48, Intelligence Memorandum entitled "The Viability of South Vietnam" dated 15 May 1964, p. 1.

47. LBJ/NSF/CF/VN/4/C9/107, Telegram from American Embassy Saigon to Department of State, serial 2220, dated 15 May 1964.

48. LBJ/NSF/CF/VN/4/C9/76, Telegram from American Embassy Saigon to Department of State, serial 2256, dated 20 May 1964.

49. LBJ/NSF/52,53/S.E.A. Memos IIb/112b, Memorandum to the President entitled "Basic Recommendation and Projected Course of Action on Southeast Asia" dated 25 May 1964, (declassified 16 March 1984), p. 1.

50. LBJ/NSF/201,202/Special Meetings/1a, Memorandum entitled "South Vietnam Action Program," (declassified 27 January 1984), p. 1.

51. Ibid.

52. Ibid.

53. Ibid.

54. LBJ/NSF/CF/VN/5/M11/37a, "South Vietnam Action Program," p. 3.

55. LBJ/NSF/201,202/Special Meetings/vol. I/4, Memorandum for Discussion entitled "Alternative Public Positions for the US on Southeast Asia for the period July 1–November 15" dated 10 June 1964, (declassified 26 January 1984).

56. Ibid., p. 4.

57. Reprinted in *Pentagon Papers, Senator Mike Gravel Edition*, 4 vols. (Boston: Beacon Press 1971), II:459.

58. LBJ/NSF/CF/VN/6/M13/55a, Memorandum to the Assistant Secretary of Defense (ISA) entitled "Military Planning in Support of NSAM 288" dated 25 June 1964, (declassified 25 March 1981), p. 7.

59. Ibid.

60. For an influential discussion of the Chinese intervention in the Korean War see Allen Whiting, *China Crosses the Yalu*, (Santa Monica, Ca.: Rand 1960).

61. Ibid., p. 8.

62. Ibid.

63. Ibid., p. 10.

64. Ibid., pp. 12–20.

65. LBJ/NSF/52,53/SCM II/61a, Telegram from COMUSMACV to JCS dated 1 July 1964 mentions 34A successes.

66. LBJ/NSF/CF/VN/6/M13/13,18,19,20, Memoranda for White House Situation Room "Reports of Significant RVN Combat Operations" 12, 13, 15 July 1964.

67. LBJ/NSF/CF/VN/5/C10/17, Telegram from USOM to Department dated 28 May 1964, p. 1.

68. LBJ/NSF/CF/VN/6/M13/14a, Telegram from Ambassador Taylor to Secretary of State dated 15 July 1964, reported to President Johnson with memo from McGeorge Bundy describing it as "interesting" (6/M13/14).

69. LBJ/NSF/CF/VN/6/M14/208,210, Memorandum for the President from the DCI entitled "Probable Communist Reactions to Certain US or US-Sponsored Courses of Action in Vietnam and Laos" dated 28 July 1964.

70. Ibid., p. 2.

71. Ibid., p. 3.

72. Ibid.

73. Ibid.

74. LBJ/NSF/CF/VN/1/C1/12, Telegram to JCS from CINCPAC entitled "Situation in SVN (7 Dec. 63)" dated 10 December 1963, (declassified 3 November 1983), p. 2.

75. LBJ/NSF/CF/VN/1/C1/7b, Telegram from COMUSMACV to Bundy, Rusk, Ball, Harriman, Hilsman, McCone, Helms, Adm. Felt and Gen. Taylor dated 4 December 1963, (declassified 24 May 1983), sec. 2, p. 2.

76. LBJ/NSF/CF/VN/6/C14/144, Telegram to JCS from COMUSMACV entitled "Current Appreciation of Situation in I Corps" dated 21 July 1964, p. 2.

77. LBJ/NSF/CF/VN/1/C1/5, Telegram from McNamara to Felt entitled "SVietnam Infiltration" dated 21 December 1963, (declassified 24 April 1984).

78. LBJ/NSF/CF/VN/6/C14/138, Telegram from Secretary of Defense to American Embassy Saigon dated 16 July 1964; 8/C17/63, Telegram from JCS to CINCPAC entitled "Control on the Mekong and Bassac Rivers and Associated Waterways" dated 10 September 1964, constitute good examples.

79. LBJ/NSF/CF/VN/6/C14/147, Telegram from COMUSMACV to JCS/DIA entitled "Estimate of Viet Cong Organization Strength" dated 18 July 1964, p. 1.

80. Ibid., p. 4.

81. LBJ/NSF/CF/VN/8/M17/90,90a,90b, Joseph Zasloff, *The Role of North Vietnam in the Southern Insurgency*, (Santa Monica, Ca.: Rand, July 1964) plus covering memo by Curtis LeMay to the JCS.

82. Department of State, "A Dangerous Game: North Vietnam's Continuing Aggression Against South Vietnam" dated 15 February 1965, (declassified 19 June 1984), p. 47.

83. Ibid., p. 72.

84. LBJ/NSF/CF/VN/6/C14/52, Telegram from American Embassy Saigon to Department of State serial 213 flash, dated 25 July 1964, sec. 1, p. 1; see also American Embassy telexes 180, 184, 186, 201 which deal with the "March to the North" theme as well as the Mission weekly report, serial 161, dated 21 July 1964 at LBJ/NSF/CF/VN/6/C14/90.

85. LBJ/NSF/CF/VN/7/M15/137, Telegram from Taylor to the President and Rusk, serial 377, dated 10 August 1964.

86. LBJ/NSF/CF/VN/8/M17/98, SNIE 53-64, entitled "Chances for a Stable Government in South Vietnam" dated 8 September 1964, p. 1.

87. LBJ/NSF/CF/VN/8C17/37, Telegram from American Embassy to Department of State, serial 698, dated 1 September 1964.

88. LBJ/NSF/CF/VN/8/M17/107, Second Draft Memo by William Bundy entitled "Possible Courses of Action for South Viet-Nam" dated 5 September 1964, p. 1.

89. Ibid., pp. 6–7.

90. Ibid., pp. 9–10.

91. Ibid., p. 8.

92. Ibid., p. 13.

93. JCSM 639-64, Memorandum for the Secretary of Defense entitled "Actions Relevant to South Vietnam" dated 27 July 1964, (declassified 9 April 1984), pp. 1–6 plus annex.

94. Bundy Second Draft Memo dated 5 September 1964, p. 17.

95. Ibid.

96. Ibid., p. 18.

97. JCSM 639-64, p. 8.

98. Bundy Second Draft Memo dated 5 September 1964, p. 18.

99. LBJ/NSF/CF/VN/7/C16/130, Telex from CINCPAC to JCS entitled "Plan-

ning for Cross Border Operations" dated 19 Aug. 1964; 8/C18/114, Telex from CINCPAC to JCS entitled "Cross Border Operations into Laos" dated 21 Aug. 1964.

100. LBJ/NSF/CF/VN/8/C18/116, Telex from COMUSMACV to JCS entitled "Cross Border Operations" dated 22 September 1964 presents an excellent example of the genera.

101. LBJ/NSF/CF/VN/8/C18/117, Telex from CINCPAC to operational elements, dated 20 September 1964.

102. LBJ/NSF/CF/VN/8/C18/35, Telegram from American Embassy Saigon to Department to State, serial 913, dated 19 September 1964.

103. LBJ/NSF/CF/VN/9/M20/142, Telegram from American Embassy Vientiane to Department of State, serial 581, dated 6 October 1964.

104. LBJ/NSF/CF/VN/9/M18/277, Telex from CINCPAC to JCS, entitled "DE-SOTO Patrol Ops," dated 23 September 1964.

105. LBJ/NSF/CF/VN/10/C21/78 dated 28 October 1964.

106. LBJ/NSF/CF/VN/8/C18/134, Telex from CINCPAC to operating elements entitled "Use of Lazy Dog and CBU-2A in SEAsia" dated 26 September 1964.

13.
Doctrine of Predestination

Militarily, the attack on the Bien Hoa airbase was a very minor affair for the attackers. The Viet Cong had fired some thirty 81mm mortar rounds against the base over the period of approximately thirty minutes during the night of 31 October.[1] As a result, four Americans were killed and thirty wounded, of whom nineteen required hospitalization. Five American B-57 light jet bombers were destroyed and thirteen more damaged, while three VNAF piston engine fighter-bombers were destroyed and two more damaged. In a possibly related action, a district capital was mortared approximately six hours later, killing one American.[2]

Inspection of the shell fragments showed the rounds to be of American manufacture, meaning they could have been captured from the Americans in Korea, the French in the earlier Indochinese War, or the ARVN forces in the preceding years. In a press conference the day after the attack, General Westmoreland did his best to convey the impression that no ammunition of that kind had been used in ARVN or issued to ARVN since the 1962 MACV build-up.[3] The impression that MACV wished to convey was that the only possible source of the ammunition was the People's Republic of China which meant that it had to have been infiltrated.. Unfortunately, neither at the time nor later did the question of acquisition from former French stocks come up. It is impossible now to determine whether or not it was more likely that the offensive mortar rounds came from stocks captured from security forces in Indochina at some previous time as opposed to being infiltrated from the North. The question is material only in that the failure to establish origin with any degree of certainty was quite illustrative of the American conviction that the rounds, like the plan and impetus for the attack, came from the North. It seemed quite impossible to MACV or the decision makers in Washington that the Viet Cong might well have planned and executed this attack as a matter of local initiative and on the basis of local resources. Doctrine and world-view alike said the locals were only obedient subordinates of the Hanoi puppetmasters.

Unlike doctrine and worldview, military logic indicates, and should have indicated at the time, that the attack had been a local matter decided upon by the regional Viet Cong leadership. They would have thought themselves most likely to become the targets of the Bien Hoa based bombers; not those forces located in North Vietnam or along the trails of the Laotian panhandle. It would have been in the normal order of military expectations that the local mainforce would have wished to remove this potential threat as well as to cause a loss of morale among the local ARVN and lower American confidence in the ability of the South Vietnamese to protect the aircraft. Additionally, the CIA had detected no signs that the North was directing, or at any time following the middle of August even contemplating, that type of reaction to the airstrikes.[4]

Moreover, the never ending deterioration in South Vietnam would have been an additional inducement to the local Viet Cong leadership to essay a dramatic and demoralizing action such as the Bien Hoa attack. It would serve to demonstrate the relative strength and aggressiveness of the Viet Cong, sow further defeatism and despair among the defenders, and give the Americans a very hard set of choices. All of these factors and inducements were well noted by the intelligence community roughly a month before the attack.

> The likely pattern of this decay will be increasing South Vietnamese defeatism, paralysis in the leadership, friction with the Americans, exploring of possible lines of retreat with the other side and a general petering out of the war effort. Viet Cong pressures will meanwhile continue to increase—military action, terrorism and political agitation. . . .[5]
>
> . . .
>
> The Viet Cong have apparently decided that heightened efforts on their part will reduce the country to near anarchy and the government to impotence, bringing an early "victory" in the form of a negotiated truce and a "neutralist" government dominated by their National Liberation Front.[6]

The Agency concluded:

> We can expect an erosion of those elements of strength and prom-
> ise which have justified US policy decisions since 1961. This does
> not mean that the US position in South Vietnam is hopeless. We
> still have some time. But, in that time the US will have to face a
> host of serious new problems: among them, the scale and nature of
> US military commitment in the Indochina area. . . .[7]

Given this intelligence matrix, it beggers the imagination that the United
States was so fixated upon the model of external control of the insurgency
that the possibility of the Bien Hoa type of attack was not seen as the
primary threat confronting American interests in the country.

When this intelligence picture is linked with the military logic of the
situation, it is difficult to fathom how the U.S. officials were unable to
tear their attention from the fatal attractiveness of the North. The Southern insurgents were not naive babes in the revolutionary woods; they could
well determine for themselves that a very dramatic attack on a high vis-
ibility, high value target, such as an airbase crowded with American aircraft, would serve perfectly to exacerbate every one of the latent and
developing stresses in the South Vietnamese government as well as between the Americans and their hosts. When it is considered that the local
mainforce guerrilla leadership had the better part of twenty years' experience with insurgent warfare, it is quite easy to credit both their will and
their ability to remove, through vigorous offensive action, the aircraft that
had been an annoying presence in recent months. It was firmly believed,
without any appreciable evidence of any nature at all, that the attack came
from the North and the punishment must be directed there.

That punishment would be forthcoming was undoubted. The dust had
scarcely settled and the fires been extinguished when the plans for an
immediate and appropriate tit-for-tat response were in the works. The
American Embassy in Saigon was immediately belligerent with Maxwell
Taylor at his paratrooper best:

> VC attack on Bien Hoa is a deliberate act of escalation and a change
> of the ground rules under which they have operated up to now. It
> should be met promptly by an appropriate act of reprisal against a

DRV target, preferably an airfield. Since both US and GVN have been victims of this attack and since the ultimate objective should be [to] convince Hanoi to cease aid to VC (and not merely lay off us), the retaliatory action should be made by a combined US/VNAF effort. Immediate objective would be to reduce probability of similar attacks on other crowded US facilities such as Danang and Tan Son Nhut and to offset the depressive effect of this action on the new government to which this attack is an affront on its national day.[8]

This was followed almost immediately by another wire in which Taylor urged that the U.S. tit should be as close to the Viet Cong tat as possible, that the attack should be mounted from South Vietnamese airfields rather than American aircraft carriers and that the VNAF must participate.[9] Additionally, he strongly recommended that:

any strikes approved be viewed as the inauguration of a new policy of tit for tat reprisals in retaliation for major Viet Cong depredations. I recommend that, immediately following completion of strikes that US and GVN jointly announce that such retaliation will henceforth be the rule, making our statement broad enough to cover major acts of sabotage, terrorism, destruction of industrial facilities and the interruption of arterial rail and highway communications.[10]

Two days later, in a somewhat more measured form, Taylor gave supporting reasons for his pugnacious recommendations which, if accepted, would constitute a major change in the nature and scope of the war.

I am in complete agreement with the thesis that the deteriorating situation in SVN requires the application of measured military pressures on DRV to induce that government to cease to provide support to VC and to use its authority to cause VC to cease or at least moderate their depredations.[11]

Taylor did conclude that the danger of overdoing the attempts at coercing Hanoi were at least as great as underdoing it, for it was essential that the North Vietnamese government not be pushed so far that they would be totally unwilling to cooperate in some sort of negotiated or tacit settlement of the conflict.[12]

Taylor's telegrams had embodied all the critical operational choices open to the United States, as well as the inbuilt dilemmas. The essential problem was twofold: how to deter further attacks from the Viet Cong and how to have a favorable impact upon the will, morale and stability of South Vietnam. In addition, there were the purely military problems of protecting the American assets in South Vietnam. It could be assumed that the punitive and coercive airstrikes would have the desired tranquilizing effect, but that was a dangerous assumption. The aircraft could be removed from South Vietnam to bases in the Philippines or Thailand, if the diplomatic details could be worked out, or the airstrikes both within and without South Vietnam could be mounted from aircraft carriers in the South China Sea, but the withdrawal of the aircraft would have a bad effect upon the very precarious morale and will to combat within the Government and Armed Forces of South Vietnam. Or, U.S. ground combat troops could be introduced to provide local security at American facilities, but that would constitute a significant upping of the ante.

The Joint Chiefs were in the process of preparing the contingency plans for the last option even before the retaliatory strike had been launched. Within hours of the attack the JCS ordered CINCPAC to "sail Marine Special Landing Force towards Danang" with the explicit reservation that the force be held in an over-the-horizon position and landed only on instructions from the Joint Chiefs.[13] In addition, CINCPAC was directed to prepare for the air movement of "appropriate Army and Marine units from Okinawa" to provide enhanced security at the airfields used by American bombers."[14] COMUSMACV concurred quickly in the alerting of the Fleet Marine Force and in preparing to move these to South Vietnam commenting, "The actual deployment of these forces to SVN should not, of course, be undertaken except in the context of wider decisions."[15] Importantly, General Westmoreland, in commenting on the retaliatory strikes, stated that the United States knew of no Viet Cong targets within South Vietnam, "the attack of which would constitute appropriate reprisal."[16] Not only did this assessment indicate the American fixation upon the North as the wellspring of all insurgent direction and strength, it also demonstrated some of the weaknesses in U.S. operational doctrine and techniques. Westmoreland made one of the latter quite explicit by mentioning the ongoing difficulty of target acquisition in the South, but hastened to request additional aircraft to service the targets which could not yet be found.[17] Later the same day, Westmoreland moderated his position somewhat, in that he now opposed the movement of U.S. combat troops to South Vietnam for the purpose of providing security to the airfields as, "we hesitate at this juncture to admit by such action that the host government can not defend bases used by the US and to take the big step in committing organized US ground units in combat with the VC."[18] Indicating a degree of confusion concerning the nature and magnitude of the threat confronting the American facilities, Westmoreland suggested that an army or marine company strength force be provided at each airfield used by the United States and reminded his superiors that he had already requested two batteries of Hawk antiaircraft missiles for installation at Danang.[19] What utility the missiles had in confronting a ground attack, the General failed to mention.

Resisting the pressures for retaliation and recognizing finally the impossibility of adequately defining a tit-for-tat policy, a decision was made at the highest levels to defer a reprisal attack for the moment.[20] American policy makers had been moved by the Bien Hoa incident to perform a partial reevaluation of policy as they searched for a new mix which would reinforce governmental stability in South Vietnam, deter or preclude any further attacks, and act to coerce the North. It had been acknowledged that simple reprisal airstrikes were an incorrect option; there existed a temporary vacuum.

Another high-level meeting on 2 November reaffirmed the basic disinclination for an immediate response to the Bien Hoa attack. Instead a major planning operation was initiated with the goal of developing further comprehensive scenarios "for wider action taking account of current circumstances and interim actions required avoid any impression [of] USG determination changing."[21] Underlying this new planning exercise was the substantial perception that "Hanoi may be embarking upon a series of provocative actions to test our intentions in what they believe may be a period [of] USG uncertainty."[22] Interestingly, this major premise constituted a reversal of the position taken just the day before when the Bien Hoa incident was described as being no escalation of the conflict in and of itself as "it differs only in degree and extent of damage from . . . previous incidents."[23]

In the scenario drafting process which ensued, a concensus emerged to the effect that the United States had only very few options to pursue if the overall goals remained the same as previously: protection of the reputation of the United States as a reliable guarantor of sovereignty and territorial integrity, the avoidance of the domino effect, keeping South Vietnam from communist control, "to emerge from crisis without unacceptable taint from the methods used."[24] The situation within South Vietnam was perceived as having reached such a state of desperation that little progress was likely despite the best American efforts. It was not argued that the United States simply abandon any programs, but that little progress should be expected for at least several months. Of course, U.S. advisory and training efforts would continue with ARVN. No one appeared to question the possibility of training an army which was also engaged in constant combat operations. The United States should have learned this in Greece or Korea where the attempt to train and fight simultaneously almost lost the war for the government forces.

The major focus of the United States was to be upon coercing North Vietnam to end the support of the Viet Cong, or, failing this, to interrupt the lines of supply. In this area three option packages were identified. The first was the continuation of the present course, with its reliance upon limited and covert activities conducted by South Vietnam with U.S. assistance against targets in Laos and portions of North Vietnam. A second set of options involved the application of immediate and very intense pressure on North Vietnam by the United States, until the North agreed to meaningful negotiations. The final set was named by McNaughton, who gave it the fullest explication, "progressive squeeze-and-talk." This, the package chosen, must have seemed quite familiar to the readers of his memo:

> Present policies (within SVN) plus an orchestration of (a) communications with Hanoi and (b) a crescendo of additional military moves against infiltration targets, first in Laos and then in the DRV, and then against other targets in North Vietnam. This scenario should give the impression of a steady, deliberate approach. It would be designed to give the US the option at any point to proceed or not, to escalate or not and to quicken the pace or not.[25]

This constituted another example of the "Goldilocks" method of option presentation, coupled with the obvious fact that the preferable option was nothing but the McNamara report package without the tit-for-tat feature. Quite unsurprisingly, it served to govern U.S. policy for the next several months. It was, after all, the "least-worst" strategy.

It was reasoned that, if the flow of infiltrated men and materiel could be reduced either en route or at its source, then the almost hopelessly inept ARVN could deal with the Viet Cong whose combat capability and effectiveness would have been measurably impaired by the shortage of supplies and reinforcements. It followed that with the improvement of the situation on the battlefield, the Vietnamese government and people would take heart, and morale, along with its concomitant, the will to persevere, would improve. This would lower the lamentable tendency of the Vietnamese to split into factions on a variety of religious, ethnic, political and local grounds. With the improvement in societal and political cohesion, the nation building component of the pacification programs would be enhanced as the society, polity and economy would be better able to absorb productively the massive American aid. As a collateral bonus of no small importance, the improvement would allow the U.S. commitment to be better sold to the American public, and it would likewise be easier to achieve a consensus among America's allies that the commitment was supportable. Or, so the logic tree ran in the minds of the Washington decision makers.

Before embarking on the new infiltration interdiction program it would be necessary to gain a measure of public support in the campaign by publicizing the amount and importance of infiltration to the insurgent forces.[26] This proved to be a task of much greater difficulty than initially envisaged, primarily due to the inherent problems in obtaining hard data on the numbers of infiltrators and the quantity of infiltrated materiel, let alone assessing on any basis other than frank guesswork the importance of either to the combat efficiency of the Viet Cong. In large measure the problem was dictated by the nature of the terrain and vegetation in the areas thought to be used for infiltration. A common theme at all the meetings of personnel from the Saigon, Vientiane and Bangkok Embassies in the Southeast Asian Coordinating Committee (SEACORD) was the difficulty of assessing the results of the airstrikes in the Laotian corridor. From the November 1964 meeting, where poststrike photos were assessed in connection with the HARDNOSE operations onwards, the problem of accurately measuring damage not only to some types of fixed targets such as bridges and barracks but also to mobile targets like infiltration parties was a central concern.[27] Another significant problem arose from the fact that much of the raw data concerning infiltration came from the reports of prisoner interrogations conducted by South Vietnamese personnel. Not to put too fine a point on the matter, the results were not verifiable and not trustworthy.

Nonetheless, prisoner and defector interrogations continued to be the primary source of information for both MACV and CIA estimates of infiltration in the fall of 1964 as they had been previously. It was not until December of 1964 that the CIA finally produced a comprehensive intelligence memorandum on the subject of infiltration.[28] In this study the Agency relied very heavily on a previously prepared MACV report for the raw numbers. The essential points made were: the overwhelming majority of the insurgent force was locally recruited; much of the Viet Cong leadership and technical personnel, however, was provided by infiltrators. The minimum aggregate number of infiltrators during the five years since 1959 was 19,000, based upon interrogation reports which had been validated by captured documents; but the figure may have run as high as 34,000, if probable but unconfirmed reports were to be allowed.[29] In assessing the effect of these infiltrators, the CIA emphasized that interrogation reports indicated the personnel introduced to South Vietnam in this manner were specialists in communications, logistics and heavy weapons as well as cadre and trainers for the newly recruited Viet Cong battalions.[30] In effect, the infiltrators from the North were providing the same military assistance as the Americans attached to ARVN. Mirror-imaging struck again.

The problems of documenting the amount of weapons and materiel and its contribution to Viet Cong combat effectiveness were much greater than the calculations concerning manpower. The South Vietnamese were simply not capturing enough weapons or equipment from the insurgents to allow much of a dog and pony show for the press, let alone a good-quality analysis of the substantial matters. Even as late as February 1965, in response to frantic inquiries from John McNaughton, MACV was able to produce only four weapons of Chinese manufacture in addition to the ten shown previously to Secretary McNamara.[31] There can be no doubt that the Viet Cong did not depend much upon infiltrated weapons and munitions at this time, although there is strong reason to believe that their dependence grew in later months and years.

A close scrutiny of the CIA weekly situation reports, as well as the MACV and USOM daily or weekly summaries, indicate persuasively that not only did the tempo and size of Viet Cong initiated actions increase through the last quarter of 1964 and the first half of 1965, so also did their use of more sophisticated weaponry and tactics, tactics which indicated an improved communications, command and control structure.[32] While impossible to quantify or to document with finality, the tactically experienced combat commander could form no other impression than that the infiltrated personnel and materiel were increasing constantly during the same period of time that the United States was escalating the infiltration interdiction campaign. This impression is borne out by the analysis of the weapons employed by the Viet Cong in early 1965: the number of infiltrated arms of Chinese manufacture was clearly increasing despite, or perhaps because of, the American aerial campaign designed to halt their influx.[33] In short, the clear impression one receives is that the more the United States attempted to stop infiltration, the more it increased. The American escalation, far from stopping the North, served to stimulate an equal and opposite Northern escalation. Newton had been read by Ho.

The Americans debated the questions of how best and when best to make public the data on infiltration. The various RLAF, FARMGATE and YANKEE TEAM aircraft bombed, strafed and reconnoitered the Laotian corridor infiltration routes. The Viet Cong increased in strength and capability. And President Johnson finally formalized both the infiltration interdiction program and the graduated military policy program on 2 December.[34] In addition to the further intensification of the existing aerial operations within the Laotian corridor, his memorandum provided for the "possible initiation of strikes a short distance across the border against the infiltration routes from the DRV."[35] This authorization took effect thirty days after promulgation and initiated a "transition phase" leading up to the second step of graduated military pressures against North Vietnam.

> Thereafter, if the GVN improves its effectiveness to an acceptable degree and Hanoi does not yield on acceptable terms, the US is prepared—at a time to be determined—to enter into a *second phase* program, in support of the GVN and RLG, of graduated military pressures directed systematically against the DRV. Such a program

would consist principally of progressively more serious air strikes of weight and tempo adjusted to the situation as it develops (possibly running from two to six months) and of appropriate US deployments to handle any contingency. Targets in the DRV would start with infiltration targets south of the 19th parallel and work up to targets north of that point. This could eventually lead to such measures as air strikes on all major military related targets, aerial mining of DRV ports and a US naval blockade of the DRV.[36]

The goal of this graduated program was stated as being the coercion of North Vietnam to the negotiating table. This program and the goal to which it was pointed were soundly within the American understanding of Clausewitz. Both were well within the prescriptions of U.S. military doctrine. The only possible objection which could be raised, given the American approach to guerrilla war, was that the program was not robust enough, quickly enough. Surprise and weight of attack were being sacrificed to diplomatic and political niceties. Of course, it hardly needs mention that nothing in historical experience justified the program or indicated that the goal was at all related to the actualities of American policy in South Vietnam.

In addition to the carefully drafted instructions for proceeding from "phase one" to the "transition phase" to the "second phase," the concept of reprisal actions was resuscitated. If the VC were to attack any one of a number of types of targets including airfields, Saigon, provincial or district capitals, fuel dumps, bridges, railroad lines, U.S. citizens or other "spectaculars" as the mining and sinking of the aircraft transport ship *Card* in the Saigon river months earlier, the reprisal attack of one or more selected targets in North Vietnam was authorized.[37] This retaliatory raid should occur within twenty-four hours of the provocative action and should be executed by GVN forces to the maximum extent possible. A list of deferred options was also presented. These actions would not be authorized for the period of the first phase but might possibly be for the transitional phase.[38] The original McNamara options had now been officially reified, including an appropriately provocative resumption of the DESOTO patrols which would now be intended to act as bait for attack so that reprisals might be undertaken rather than their former roles of intelligence collection and flag showing.

In the first month of the "first phase," the United States had precious little to show for its efforts except a continued increase in infiltration demonstrated by Viet Cong actions; including a bombing of a barracks containing American personnel on Christmas Eve, for which retaliation was delayed so long that it was not considered proper to go ahead with it.[39] Beyond that, the results were disappointingly minimal. The SEA-CORD meeting on 6–7 January 1965 reported:

> We consider that US YANKEE TEAM and BARREL ROLL and RLAF T-28 operations in Laos corridor have had only minimal effect upon Viet Minh/Viet Cong infiltration effort directed against South and upon Hanoi's willingness to continue this effort.[40]

The effect on morale in the South had not been all that had been hoped, as was mentioned by William Bundy in a briefing for Secretary Rusk prior to a meeting with the President:

> I think we must accept that Saigon morale in all quarters is very shaky indeed, and that this relates directly to a widespread feeling that the US is not ready for stronger action and indeed is possibly looking for a way out.[41]

The conclusion was that the United States must take some sort of stronger action in order to signal to their allies in the GVN that they were seriously seeking victory, which had been one of the purposes of the infiltration interdiction program.[42]

If there were to be any actions to improve the morale and determination of the Government of Vietnam, they would not be forthcoming from the Vietnamese Army. No matter how optimistically couched the situation reports might be, the reality was all too apparent by the turn of the year. The Viet Cong, more than ever before, held the initiative, and were employing it with increasing audacity and competence. Even though the struggle now more closely resembled a conventional instead of a guerrilla war (and it was conventional war for which the ARVN units had been best trained by the American advisers), they were but rarely able to match the Viet Cong opponent. A large number of reasons might be, and were, adduced to explain or justify this battlefield ineptitude, but two salient features dominate the situation reports and intelligence appreciations of the day. The best of the Vietnamese Armed Forces, those elite units such as the rangers and paratroopers which could have continued to carry out morale building, aggressive operations such as had the LOK in Greece or the Scouts in the Philippines, had degenerated into "coup troops," armed retainers of the rival factions in the ever changing Saigon government. The "straight leg," regular infantry battalions of ARVN were simply too ponderous, too slow and too hesitant to meet the confident, aggressive and well-led Viet Cong mainforce units on anything resembling even terms. The Americans, by having failed to train the Vietnamese forces to fight insurgent guerrillas and by creating an escalation of external support through poorly considered and ill-advised attempts to interdict by air, had assured the increase of Viet Cong combat efficiency to the point that, when the conflict entered an essentially conventional warfare phase, ARVN was on the defensive and had been wasted in its morale.

Neither was there any joy to be found in the area of pacification. Despite an impressive number of plans and a bewildering number of changes in the program name, the fact remained that there was no successful pacification and rural stabilization program either in place or on the horizon by the dawning of 1965. The shambles of the original Strategic Hamlet Program had not been cleaned away; the impressive and at times insightful discussion and rhetoric about approaches to pacification, most notably the "oil spot" model, had produced much traffic on the international radio and cable links and a great deal of discussion in the corridors and offices of the Pentagon, the State Department and the White House, but nothing in the field. The failure of pacification and rural stabilization, the attempts at defeating the Viet Cong by segregating them from their potential support base through the combination of population control and the reduction of grievances, had occurred because of the recurrent, indeed never ending, chaos at the governmental center. It was facilitated by the extreme reluctance of the Americans to recognize the essentially decentralized nature of Vietnamese society. Throughout this period, the tendency was to look to the center for the implementation of centralized plans regarding everything from the mobilization of the citizenry and the economy to the institution of land reform and pacification programs. While it was much more efficient and businesslike to work from the center out, this approach was antithetical to the severely localistic and particularistic nature of the rural Vietnamese society. The inevitable result was that Viet Cong political cadres had a wide open venue for the propagation of the insurgency and the formation of new guerrilla units.

In a very real sense, what resulted was a reverse oil spot model, with the Viet Cong mainforce units displacing and defeating the ARVN; Viet Cong political cadres working out from previously held areas to newly opened territory, there to develop support and to undertake governmental functions. Finally, as the new territory was organized, the recruiting of a local, part-time guerrilla force provided the necessary means of self-defense against any potential encroachments by the Saigon government. Quite obviously, some of the major Viet Cong battalion size operations in the last portion of 1964 and first months of 1965 were "clear and hold" in intent and result. After the initial armed action, the effective and energetic Viet Cong cadres needed little time to secure the necessary degree of peasant agreement to establish the new order along with a new resource base for manpower, intelligence and logistics.

Given this backdrop, it was to be expected that the United States sought to make its aerial interdiction efforts more effective. The January SEACORD meeting recommended extending the BARREL ROLL armed "reconnaissance" program in the Laotian corridor into the hours of darkness and, further, that the daylight BARREL ROLL flights drop armed reconnaissance as a priority so as to better service planned primary and secondary targets.[43] It was not remarkable that the Viet Cong undertook another successful strike against the U.S. compound and airfield at Pleiku within the month.

This attack, which came at the end of the already customary Tet truce, killed eight Americans and destroyed five U.S. aircraft. It served dramatically to highlight the increasingly vigorous nature of guerrilla operations. The upsurge in the tempo of guerrilla-initiated actions, as well as the continued inability of a stable government to coalesce in Saigon, served to convince the CINCPAC Admiral Ulysses Sharp, that the situation had deteriorated to such an extent that all American dependents should be evacuated without delay. He stressed that the problem could no longer be "treated primarily from a political point of view but must be decided on the basis of the actual and growing danger to American lives."[44] The question of evacuating American dependents had been discussed for months, typically in terms of its psychological impact upon either the

South in terms of undermining morale, or Hanoi in terms of signaling a clearing of the decks, or a similar indication of resolve. Admiral Sharp was acquainted with the nuances of psychology which had entered these previous discussions. His decision to make the recommendation was motivated by the desire to put the United States "in [a] position [to] be able take offensive action without worrying about reprisals on military dependents."[45]

The pressure for offensive action by the United States increased in the immediate wake of the Pleiku attack. From Hawaii, Admiral Sharp was flexing his muscles, urging that the retaliation for the Pleiku attack be used as the opportunity "to step up on a continuing basis, military pressure against DRV."[46] Specifically, he recommended the release of U.S. aircraft to participate with the SVNAF inside South Vietnam, as the increase in the scale of Viet Cong activities had resulted in more profitable targets; the resumption of DESOTO patrols; initiation of medium and low level reconnaissance flights over North Vietnam, both to develop intelligence and to have a psychological impact on the North's leadership; and the use of U.S. aircraft for armed reconnaissance in southern regions of the North.[47] The view of CINCPAC was speedily endorsed by General Westmoreland, who agreed with all the recommended actions and pointed out that his superior had apparently forgotten that COMUSMACV already had the authorization to employ American jet aircraft within South Vietnam under certain conditions and that he intended "to use that authority."[48] On the civilian side, pressure was coming from the President's National Security Advisor, McGeorge Bundy.

Bundy had just returned from a brief, but intensive, series of meetings in Saigon with the leadership of the Embassy and MACV, in which a comprehensive agenda had been considered by the resident first team in conjunction with the top-echelon visitors. Bundy's intellectual exercise had been interrupted by the first report of the Pleiku attack and he was most disturbed.[49] His perceptions were summarized at the start of a lengthy memo to the President:

> The situation in Vietnam is deteriorating, and without new US action defeat appears inevitable—probably not in a matter of weeks or perhaps even months, but within the next year or so. There is still time to turn it around, but not much.[50]

In this observation, Bundy was supported by the most recent CIA SNIE, which focused on the question of short-term prospects in Vietnam. The Agency stated flatly that the opportunity was fleeting and the odds were against success.[51]

Unlike the CIA, Bundy saw a number of factors which gave reason for optimism. Among these he listed the improving efficiency of ARVN in open combat, the ability and zeal of the American advisors and the intrinsic toughness and resiliency of the Vietnamese people. Underlying these were the saturnine realities that the social fabric of Vietnam and the political integrity of the government had been worn quite thin. Bundy and the CIA agreed that the problem of governmental stability was central to the problem, but where the Agency saw no way of solving that issue, Bundy did. The way was the policy of sustained reprisal. For this approach, no strong and well-supported central government was required.

> For immediate purposes—and especially for the initiation of reprisal policy, we believe that the government need be no stronger than it is today with General Khan as the focus of raw power while a weak caretaker goes through the motions. Such a government can execute military decisions and it can give formal political support to joint US/GVN policy. That is about all it can do.[52]

Bundy's plan for the future, which had been concurred in by Maxwell Taylor, General Westmoreland and the country-team, used the offensive power of U.S. aircraft to coerce Hanoi and increase South Vietnamese morale, after which the development of a central government would become possible given the decrease in Viet Cong competence in combat. After the central government was stabilized, it would again be possible to undertake an effective pacification program.[53] Bundy concluded by restating the argument that increased air operations were necessary for their psychological effect upon a war weary and cynical population and a demoralized leadership.[54]

Bundy was craftily repackaging old wine in relabeled old bottles. No matter how packaged, the proposed program constituted a significant escalation in the conflict, an escalation that had been presaged in a meeting between the President, Bundy and Secretary McNamara on 27 January. In the memorandum setting up the agenda for that conversation, Bundy stated that he and McNamara preferred the alternative in Vietnam which involved the use of American "military power in the Far East and to force a change of Communist policy."[55] It deserves mentioning that Bundy informed the President that Secretary Rusk did not agree with this option, believing that the consequences of too much escalation were as calamitous as too little and that the U.S. should seek a way of making present policy work.[56]

The major features of the sustained reprisal policy were essentially clones of the previous programs: gradual increase in the level of force applied and in the tempo of operations coupled with an emphasis upon the notion of continuous operation.[57] This plan differed from its immediate predecessor both in the admission that the period of confrontation might be quite protracted and that the level of violence necessary might far surpass that projected in December. Bundy warned of the possibility of involvement with the People's Republic of China, a possibility which the CIA, generally the most pessimistic of the intelligence community members, deprecated, except in the event that the United States engaged targets quite close to the Chinese border.[58]

Bundy's scheme was not realistic in its underlying assumptions. In order to be effective, three prerequisites had to be met: the North had to have the capability to control infiltration and the activities of the Viet Cong attributed to it by the Americans; the North Vietnamese had to have values and an understanding of strategic goals and costs which fit the "Prisoner's Dilemma" and "least worst" models upon which U.S. planning was so firmly based; the government and population of North Vietnam had to be susceptible to moral as well as physical damage being inflicted by U.S. airpower. Even if the first criterion were to have been met, there can be no doubt that the latter two were not. That unpleasant reality should have been plain to the Americans.

Bundy was quite sanguine concerning the effects expected as a result of the sustained reprisal program. In evaluating the effects he explicitly stated that the two "immediate and critical targets are in the South—in the minds of the South Vietnamese and in the minds of the Viet Cong cadres."[59] Why McGeorge Bundy believed that this unique, indirect application of the hoary Douhet argument concerning the inability of civilians and governments to withstand the psychological effects of air raids, which had proven so completely wrong in World War II, would now prove effective eludes understanding. Equally elusive of explication was Bundy's conclusion, in which he introduced the notion that *Luftschreckheit* applied at a distance from the battlefield constituted a new means of counterinsurgency:

> We cannot assert that a policy of sustained reprisal will succeed in changing the course of the contest in Vietnam. It may fail, and we cannot estimate the odds of success with any accuracy—they may be somewhere between 25% and 75%. What we can say is that even if it fails, the policy will be worth it. At a minimum it will damp down the charge that we did not do all that we could have done, and this charge will be important in many countries, including our own. Beyond that, a reprisal policy—to the extent that it demonstrates US willingness to employ this new norm in counterinsurgency—will set a higher price for the future upon all the adventures of guerrilla warfare, and it should therefore somewhat increase our ability to deter such adventures. We must recognize, however, that that ability will be gravely weakened if there is failure for any reason in Vietnam.[60]

Implementation was recommended to commence with the reprisal action for the Pleiku attack, followed by the evacuation of American dependents. The President agreed.

In Saigon the decisions were met with joy on the part of the Embassy. Taylor telegraphed his appreciation on 9 February, along with a lengthy comment upon the sequencing of the program of graduated response.[61] The Viet Cong commented on the situation on 10 February by bombing the U.S. billet at Qui Nhon, killing or wounding most of the forty-five occupants.[62] This was followed immediately by intensive retaliatory attacks on the North, in keeping with the new program. It should be mentioned that a special reporting program called FISHNET was established to provide daily summaries of all Viet Cong-initiated actions in five designated categories, so as to provide Washington with the necessary basis to authorize continuation of the reprisal raids.[63]

As the use of U.S. air power increased to the North, the pressure to expand its use in the South grew as well. General Westmoreland had possessed for some time the authorization to employ U.S. jet aircraft in direct combat support of ARVN, under certain defined situations involving very lucrative targets of a time sensitive nature which could not be adequately attacked by Vietnamese aircraft. With the increase in the size of Viet Cong operations came greater opportunity to exercise this authorization.[64] There is no doubt that General Westmoreland interpreted the rather vague guidelines as loosely as possible. In short order U.S. jet fighter-bombers flew nearly one hundred sorties and dropped over 270 tons of bombs.[65]

This activity was justified by General Westmoreland:

> The strength, armament, professionalism and activity of the VC have increased to the point where we can ill afford any longer to withhold available military means to support the GVN counterinsurgency campaign. To date, US policy has curtailed or denied the use of certain highly effective weapons systems. Although some restrictions have been relaxed in the past several months, further release and delegation of authority is essential as re-equipped and reinforced VC step up war.[66]

He went on to request enhanced delegated power to employ U.S. jet aircraft in airstrikes against the Viet Cong in South Vietnam. He stated:

> We have evidence that few jet strikes in SVN thus far delivered have had a salutary morale effect on GVN forces and probably opposite on VC morale. While impact on VC is difficult to measure at this early stage, damage could be substantial.[67]

In entering this blithely unsupported assessment, the General was ignoring the experiences in Greece and Korea alike where it was found that guerrillas withstood aerial bombardment as well as did regular troops and that, when they were well covered and camouflaged, the damage done them was not in keeping with the effort. He also ignored the pioneering experience in Nicaragua where the marine pilots reported results all out of keeping with realities. Given the terrain and cover in South Vietnam as well as the combat experience of the insurgent leadership and cadre, it would have been debatable that the increased load carrying capability of jet aircraft or the marginally enhanced lethality of the munitions employed could have an end result markedly different from those seen in

Greece, Korea and the Philippines. Likewise, it is highly dubious that the fighter-bomber pilots of the 1960s were any less likely to overstate the observed effects of their munitions than had been the case with their predecessors in Nicaragua thirty years earlier. Not mentioned by the General in this request, but considered in other dispatches, was the obvious probability that the increased employment of U.S. jets would excite the Viet Cong to the extent that they would seek again to attack the bases used by American aircraft by employing their two best methods, mortars and sappers. These were the highly skilled Viet Cong sabotage experts who, stripped to loin cloths and bodies covered with oil, would wiggle noiselessly through barbed wire and mine fields to plant satchel charges and generally raise merry and quite effective hell in American and South Vietnamese installations.

CINCPAC and JCS were concerned about the provision of improved security to the high risk U.S. facilities in South Vietnam as well. As early as 12 February, hard on the heels of the decision to escalate the U.S. air effort as well as of the Pleiku and Qui Nhon attacks, the Joint Chiefs had recommended the deployment of a marine brigade to South Vietnam. Within two days CINCPAC agreed, pointing at the sizable and exposed concentration of U.S. and GVN aircraft at the Danang airbase as well as the obvious vulnerability of Danang to a determined infiltration or attack effort by the Viet Cong. In the same dispatch, unfavorable mention was made not only of the loyalty of certain ARVN troop elements, but the general ability of the South Vietnamese forces to repel any sort of determined attack on the Danang facility.[68]

Ambassador Taylor disagreed with the deployment of marines, citing the reversal of a long-standing policy "of avoiding commitment of ground combat troops in SVN."[69] Taylor also mentioned the increase in friction with the Armed Forces and Government of South Vietnam as well as the local population which could be expected to follow the introduction of more American personnel. Having delivered himself of his doubts, Taylor then examined potential missions for the marines, were they to be landed at Danang. Several seemed promising: the provision of local or perimeter security to the Danang airbase led the list, closely followed by "a more ambitious mission," the use of the marines in a mobile role designed to keep the Viet Cong at a sufficient distance from the base to preclude a repetition of the Bien Hoa type mortar attack as well as "to make a positive contribution to pacification of area."[70] He cautioned that, due to the range of mortars and similar weapons, even were the entire brigade to be deployed, it could not provide absolute security and that limiting the mission to the protection of the base against sapper attack would require fewer marines and would be more likely to prove successful. He estimated that a battalion would be sufficient to undertake that role. He also warned that while the use of the marines in a mobile and offensive role against the Viet Cong had a greater appeal than putting them on a static and defensive posture, there were definite problems in the employment of Caucasian soldiers in a counterinsurgency role in Asia.[71] CINCPAC commented in a rather stuffy fashion. "The Marines have a distinguished record in counter-guerrilla warfare."[72] After reminding JCS that there was a Marine Battalion Landing Team afloat on a six hour reaction time and another afloat with a forty-four hour reaction time, CINCPAC concluded by urging the incremental deployment of the brigade, one battalion at a time plus necessary logistics support and a marine air squadron.[73] Subject only to the proforma concurrence of the South Vietnamese government, it was decided by the President to authorize the landing of a marine brigade at Danang.[74]

The air war against the North and the supposed infiltration routes had been undertaken to make sure that U.S. ground combat troops were not needed to stabilize the situation in South Vietnam. Because the North and the Viet Cong had reacted to the American escalation in a natural, predictable and militarily correct, but not anticipated, manner by increasing both the level of infiltration and the intensity of ground combat operations, U.S. ground troops were now necessary to protect the air war.

The landing of the marines did not change the focus upon the air campaign or the drive toward the creation of an effective pacification program. The two were seen as being interlocking. At the last SEACORD meeting prior to the initiation of the sustained reprisal program, a direct linkage was finally made between the ability of North Vietnam to increase the pace of infiltration and the increase in American air strikes.[75] The situation had not changed by 7 March when a party headed by the Army Chief of Staff, Gen. Harold Johnson, met with the Mission Council. The failure of the pacification program was seen as resulting from the inability of the U.S./GVN to provide adequate security to the rural population; without security the rest of the pacification operations were ineffective.[76] Taylor stated that the reason the Viet Cong had continued to increase in combat effectiveness was the inability to stem infiltration.[77] He asserted:

> The continued support of VC from DRV is heart of infiltration problem. If frontiers cannot be closed from the inside—and we are convinced that they cannot—then only way to stop infiltration is to get Hanoi to order it to stop. Such is fundamental justification for BARREL ROLL and ROLLING THUNDER operations. They constitute our principal hope of ending infiltration—and end it we must if incountry pacification is to succeed.[78]

Having lost all hope of controlling its borders, South Vietnam must enforce its territorial integrity by American bombing of North Vietnam. Then, and not until then, pacification would prove successful.

In order to change this unfortunate situation, Taylor offered several recommendations as representing a consensus of the meeting's participants. Some were quite unremarkable, such as the increase of the training effort and improving the mobility of the present ARVN forces. Others were essentially escalatory but well within the current strategic and operational thinking, such as increasing the tempo of the ROLLING THUNDER and BARREL ROLL operations and employing U.S. Navy resources in enhancing the coastal surveillance capabilities of the Vietnamese navy. One was both new and escalatory: "Use of US manpower to offset present shortage in Armed forces of GVN."[79] Although subject to various interpretations, the last recommendation was directed primarily, but not strictly, at the idea of using U.S. combat forces. The original objections expressed by Maxwell Taylor concerning the use of the marines as counterguerrilla warriors must have been reduced by something, but no explanation was given.

His reluctance resurfaced two weeks later when commenting upon a request entered by General Westmoreland to land the third battalion increment of the marine brigade. In this context, he analyzed the proposal made by Chief of Staff Johnson to either deploy U.S. combat units amounting to a division equivalent to assume responsibility for Bien Hoa, Tan Son Nhut, Nha Trang, Qui Nhon and Pleiku or to deploy an equivalent sized combat force to assume responsibility for the highlands area of the II Corps Tactical Zone (CTZ).[80] While agreeing with General Johnson that this commitment would free a significant number of ARVN maneuver battalions for offensive operations, Ambassador Taylor was more concerned about the negative side of U.S. ground combat force employment. He mentioned a number of drawbacks which accrued to the use of U.S. combat troops, including the perception that the number of ARVN units released would not significantly affect the manpower shortage.[81] After offering general grounds for objection, Taylor examined the alternative missions outlined by General Johnson, with the conclusion that the II CTZ option would unnecessarily expose the force due to its lengthy and indefensible lines of communication, while the security mission at the various airfields and communication centers would constitute "a rather inglorious static defensive mission unappealing to them and unimpressive to the Vietnamese."[82] In neither mission, Taylor seems to have been saying, was the payoff worth the play.

Taylor's objections and analyses may have been right in theory, but they were far outweighed by the lack of immediate and demonstrable success in the enlarged use of U.S. air power both inside South Vietnam and without. The first attempt to analyze the impact of the new reprisal program came on 8 March when the CIA Deputy Director for Intelligence, Ray Cline, sent a special memorandum on the subject to McGeorge Bundy.[83] After stating that it was simply too soon to assess the results of the enhanced military pressure on North Vietnam, Cline sailed on blithely to paint a rosy-hued view of the results. He emphasized the reported improvement of Southern morale, the lack of an overt military response from the North or from the People's Republic of China. Not until the end of his effort did he bump reluctantly against a gloomy, but very central reality, the guerrillas continued to have the initiative and dominated large areas of the countryside previously under nominal Saigon control.[84] Obviously, the virtually unrestricted deployment of U.S. jet aircraft against the Viet Cong had not proven decisive. A report by General Westmoreland which went to the President detailed ten major activities, with the conclusion that the "inaccessibility of the areas struck, dense jungle canopy and brief time elapsed [since 19 February, the start date for the new policy] account for the paucity of poststrike intelligence."[85]

By the middle of March, intelligence on the Viet Cong order of battle and combat capabilities demonstrated no slackening and, inferentially, that the air campaigns had been without effect.[86] The trends were no longer simply alarming, they were potentially disastrous. The CIA concluded that the Viet Cong were able now to mount "up to ten regimental level attacks almost simultaneously."[87] Additionally, the Viet Cong now had the advantage in firepower to the extent that simple numerical parity was not sufficient to ensure ARVN victory.[88] CIA also commented upon the depleted state of the ARVN general reserves, concluding that they were clearly insufficient.[89]

Within the White House staff, pressure was building against the arguments advanced by Maxwell Taylor. Central to this was the person of Chester Cooper, who had moved over to the National Security staff from the CIA. Cooper had a long-standing acquaintanceship with Vietnam and was blessed with a singularly able and stylish pen. At times his memos glow and at times they amuse, but they were always convincing. He turned his attention to the problem of Taylor's objections to the deployment of U.S. ground combat units at a time when it was becoming increasingly obvious that without such the war was lost. On 10 March he recommended to McGeorge Bundy that the United States continue bombing the North, continue bombing the Viet Cong, and introduce U.S. troops across the southern edge of the Demilitarized Zone (DMZ).[90] He also introduced one new idea, the decentralization of the pacification efforts, noting that "their success or failure does *not* depend on how effective the government happens to be in Saigon."[91] He also attractively restated the old, and still not feasible notion of the United States waging guerrilla warfare in areas under tight Viet Cong control. With the argumentation offered by staff members like Cooper, coupled with the reality that the Viet Cong were still gaining vigor in the field and the concomitant that the most ambitious pacification efforts would not work until the insurgents had lost military dominance, as well as the pervasive doctrinal ambiance which emphasized the idea of destroying the opponent's army in the field or his will and ability to fight, the tide had definitely been set in favor of using American troops in a major offensive role.

Psychological operations were at the center of the new plan for nonmilitary actions, which was emerging from the State Department with assistance from other agencies, most notably the CIA.[92] This lengthy, indeed exhaustive, set of forty-one proposals and concomitant discussion constituted the most complete explication of the nonshooting portion of the Vietnamese conflict during this early period. Notable among the basic proposals were those regarding the decentralization of the pacification effort.[93] The Americans had finally realized that the basic structure of Vietnamese society not only allowed decentralization or the comparative ignoring of the Saigon government, it practically required it. Of a more controversial nature would be the CIA discussion of the decentralization proposal.[94]

Embedded within the CIA analysis was a discussion of the Quang Ngai Special Platoons, which were the germ of the so-called Phoenix Program. The idea was presented as another form of revolutionary development coupled with protection of the rural community through disrupting the Viet Cong infrastructure. In short, the CIA proposed to establish a type of anti-Viet Cong but not necessarily pro-Saigon guerrilla force, notionally operating under the authority of the provincial chief. Like the Voluntarios in Nicaragua, this was an idea rife with potential for success and ripe with the possibility of egregious abuse.

Most of the other ideas were, as the memorandum stated, new expressions for old programs. Certainly this description is correctly applied to the updating of the old Strategic Hamlet Program, but the new attempt mandated slow rates of development and sought to lower the potential for both self-destructive gigantism and megalomanic abuse. The role of military civic action was delineated, with an emphasis upon limited programs or projects designed to reduce duplication of effort. Basic economic, transportation and educational development matters were all covered by specific and carefully detailed proposals as were the general subjects of police, intelligence and internal security. In connection with this latter area, the CIA discussion served to highlight the number of potential intelligence sources which were not being used because of inadequacies in the ARVN and GVN system for treating prisoners, encouraging civilian informers and inciting desertions from the insurgent forces and mass support base.[95] From this, an inferential insight into the problems of finding the Viet Cong might be obtained, particularly when compared with the Malayan situation. It deserves mention that the "Forty-one Point Program" explicitly opposed any consolidation of the various pacification programs under MACV. Rather, pacification program responsibility would remain divided among USOM, USIA and the CIA.[96]

When the new pacification proposals were brought up for discussion at the highest levels on 1 April 1965 it was in conjunction with certain recommendations for increases in the military program, including the "Twenty-one Point Military Program" of General Harold K. Johnson, and against a background of continued stalemate.[97] While the situation was seen to have improved, in that morale was no longer deteriorating in South Vietnam, the tide was still flowing full for the Viet Cong in the country-side.[98] In addition:

> Hanoi has shown no signs of give, and Peiping has stiffened its position within the past week. We still believe that attacks near Hanoi might substantially raise the odds of Peiping coming in with air. Meanwhile we expect Hanoi to continue to step up its infiltration both by land through Laos and by sea. . . . However, . . . the pressure of our present slowly ascending pace of air attack on North Vietnam cannot be expected to produce a real change in Hanoi's position for some time, probably 2–3 months, at best.[99]

While the approval of the "21-Point," "41-Point" and the CIA "12-Point Covert Action" plans were all recommended, as was the deployment of an additional 18,000 U.S. logistics and support troops, the recommendation for the commitment of combat forces was deferred.[100] It is significant that this deferral occurred despite the reversal of position by Ambassador Taylor, who as of 27 March had decided that the Marines could use enclaves like that at Danang to "sally forth and engage in operations" while recognizing that some successes in the field would reinforce the air campaigns in accelerating the decision of the North Vietnamese leadership to "mend their ways."[101] It is possible that this signified not so much a reluctance to commit more ground combat forces, as the first deployment had been the most difficult both politically and psychologically, but rather a continued faith in the potential efficacy of ever escalating air strikes. Were this the case, the support for the belief was both ambiguous and filled with the potential for misinterpretation through the ministrations of undue optimism.[102]

There was no immediate or universal agreement as to either the adequacy of the decisions achieved in the meeting of 1 April or the nature of the role assigned to the Marines already in South Vietnam. The next day the Director of Central Intelligence, John McCone, expressed reservations over shifting the marines to a mission of active operations against the Viet Cong.[103] McCone did not want to use gentler measures on the ground in South Vietnam, but he wanted harsher actions in the sky over North Vietnam. He believed that, unless the United States increased the bombing significantly, Hanoi would simply attack the marines in costly actions hoping to sap the American will. He reiterated that the American bombing to date had not softened the Northern control of the guerrilla war. He concluded, "the strikes to date have hardened their attitude."[104] His conclusion was "we must hit them harder, more frequently and inflict greater damage."[105] The logical inconsistency of the analysis and the recommendation escaped him and his contemporary readers.

Despite McCone's reservations, the decision to authorize offensive marine operations was made without any dramatic escalation in the air war. The Embassy was informed of this decision on 3 April in a telegram which explicitly stated that the "mission of Marine elements expanded to include engagement in counterinsurgency operations."[106]

Within days, Taylor was enthusiastically reporting to Washington not only about the plans for enhancing the logistics capabilities of MACV as agreed previously, but the desire to increase the American combat force.

If the Marines demonstrate effectiveness in operating out of Danang in an offensive counterinsurgency role, other offensive enclaves may be established along the coast and garrisoned with similar brigade-size contingents for employment similar to the Marines. General Westmoreland is very anxious to establish such a force as soon as possible in the Bien Hoa-Vung Tau area.[107]

Having lost all of his former inhibitions concerning the use of American troops in an active counterinsurgency role, Taylor urgently recommended that the logistic preparations be undertaken immediately to support yet another brigade in Qui Nhon.[108] The old paratrooper was no longer concerned about the unsuitability of white faced troops in the Asian jungle as he had been only a few weeks earlier.

Two days later Ambassador Taylor was again imitating Hamlet, expressing reservations concerning the rush to employ U.S. combat units in South Vietnam. He saw only three reasons to bring in more troops: the need to perform essential security tasks beyond the present capability of ARVN to undertake; the need to execute essential security tasks more rapidly than ARVN could do without American assistance; to prepare for "possible future crises and contingencies."[109] He was still concerned that the greater U.S. presence would lead to greater frictions with the GVN and that the larger and more visible American contingent would serve to facilitate hostile propaganda branding the war as an American creation. Taylor warned that these possible repercussions would cause the American combat troop deployments to have the effect not of expediting victory but of retarding it. He also was quite critical of wasting the "specialized mobility of Marines and airborne troops" by committing them "prematurely to restricted land areas."[110]

The situation in Vietnam, or at least in the American Embassy, became tense when on, 15 April 1965, the Defense Department sought to institute a number of experiments in the South.[111] The new measures included encadrement of ARVN troops into U.S. units, the introduction of U.S. troops into Qui Nhon and Bien Hoa-Vung Tau, a U.S. style recruiting campaign for ARVN, and the "introduction into the provincial government structure of a team of US Army Civil Affairs personnel."[112] Taylor was furious. In the most hotly worded dispatch of his tenure as Ambassador, he lashed out at the Washington policy makers for having already overloaded the Embassy and the still infant government of Prime Minister Quat with "a 21-Point Military Program, a 41-Point Non-Military Program, a 16-Point USIS Program and a 12-Point CIA program . . . as if we can somehow win here on a point score."[113] His anger concerning the proposed introduction of Army Civil Affairs people and the removal of civilian advisors who had the advantage of long-term familiarity with the local situation and personalities was quite obvious and quite justified. McNaughton was flatly wrong in desiring to replace the experienced civilian provincial advisors with newly minted Army Civil Affairs officers. The Defense Department had chosen to ignore some of the most basic lessons of previous insurgent wars. Fortunately, Taylor's quick and angry reaction stopped the potentially dangerous experiment.

At MACV, confusion was rampant in the matter of deciding what sort of mission should be undertaken by the new U.S. combat troops. On 10 April, General Westmoreland issued orders to the marines, which permitted offensive operations but emphasized the security mission at the Danang area airfields.[114] This was not at all satisfactory to Admiral Ulysses Sharp, who quite brusquely countermanded this orientation by ordering

MACV to insert instructions explicitly authorizing offensive operations.[115] CINCPAC Sharp was also unhappy with the apparent dilatoriness of Westmoreland in entering the offensive stage of operations. He sharply directed Westmoreland that "this is not what our superiors intend. Recommend you revise your concept accordingly."[116] This more aggressively minded stance was in keeping with the Joint Chiefs' position. The JCS also demonstrated their commitment to the classic doctrinal objectives of finding, fixing and destroying the enemy by conventional tactics and air support in their memoranda to decision makers and subordinates alike.[117]

Reacting to this confusion between the view from the JCS and the less than robust response from MACV, Taylor sought clarification on the mission envisioned for the American combat troops. His rehearsal of the many telegrams, the bulk of which were contradictory in nature, well substantiated his perception of confusion. He concluded:

> Faced with this rapidly changing picture of Washington desires and intentions with regard to the introduction of third country (as well as US) combat forces, I badly need a clarification of our purposes and objectives. Before I can present our case to GVN, I have to know what that case is and why.[118]

After suggesting wording for instructions which he would like to receive, Taylor commented that the American request for an invitation from Saigon to send additional combat troops to South Vietnam might well result in a "sharp debate" with the South Vietnamese Government.[119]

The response to Ambassador Taylor's confusion was not easily made as a degree of uncertainty still persisted in Washington concerning both the air campaigns and the introduction of further U.S. ground combat troops. More consideration was given the problem of Soviet and Chinese reactions to a continued escalation of the bombing campaign in the North. McGeorge Bundy reported to the President that senior U.S. experts considered it likely that Russian or Chinese response to the continued escalation would be moderate and the possibility of either country sending "volunteers" remote. The air war had some danger of confrontation between Soviet and American combatants, as the Russians were in the process of installing new surface-to-air missiles around Hanoi.[120] This position was supported by the CIA, which added that the possibility of negotiations were remote as "the Viet Cong, the DRV and Communist China have hardened their attitudes toward negotiations, without categorically excluding the possibility under all conditions."[121] In the draft version of this CIA memorandum it was argued that the Communists would hold to their policy of seeking victory through the local military struggle in South Vietnam, provided the United States did not introduce "large additional forces."[122] In a revised text appearing the same day, a strong proviso was added "or increased US air effort."[123] This was a more than cosmetic change, as the first merely cautioned against radical growth of the U.S. combat force in the country while the second seemed to constrain the air campaign upon which so many had pinned so much hope.

The spirit of optimism concerning the bombing effort was quite widespread. The SEACORD conferees reported:

> Meeting opened with a general assessment of the air operations in Laos, SVN and DRV. . . . agreed that operations to date have been effective and morale in all three countries has been markedly raised as a result of increased tempo, and scope of BARREL ROLL, STEEL TIGER and ROLLING THUNDER missions.[124]

At the same time, Ambassador Taylor, General Westmoreland, Secretary McNamara, Assistant Secretary McNaughton, the Chairman of the Joint Chiefs, General Wheeler, CINCPAC Admiral Sharp and William Bundy from the State Department were meeting in Honolulu. The assessment of this group concerning the air strikes in the North was that "the present tempo is just about right, that sufficient increasing pressure is provided by repetition and continuation."[125]

Importantly, the group felt that the air strikes could not do the job of "breaking the will of the DRV/VC by denying them victory" alone.[126] This would require some U.S./GVN success on the ground against the insurgents. To this end it was recommended that additional combat troops, American, Korean and New Zealand, be sent to South Vietnam for a total of thirteen American battalions and four Korean and New Zealand battalions.[127] Later deployments considered, but not yet recommended, included nine battalions to Pleiku/Kontum, three marine battalions to Danang and six Korean battalions to Quang Ngai.[128] Between the continuation of the air campaign and the additional combat forces to the South,

it was believed that, while the North and the Viet Cong would not immediately capitulate, eventually the combination of lack of success in the
South and punishment in the North would prevail. This might take "a
year or two."[129]

By the end of April even the CIA was optimistic, stating that "some
downward trends appear to have been checked, at least for the moment,
and in a few cases even reversed."[130] Despite these surface changes, the
Agency hastened to warn, the underlying dynamics had not been altered;
neither had the military balance of power. Even though the essential
elements of the situation were not seen to have changed, there was a new
operational aspect under active consideration, that of a bombing pause.

The purpose of the bombing pause, as indicated by John McNaughton,
Douglas Dillon and McGeorge Bundy, was to assure that the United States
did not get itself in the box of exhausting suitable military targets in the
North without having laid the necessary political and diplomatic founda-
tions for engaging broader categories of targets. It also allowed the United
States to offer Hanoi the opportunity to negotiate without seeming to cave
in to the pressure. Finally, it served as the necessary hesitation between
an operational plateau and another escalation, placing the onus of responsibility for the escalation on the North and insurgent clients to the
South.[131] However, the major reason for initiating a pause was to enable
the observation of the North Vietnamese rail and road system so as to
judge the effects of the campaign to date and to acquire targets for the
future.[132] The several day suspension of ROLLING THUNDER, as the
bombing campaign in the North was codenamed, allowed both political
and public relations goals to be profitably pursued, while simultaneously
meeting a legitimate military need for assessment and acquisition.

After the pause, May 1965 was the month of ROLLING THUNDER.
There seemed to be a feeling throughout the National Security Staff that
the bombing operations in the North represented the last, best hope to
salvage the situation before the need would arise to use more and more
American troops. With the exception of a few days lost to weather, the
bombing campaign was mounted with vigor. The after action reports sub-
mitted by the operational elements show conclusively that after the pause,
the campaign was heavy in the sorties and ordnance dispatched, fast in
the operational tempo and, occasionally, devastating in its effect, particularly on transportation and warehouses or barracks.[133]

The reaction of the North to both the pause and the continuation of the punishment was the introduction of units of the People's Army of Vietnam (PAVN). First reported as a possibility on 2 June, the PAVN presence was verified five days later.[134] In view of the introduction of North Vietnamese regulars and the still increasing combat efficiency of the Viet Cong as well as the continued lack of ARVN competence, Admiral Sharp saw no alternative to the rapid reinforcement of the South Vietnamese effort by additional U.S. or third country ground combat forces.[135] General Westmoreland presented the same conclusion, arguing that the U.S./GVN forces might have only a tenuous numerical parity with the VC/PAVN forces operating in South Vietnam; the best case situation gave the force ratios as 1.41 allies to 1 insurgent and the worst case was .98:1.[136] Since no one was aware that, historically, force or tie-down ratios were so much pernicious nonsense, this was a truly alarming revelation, particularly given the seemingly inexhaustible strength of the Viet Cong and, now, the certainty that Hanoi's troops had entered the war in the South.

By mid-month General Westmoreland was able to prepare and send to Washington a concept of future operations which showed how MACV intended to use additional combat troops. After reviewing the situation in each of the four Corps Tactical Zones and indicating the probable deployment of new troops, he concluded:

> The VC are destroying battalions faster that they can be reconstituted and faster than they were planned to be organized under the buildup program. The RVNAF commanders do not believe that they can survive without the active commitment of US ground combat forces. The only possible US response is the aggressive employment of US troops together with Vietnamese general reserve forces to react against strong VC/DRV attacks.[137]

While left unstated in detail, the concept of operations revolved about the use of multibattalion forces in wide sweeps, spoiling attacks and search and clear missions. The Embassy confirmed the generally pessimistic assessment which had been offered by COMUSMACV, even to the extent of validating the force ratios, and the understrength and overstressed nature of the ARVN forces.[138]

Further confirmation of the dangerous state of affairs was presented to the White House by a Chester Cooper memorandum assessing the effective degree of mobilization in South Vietnam against the insurgency. Basing his conclusions upon CIA information, Cooper stated flatly that despite the alleged slackening in Vietnam, that the South "had been mobilizing at near peak capacity since mid-1961."[139] In annexes to the same report, CIA information demonstrated that the most reliable indicators, such as weapons lost by security forces as compared with weapons captured from the insurgents, were consistent with the most pessimistic interpretations of the Viet Cong supremacy on the battlefield, and further, that the supremacy was growing weekly. By the end of May the ratio was nearly 10:1, the worst it had ever been.[140]

The battlefield dominance of the Viet Cong resulted in the first employment of the largest strategic bombers in the American inventory in what were essentially tactical roles. In the third week of June the ARC LIGHT strikes commenced. These involved the bombing of Viet Cong troop concentration areas by B-52 aircraft, employing conventional iron bombs. ARC LIGHT I, with thirty aircraft on 17 June, was followed by the almost immediate authorization of ARC LIGHT II, a decision which bothered Ambassador Taylor. He wondered whether this marked an exception to the policy agreed upon previously or did it mean that the White House had inaugurated a new, implicitly escalatory program?[141] The answer to this, although Taylor did not receive it for some time, was obvious from the minutes of the meeting at which ARC LIGHT II was approved: McNamara wanted to proceed with the use of B-52 bombers and "most of us agree."[142] Any problem with ARC LIGHT was seen to fall in the area of public relations, not the correctness of the military decision.

Only one voice was raised against the consensus which saw bombing as a solution. George Ball, the Undersecretary of State, in a remarkably insightful memorandum, showed not only a unique appreciation of the inefficacy of bombing, but an even more unique understanding of the nature and character of the Viet Cong insurgency and the realities of Vietnamese society. He argued against bombing and the precipitate introduction of more American combat troops.[143] Probably due to his service during World War II with the United States Strategic Bombing Survey in Germany, Ball was unusually sensitive to the ineffectiveness of aerial bombardment and equally well equipped to demonstrate how the bombing in the North had been fruitless.[144] Commenting on the use of American ground troops, Ball argued that further American troops should not be sent until those already in South Vietnam had demonstrated that they could both find and defeat the guerrillas.[145] Finally, he accurately stated that:

> *The Viet Cong—while supported and guided from the North—is largely an indigenous movement.* Although we have emphasized the Cold War aspects, the conflict in South Vietnam is essentially a civil war within that country. [emphasis in original][146]

In conclusion, Ball demonstrated that if the game were not worth the candle, we could simply leave Vietnam without undue cost in the international community and with profit at home. This minority opinion was completely ignored in the rush to find a solution to the still precarious situation in South Vietnam within the capacities of American doctrine and forces.

Pressure for additional troop commitments was growing in Saigon. Ambassador Taylor reported a conversation with the latest South Vietnamese head of state, General Nguyen Ky, whose major point was the "need for additional US ground combat forces."[147] Two days later, approval was given to land two additional marine battalions at Danang.[148] This, Taylor reported, was not enough "to make mileage from the Ky government. . . ."[149] More of a solution was needed.

As had been the case before, one was quickly forthcoming from the Secretary of Defense. First drafted on 26 June and revised on 1 July, this plan, which was ultimately presented to the NSC on 27 July, called for an increase of U.S. troop strength to the level of thirty-four battalions coupled with ten battalions from New Zealand and Korea.[150] The ARC LIGHT operations would be boosted to the level of 800 sorties per month, and operations against North Vietnam would be intensified, with the intent being the complete blockade of war supplies entering the country. In addition to the blockade, which would be enforced by the mining of Haiphong and the destruction of the rail and road lines to China, strikes against the internal lines of communication would be increased, as would the operations against such targets as dams, bridges and ferries. Sanguine politically, the McNamara plan was guarded in assessing the purely military aspects of the war, mentioning that success in the South depended upon the ability of the Vietnamese to hold on to their fighting spirit and on "whether the US forces can be effective in a quick-reaction reserve role, a role in which they have not yet been tested."[151] In conclusion, he reported the CIA assessment of the situation which obviously matched his own: the North and the Viet Cong would not give in at all until they were convinced that the idea of quick victory was no longer possible and that the United States could, and would, continue to inflict unacceptable punishment on the North and the Viet Cong alike.

While not approved in its entirety at this time, the McNamara plan did form the central axis of the ensuing escalation ground combat troop strength in the South, as well as the expansion of air operations in the North. The plan presented to the NSC had been well outlined in a series of memoranda for the President by both Secretary McNamara and McGeorge Bundy. There can be no doubt but that U.S. military doctrine and force capabilities had been discussed. As the Secretary to the NSC, Bromley Smith, reported in the minutes, "there was no response when the President asked whether anyone in the room opposed the course of action decided upon."[152]

NOTES

1. LBJ/NSF/CF/VN/10/C21/90, Telegram from COMUSMACV to CINCPAC/ JCS, serial MA J-312 12900, dated 1 November 1964.

2. Ibid., p. 2.

3. LBJ/NSF/CF/VN/10/C21/86a, Telegram transcript of Westmoreland. Press Briefing dated 1 November 1964, sec. 1, p. 2.

4. LBJ/NSF/CF/VN/8/M17/103, Intelligence Memorandum entitled "Communist Reaction to Increased US Pressure Against North Vietnam" dated 9 September 1964.

5. LBJ/NSF/CF/VN/9/M18/249a, Draft SNIE entitled "Deterioration in South Vietnam" dated 28 September 1964, p. i; this SNIE was sent with a cover memo to McGeorge Bundy by Marshall Carter, DDCI on 28 September 1964 (9/M18/249).

6. Ibid., p. 5.

7. Ibid., p. 7.

8. LBJ/NSF/CF/VN/10/C21/54, Telegram from American Embassy to Secretary of State, serial 1357, dated 1 November 1964.

9. LBJ/NSF/CF/VN/10/C21/51, Telegram from American Embassy to Secretary of State, serial 1360, dated 1 November 1964.

10. Ibid., p. 2.

11. LBJ/NSF/CF/VN/10/C21/46, Telegram from American Embassy to Secretary of Defense and JCS, serial OSD 251, dated 3 November 1964.

12. Ibid., p. 3.

13. LBJ/NSF/CF/VN/10/C21/178, Telegram from JCS to CINCPAC, serial JCS 1449, dated 31 October 1964.

14. Ibid.

15. LBJ/NSF/CF/VN/10/C21/89, Telegram from COMUSMACV to JCS/ CINCPAC, serial MACJOO-12862, dated 1 November 1964.

16. Ibid.

17. Ibid.

18. LBJ/NSF/CF/VN/10/C21/173, Telegram from COMUSMACV to JCS/ CINCPAC, serial MACJOO-12962, dated 2 November 1964.

19. Ibid.

20. LBJ/NSF/CF/VN/10/C21/70, Telegram from Department of State to American Embassy Saigon, serial 978, dated 1 November 1964.

21. LBJ/NSF/CF/VN/10/C21/69, Telegram from Department of State to American Embassy Saigon, serial 988, dated 2 November 1964.

22. Ibid.

23. LBJ/NSF/CF/VN/10/C21/70, p. 1.

24. LBJ/NSF/CF/VN/10/M21/201a, Memorandum from John McNaughton to Secretary McNamara also distributed to Secretary Rusk, McGeorge Bundy, William Bundy, Michael Forrestal and William Sullivan, entitled "Action for South Vietnam" dated 7 November 1964, p. 1.

25. Ibid.

26. LBJ/NSF/CF/VN/10/M21/201b, Memorandum from William Sullivan to William Bundy entitled "Courses of Action in South Vietnam" dated 6 November 1964, p. 3.

27. LBJ/NSF/CF/VN/10/C21/32, Telegram from American Embassy Saigon to Department of State, serial 1415, dated 6 November 1964, (declassified 9 November 1980), sec. 1, p. 1, sec. 2, p. 1.

28. LBJ/NSF/CF/VN/11/M23/116, Intelligence Memorandum entitled "Infiltration of Military and Technical Personnel from North to South Vietnam" dated 3 December 1964.

29. Ibid., pp. 1–2.

30. Ibid., pp. 6–7.

31. LBJ/NSF/CF/VN/13/C28/20, Telegram from MACV to OSD/ISA, serial MAC 0704, dated 11 February 1965.

32. LBJ/NSF/CF/VN/10-17 passim.

33. CIA Intelligence Memorandum entitled "Chinese Communist Arms in Viet Cong Hands Increasing" dated 1 March 1965, (declassified 3 June 1980).

34. LBJ/AF/MP/2/7/53 & 53b, Memorandum from the President to Secretary McNamara, Secretary Rusk and DCI McCone together with "Position Paper on Southeast Asia" dated 2 December 1964.

35. Ibid., p. 2.

36. Ibid.

37. Ibid., p. 5.

38. Ibid., p. 6.

39. LBJ/NSF/CF/VN/12/M25/141, Memorandum by McGeorge Bundy entitled "Pros and Cons of a Reprisal Raid against North Vietnamese Barracks at Vit Thu Lu (Target 36)" dated 28 December 1964.

40. LBJ/NSF/CF/VN/12/M25/111c, Telegram from American Embassy Saigon to Department of State, serial 2077, dated 7 January 1965, (declassified 4 September 1980).

41. LBJ/NSF/CF/VN/12/M25/131, Memorandum from William Bundy to Secretary of State Rusk entitled "Notes on the South Vietnamese Situation and Alternatives" dated 6 January 1965, p. 1.

42. Ibid., p. 4.

43. LBJ/NSF/CF/VN/12/M25/111b, Telegram from American Embassy Saigon to Department of State, serial 2073, dated 7 January 1965, (declassified 4 September 1980), p. 4.

44. LBJ/NSF/CF/VN/12/C26/24, Telegram from CINCPAC to JCS and COMUSMACV dated 27 January 1964.

45. Ibid.

46. LBJ/NSF/CF/VN/13/C27/3, Telegram from CINCPAC to JCS entitled "Step Up of Military Pressure Against DRV" dated 7 February 1965, p. 1.

47. Ibid.

48. LBJ/NSF/CF/VN/13/C28/6, Telegram COMUSMACV to CINCPAC/JCS entitled "Step Up of Military Pressure Against DRV" dated 10 February 1964, p. 2.

49. For the agenda see, LBJ/NSF/NSC Meetings/1/3/3, Telegram from American Embassy Saigon to McGeorge Bundy, serial 2365, dated 1 February 1965, (declassified 22 November 1982).

50. LBJ/AF/MP/2/8/54, Memorandum from McGeorge Bundy to the President entitled "The Situation in Vietnam with Annex A, A Policy of Sustained Reprisal" dated 7 February 1965, p. 1.

51. LBJ/NSF/IMT/3/23, CIA SNIE 53-65, "Short Term Prospects in South Vietnam" dated 29 January 1965, p. 1.

52. Ibid., p. 4.

53. Ibid., p. 6.

54. Ibid., p. 8.

55. LBJ/AF/MP/2/8/54, Memorandum from McGeorge Bundy to the President entitled "Basic Policy in Vietnam" dated 27 January 1965, p. 2.

56. Ibid.

57. LBJ/AF/MP/2/8/54, Annex A, p. 2.

58. CIA SNIE 10-3-65, "Communist Reactions to Possible US Actions" dated 11 February 1965, pp. 10–11.

59. Ibid., Annex A, p. 3.

60. LBJ/AF/MP/2/8/54, Annex A, p. 3.

61. LBJ/NSF/CF/VN/13/C28/104, Telegram from American Embassy Saigon to Department of State, serial 2445, dated 9 February 1965.

62. LBJ/NSF/CF/VN/13/M28/222, CIA Intelligence Memorandum entitled "Viet Cong Military Activity in South Vietnam" dated 10 February 1965, p. 10.

63. For examples of FISHNET reports see LBJ/NSF/RP/I/167, 168, 169, 170, 171, (declassified 26 October 1982).

64. For an example see LBJ/NSF/CF/VN/14/C29/37, Telegram from COMUSMACV to CINCPAC dated 23 February 1965.

65. LBJ/NSF/CF/VN/14/C29/38, Telegram from COMUSMACV to CINCPAC, serial MACJ3 5704, dated 24 February 1965.

66. LBJ/NSF/CF/VN/14/C29/49, Telegram from COMUSMACV to CINCPAC entitled "Use of US Airpower," serial MAC JOO 6127, dated 27 February 1965.

67. Ibid., p. 2.

68. Summary provided in LBJ/NSF/CF/VN/14/C29/41, Telegram from CINC-PAC to JCS entitled "Deployment of MEB to Danang" dated 24 February 1965.

69. LBJ/NSF/CF/VN/14/C29/89, Telegram from American Embassy Saigon to JCS, serial 2699, dated 22 February 1965.

70. Ibid., pp. 1–2.

71. Ibid., sec. 2, p. 1.

72. NSF/CF/VN/14/C29/41, p. 2.

73. Ibid., sec. 2, p. 1.

74. Taylor was informed immediately by LBJ/NSF/CF/VN/14/C29/74, Telegram from Secretary Rusk, serial 1840, dated 26 February 1965.

75. LBJ/NSF/CF/VN/14/C29/97, Telegram from American Embassy Saigon to Department of State, serial 2712, dated 23 February 1965.

76. LBJ/NSF/CF/VN/14/C30/22, Telegram from American Embassy Saigon to Department of State, serial 2879, dated 7 March 1965, (declassified 8 January 1980), p. 1.

77. Ibid., p. 2.

78. Ibid., sec. 2, p. 1.

79. Ibid., sec. 2, p. 3.

80. LBJ/NSF/CF/VN/15/M31/194, Memorandum by Harold K. Johnson outlining "21-Point Plan" dated 14 March 1965.

81. LBJ/NSF/CF/VN/15/M31/188b, Telegram from American Embassy Saigon to Department of State, serial 3003, dated 16 March 1965, p. 2.

82. Ibid., p. 3.

83. LBJ/NSF/CF/VN/14/M30/134, 134a, Memorandum from Ray Cline to McGeorge Bundy entitled "Status Report on Vietnam after Seven Days in March" dated 8 March 1965.

84. Ibid., p. 2.

85. LBJ/NSF/CF/VN/14/M30/144, and RP/I/2/42, Telegram from COMU-SMACV to NMCC, dated 2 March 1965, (declassified 26 October 1982).

86. LBJ/NSF/CF/VN/15/M31/193, 193a, Intelligence Memorandum entitled "Strength of Viet Cong Military Forces in South Vietnam" dated 16 March 1965 with Memorandum of Transmittal from Ray Cline to McGeorge Bundy.

87. Ibid., p. 4.

88. Ibid.

89. Ibid., p. 5.

90. LBJ/NSF/CF/VN/14/M30/130, Memorandum from Chester Cooper to McGeorge Bundy entitled "Vietnam Revisited" dated 10 March 1965, (declassified 22 July 1980), pp. 3–4.

91. Ibid., p. 4.

92. LBJ/NSF/CF/VN/15/M31/181a, Memorandum for the President, entitled "Actions to Expand and Make More Effective Joint US-GVN Activities in the Non-Military Sphere in South Vietnam" dated 23 March 1965, (declassified 17 March 1980).

93. Ibid., p. 3.

94. LBJ/NSF/CF/VN/15/M31/181c, Tab. A to 15/M31/181a, (declassified 21 July 1981), pp. 1–2.

95. Ibid., Tab. A, pp. 24–28.

96. Ibid., p. 2.

97. LBJ/NSF/CF/VN/16/M32/235, Memorandum entitled "Key Elements for Discussion, Thursday, April 1, 1965 at 5:30" dated 1 April 1965.

98. Ibid., p. 1.

99. Ibid.

100. Ibid., p. 3.

101. LBJ/NSF/CF/VN/15/C31/10, Telegram from American Embassy Saigon to Department of State, serial 3120, dated 27 March 1965, pp. 2–3.

102. LBJ/NSF/CF/VN/15/M30/195, Memorandum for the President from DCI John McCone, entitled "Communist Reactions to US Air Attacks on North Vietnam" dated 12 March 1965, (declassified 15 June 1984), especially p. 2.

103. LBJ/NSF/CF/VN/16/M32/231c, Memorandum for Rusk, McNamara, McGeorge Bundy and Taylor dated 2 April 1965.

104. Ibid., p. 1.

105. Ibid., p. 3.

106. LBJ/NSF/CF/VN/16/C32/133, Telegram to American Embassy Saigon, serial 2184, dated 3 April 1965, p. 1.

107. LBJ/NSF/CF/VN/16/C32/47, Telegram from American Embassy Saigon to Department of State, serial 3332, dated 12 April 1965, p. 2.

108. Ibid., p. 3.

109. LBJ/NSF/CF/VN/16/C32/27, Telegram from American Embassy Saigon to Department of State, serial 3384, dated 14 April 1965, p. 1.

110. Ibid., p. 2.

111. LBJ/NSF/CF/VN/16/C32/157, Telegram from Assistant Secretary of Defense for International Security Affairs—ASD/ISA (J. McNaughton) to American Embassy Saigon, serial DEF 9164, dated 15 April 1965.

112. Ibid., p. 3.

113. LBJ/NSF/CF/VN/16/C32/16, Telegram from American Embassy Saigon to McGeorge Bundy and Dean Rusk (eyes only) dated 17 April 1965, (declassified 5 April 1984), p. 1.

114. COMUSMACV Telegram, serial MAC J3 11535, dated 10 April 1965.

115. LBJ/NSF/CF/VN/16/C32/162, Telegram from CINCPAC to COMUSMACV entitled "Employment of MEB in Counterinsurgency" dated 14 April 1965.

116. Ibid., p. 2.

117. An excellent example by Gen. Harold Johnson is LBJ/NSF/CF/VN/16/M32/213, Memorandum entitled "Actions Designed to Accelerate Stability in South Vietnam" dated 12 April 1965.

118. LBJ/NSF/CF/VN/16/C32/15, Telegram from American Embassy Saigon to

Department of State, serial 3423, dated 17 April 1965, (declassified 5 April 1984), sec. 1, p. 2.

119. Ibid., sec. 2, p. 2.

120. LBJ/AF/MP/3/10/126, Memorandum for the President from McGeorge Bundy entitled "The Demonologists Look at the Noise from Hanoi, Peking and Moscow" dated 20 April 1965, (declassified 17 August 1983).

121. LBJ/NSF/CF/VN/17/M33/119a plus 119 cover memo, Intelligence Memorandum entitled "Reactions to US Course of Action in Vietnam" dated 21 April 1965, (declassified 15 June 1965), pp. 1–2.

122. Ibid., p. 3.

123. LBJ/NSF/CF/VN/17/M33/120, Intelligence Memorandum (revised text) dated 21 April 1965, (declassified 15 June 1965), p. 3.

124. LBJ/NSF/CF/VN/16/C33/48, Telegram from American Embassy Saigon to Department of State, serial 3378, dated 21 April 1965, (declassified 24 July 1980).

125. LBJ/AF/MP/3/10/108d, Memorandum from McNamara to the President dated 21 April 1965, (declassified 27 August 1981).

126. Ibid.

127. Ibid., p. 2.

128. Ibid.

129. Ibid., p. 1.

130. LBJ/NSF/CF/VN/M33/92b, Special Intelligence Memorandum 12-65 entitled "Current Trends in Vietnam" dated 30 April 1965, p. 1.

131. See LBJ/AF/MP/3/10/78,78a,78b,78c,78d for the basis of this analysis.

132. LBJ/NSF/RP/III/2/178, Telegram from Secretary of Defense to American Embassy Saigon, CINCPAC, dated 11 May 1965, (declassified 10 November 1983).

133. See LBJ/RP/3/1/41, 42, 43, 45, 46, 47, 48, 49, 56, 57, 60, 65, 70, 74, 80, 86, 91, 99, 100, 102, 103, (declassified 10 November 1983), for coverage of the first two weeks of May in ROLLING THUNDER operations.

134. LBJ/NSF/CF/VN/18/C35/137, Telegram from American Embassy Saigon to Department of State, serial 4017, dated 2 June 1965; 18/C35/248, Telegram from CINCPAC to JCS, dated 7 June 1965.

135. Ibid., sec. 1, p. 1.

136. LBJ/NSF/CF/VN/18/C35/247, Telegram from COMUSMACV to Ambassador Taylor in Washington entitled "Allied vs VC Force Ratios" dated 8 June 1965, p. 2.

137. LBJ/NSF/CF/VN/18/C35/235, Telegram from COMUSMACV to CINCPAC entitled "Concept of Operations—Force Requirements and Deployments, SVN" dated 13 June 1965, sec. 3, p. 2.

138. LBJ/NSF/CF/VN/18/C35/26, Telegram from American Embassy Saigon to Department of State, serial 4265, dated 18 June 1965.

139. LBJ/NSF/CF/VN/18/M35/407, Memorandum to McGeorge Bundy from Chester Cooper entitled "GVN Mobilization" dated 16 June 1965, (declassified 14 April 1981), p. 1.

140. Ibid., Chart "Weapons Losses Tab. A, n.p.

141. LBJ/NSF/CF/VN/19/C36/28, Telegram from Taylor to McNamara and McGeorge Bundy, serial 4370, dated 24 June 1965, (declassified 6 August 1983).

142. LBJ/AF/MP/3/11/38c, "Agenda for 5:30 Meeting with the President, Wednesday, June 23, 1965," (declassified 23 August 1983).

143. LBJ/NSF/CF/VN/18/M35/349, Memorandum for Rusk, McNamara, M. Bundy, W. Bundy, McNaughton and Unger dated 29 June 1965.

144. George Ball, *The Past Has Another Pattern: Memoirs*, (New York: Norton 1982), pp. 42–62 passim; 18/M35/349, pp. 1–3.

145. LBJ/NSF/CF/VN/18/M35/349, p. 4.

146. Ibid., p. 13.

147. LBJ/NSF/CF/VN/19/C36/6, Telegram from American Embassy Saigon to State Department, serial 4422, dated 28 June 1965, (declassified 6 August 1983).

148. LBJ/NSF/CF/VN/19/C37/202, Telegram from JCS to CINCPAC, serial JCS 4893, entitled "Deployment of Marine Corps Elements" dated 1 July 1965.

149. LBJ/NSF/CF/VN/19/C36/2, Telegram from American Embassy Saigon to State Department, serial 4439, dated 30 June 1965, (declassified 6 August 1983).

150. LBJ/NSF/NSC/3/35/4, Memorandum for the President entitled "Program of Expanded Military and Political Moves with respect to Vietnam" dated 26 June 1965, revised 1 July 1965, (declassified 23 November 1982), p. 2.

151. Ibid., p. 6.

152. LBJ/NSF/NSC/3/35/2, "Summary Notes to 553rd NSC Meeting" dated 27 July 1965, (declassified 9 December 1980), p. 4.

14.

Auguries of Janus

When no one in the room disagreed, they at least tacitly accepted a course of action which had been formulated upon ignorance; ignorance, not malice, as was later charged by opponents of the war, was at the root both of the American escalation and the ultimate American failure. Doctrine preconditions the advice given to the civilian decision makers by the military as well as the military's view of its own capabilities and the nature of the war it is called upon to fight. It serves to determine, if not national policy, then the way in which that policy is to be implemented. American doctrine was neither wittingly vacant and intellectually bankrupt nor willfully mendacious. It was not the product of some coupling between Doctor Strangelove and Colonel Blimp. American doctrine was the result of intellectual limitations which combined synergistically.

The essential synergy was between a belief structure which held the creation of a true, organic insurgency to be impossible and a view of war which held the destruction of the enemy's force in the field or his will and ability to conduct war as the necessary precondition for victory. More specifically, the American view of guerrilla war held that there must be an external sponsoring power supporting and directing the guerrillas. If this support could be interdicted or interrupted, then the insurgency would rapidly collapse, particularly if a judicious mix of internal security measures and social reforms aimed at the mitigation or obviation of any underlying legitimate grievances were to be employed. Given this view, it is quite easy to understand how the American experience in wars, such as those in Greece and Korea, would emphasize matters of external support to the guerrillas and the necessity of interdicting that support. The Americans incorrectly viewed all guerrillas as partisans, as the armed auxiliaries to a conventional military force. In Greece the guerrillas had been considered to be the partisans of the Red Army located just over the horizon in Albania, Yugoslavia and Bulgaria. In Korea the partisan guerrillas were quite obviously the auxiliaries of the North Korean People's Army.

In Korea the guerrillas were not simply partisans, they were the distant early warning signs of a cross-border invasion. In the wake of the Korean War the American Army was sensitized not simply to the possibility of conventional cross-border invasion from a "Communist" state into its neighbor, but also to the probability that the first sign of an impending invasion would be partisan activity in the target country. The rise of the National Liberation Front in South Vietnam was therefore seen as validation of the correctness of training the South Vietnamese Army to defend against conventional attack as such was now imminent. The army, having been caught once in making the mistake of training an army for internal security duties when the actual threat was massive armored invasion, was not going to make the same error again. South Vietnam was not going to be another South Korea. ARVN was going to be ready and able to destroy the North's forces.

The doctrinal focus upon the destruction of the opponent's army in the field as well as its ability or will to continue the war was elevated to its place of primacy during World War II, as was the notion that air power was an effective means of occasioning this destruction. With the advent of nuclear weapons, this doctrine was modified to incorporate a calculus of strategic cost and benefit. While this concept and its concomitant, the "least worst" basis of strategic choice might have some place in the theology of nuclear war planning, it remains without merit in less cataclysmic conflicts. It is particularly without merit in situations where the opponents do not calculate cost and benefit in the same way, indeed, do not share any strategic vocabulary in common. The American fixation upon the use of aerial bombardment as a means of coercing North Vietnamese acquiescence to American policy goals resulted in the operational fugue state in which stereotyped actions were repeated unthinkingly at ever increasing amplitude, without demonstrable positive results.

The air war, while in large part the result of a doctrinal astigmatism which placed borders in the center and a political fugue which sought agreement through bombardment, was not the policy of choice. The air war was the result of the policy of choice having failed. Initially the desired way of fighting the insurgency in Vietnam was through the employment of ground forces coupled with the development of civic action and population control measures. The policy failed in large measure because an army trained and equipped on the American model was not properly configured to fight guerrilla war, as the initiators of the model found in time. Despite the theoretical elegance of the ROAD concept and regardless of the technical sophistication of the forces, their firepower and their mobility, the truth was that the big battalions were not the correct instrument to bash the bush nor were the specific doctrines developed by the army the correct way to counter insurgents.

The initial policy of choice also failed because of matters far outside American control. It was painful to the point of impossibility for Washington to admit that there were factors which could not be managed by the moral and material tools at the disposal of American ambassadors and advisors, but such was the case. There was no possibility of emulating the British in Malaya or even JUSMAPG in Greece. There was no possibility of finding a Vietnamese analogue to Magsaysay, desirable as such would have been; the specious search ultimately served to erode both pacification and population control plans, but more significantly and lethally, the stability of the government of South Vietnam.

The search for a Magsaysay underscores another fault in American doctrine, the focus upon universals. This is a fault held in common with much of the most "pure" military history. There are seeming universals in war: the Clausewitzian principles of mass, surprise, concentration and so forth. There are seeming universals in insurgent war also: intelligence, the eschewing of area denial and high-lethality weapons, the centrality of non-military measures, unity of command among others. But it is most important that the universals be modified to fit the requirements of the local situation rather than the local situation be interpretively manipulated to fit the requirements of the universals. Such an exercise in intellectual thaumaturgy and policy formulating prestidigitation breeds counterproductive results.

The American policy and the American policy makers reflected a remarkable lack of knowledge concerning Vietnamese society and politics, history and language. Given this, it is not surprising that there was no attempt made to modify the seeming universals to meet the exigencies of

Indochina. Dealing with insurgency when not in a command, but, rather, in an advisory position required a type of cooperative manipulation, a sort of political jujitsu, which was obviously lacking from the American armamentarium. Without either the ability to guide or manipulate, without a doctrine which would provide for the creation of a military instrument capable of achieving victory in the field, without a political view which would allow standing back while nature took its course, there was no option for the Americans except reliance upon the operational technique of aerial interdiction and coercion, futile as that proved from the start. No matter how futile it appeared to have been, it was necessary to continue the exercise as the only apparent alternatives were the unsupported introduction of U.S. troops or complete withdrawal.

When the ground combat troops were deployed, it was the logical result of two intersecting paths: the need to do more to improve the morale of the South Vietnamese Government and the requirement that U.S. aircraft and facilities be protected. The expansion of the mission of the troops to include aggressive combat operations was quite inevitable, although necessarily without success due to the doctrinal errors. The fear of the Johnson Administration was that the United States would be found to have done too little too late for the Vietnamese: instead they did too much, too soon.

The American Army was the incorrect instrument for fighting the conflict which had developed in South Vietnam. It was a force configured, equipped and trained according to a doctrine suitable for conventional warfare, or for warfare in the nuclear battlefield of Europe. The mechanical techniques of mobility, heavy firepower and sophisticated communications did not automatically endow the army with the necessary capabilities to successfully counter insurgent forces. The attempt to engage the insurgent forces in set-piece battles in remote areas of South Vietnam could result in the infliction of large casualties upon the guerrilla enemy, but, in and of itself, could not insure the victory of the Saigon government. At the very most, the use of conventional, big battalion tactics by the Americans would assure that the insurgents ceased assembling their forces in large concentrations, resuming instead the campaign of ultra small-scale efforts of terrorism and intimidation coupled with political agitation and propaganda which had served so well in earlier days. The American idea that guerrilla wars could be fought successfully by using what were essentially conventional forces, tactics and doctrine was plainly wrong and was not supportable from the historical record, except in the narrowest of situations. The pursuit of the grail of a true general purpose land force was an exercise in dangerous futility.

In addition to that real danger, the American doctrine and its tactical implementation would result in significant civilian casualties or social dislocation. Either of these would simply provide grist for the insurgents' propaganda mill. The dependence upon heavy firepower central to U.S. doctrine, particularly the emphasis upon the employment of artillery and aerial bombardment in harassment and interdiction or area denial missions, worked to assure that neutral or potentially friendly civilians would be caught in the middle and converted into either rootless refugees or insurgent activists. This much at least was obvious from the previous insurgencies. Army concepts of civic action and psychological operations were quite irrelevant to the requirements of the South Vietnamese conflict, being either too minor in impact or too far outside the expectations and needs of the civilian population. In short, any U.S. Army civic affairs programs would have been quite unable to undo the negative effects of the army's artillery fire and air support upon the affected population. The concept of insurgent warfare held by the army at all command levels bore no resemblance to the actual requirements of South Vietnam. The incorrectness of the army's conceptualizations was to be seen in the constant failure of the American-trained, -equipped and -advised ARVN to effectively come to grips with the Viet Cong insurgents. There was no reason to believe that the Americans would have done any better no matter how many more casualties they inflicted upon the guerrillas and their supporters.

Ultimately, success in insurgent warfare is not dependent upon the mere killing of insurgent combatants. The formulations of Clausewitz are quite often irrelevant to the realities of the primarily political insurgent conflict. Without the well-defined military unit structure and with a set of tactics and operational principles dependent upon small actions and the erosion of confidence in the efficiency and fairness of the government in power, the insurgent forces are not as susceptible to destruction in the field or demoralization at the command level as the conventional armies considered by Clausewitz and his American successors. Destruction, annihilation and demoralization are almost irrelevant to the task of eroding the insurgents' base of support among the civilian population or the isolation of the fighters from the politically oriented segment of the insurgent movement.

The marines had a more viable counterinsurgency doctrine but were not able to consistently enact this doctrine or extend it operationally beyond a narrow geographic area and a short period of time. The reasons for the lack of influence exercised by marine doctrine are many and, ultimately, speculative, but the effect was that there were no alternatives to the formulations the army and air force presented. Even if the marines' approach to counterinsurgency had been better presented to the decision makers of the Johnson Administration, it is doubtful that they would have had any impact. The marine doctrine, as developed from the Banana War experiences, was not particularly attractive as it held no promise of rapid or facile success. The marines contemplated protracted low-intensity conflict with equanimity, but the Johnson aides, advisors and Secretaries could not do likewise. Vietnam was an annoying distraction to be liquidated with speed and exemplary effect so that the major business of defense and national security could be attended to without further delay. Additionally, the condign and salutory handling of North Vietnam would preclude the further employment of the war of national liberation gambit by the puppetmasters of the Kremlin and Peking; so time was of the essence from the Washington perspective. The existence of political opposition to the U.S. commitment also worked against the adoption of the protracted conflict-oriented Marine Corps perceptions and in favor of the aerial interdiction and border closure tactics which were seen as promising emulation of the success in Greece.

The emphasis upon speed and low cost, at least in terms of manpower and potential American casualties, combined with the notion of mutual rationality to produce the slow paced escalation of the air campaign. This, in turn, provided both time and impetus for insurgent responses directed against their U.S. tormentors. The American planners were fatally incorrect in positing a mirror image of cost-benefit analysis in Hanoi and Washington. They were also horribly wrong in assuming that the North Vietnamese would reply to air strikes with air strikes rather than assuming that the Viet Cong, with or without the authorization and assistance of Hanoi, would attack the American aircraft and bases directly using the weapons and tactics in which they were strongest and most experienced.

The hubris resident in these twin, mirror image, assumptions well merited the nemesis it received. The nemesis was the North Vietnamese ability to match every American escalation. Ironically, while American leaders successfully represented every increase in the American commitment to have been caused by the Viet Cong and Hanoi having upped the ante, the reality was the opposite. The United States imitated every escalatory cycle through 1964 and 1965. As has been seen, the bombing of unused infiltration routes and the supposed Northern terminals caused the North to jam the traffic on the South-bound lanes of the Ho Chi Minh Trail. The American retaliation for Viet Cong attacks led to increased counter-retaliation which necessitated the very introduction of ground combat forces which the use of air strikes was supposed to prevent.

The American military did not understand the nature of insurgent war generally or the character of the conflict in South Vietnam in particular. It is not surprising that the same can be said of the civilians of the Defense Department or National Security Council. Neither is it remarkable that McGeorge Bundy, Robert McNamara or Lyndon Johnson did not understand the nature of the conflict to which they slowly and quite logically committed American materiel and American lives. It is not surprising that the doctrine and plans upon which the commitment were founded brought failure.

The combination of ideology and unquestioning acceptance of the Clausewitzian priority upon destruction combined to preclude developing more penetrating and accurate appreciations of the insurgent challenge and profitable responses to that challenge. This combination represented a central, systemic failure. A failure which obviated the most noble of intents and rendered impotent the most powerful of military forces: A failure which gave each marine and paratrooper who landed in South Vietnam in the spring of 1965 an invisible white flag. A failure which would be transmitted by the training components of the "Vietnamization" program to the South Vietnamese Army and, ultimately, help to bring about the defeat of that army. A failure which almost inevitably assured that the next eight years would simply constitute a prolonged, agonizing and bloody anticlimax. A failure which continues to influence in an erosive way American national security affairs to the present day.

BIBLIOGRAPHY

I. ARCHIVES

The following archives and, where relevant, collections within an archive have been consulted or cited.

Army Military History Research Collection

Lyndon Baines Johnson Library (LBJ)
  National Security Files (NSF):
    Country File, Vietnam
    National Security Council Meetings
    International Meetings and Travel
    Lodge/Rusk/LBJ Correspondence
  Aides Files

John Fitzgerald Kennedy Library

MacArthur Memorial Bureau of Archives
  RG 3 Southwest Pacific Area HQ, 1942–1945
  RG 5 Records of Supreme Command, Allied Powers
  RG 6 Records of Far East Command HQ, 1947–1951
  RG 7 Records of United Nations Command, 1950–1951
  RG 8 Records of U.S. Army Forces in Korea, 1947–1948

Marine Corps Historical Center

National Archives
  Civil Archives, Diplomatic Branch
    Record Groups 59, 84, 353
  Military Archives, Modern Military Branch
    Record Groups 107, 218, 226, 263, 319, 330, 334, 407
  Military Archives, Navy and Old Army Branch

Record Groups 38, 80, 127, 395
Naval Historical Center, Operational Archives
Department of State, Foreign Affairs Document and Reference Center
Harry S. Truman Library
   Official File, Truman Papers
   President's Personal File
   President's Secretary's File
Although not strictly speaking an archive, the Library of the Department of Defense has proven to be an important source of critical documents relating to the Joint Chiefs and Army operations.

II. GOVERNMENT PUBLICATIONS AND DOCUMENTS, U.S.

Department of Defense

Office of the Secretary of Defense, *US-Vietnam Relations, 1945–1967.* Washington, D.C.: House Committee on Armed Services Committee Print, 1971.

Department of the Army, Field Manuals (FMs)

6-20-1. *Field Artillery Tactics.* 1962.
6-20-2. *Field Artillery Tactics.* 1962.
7-10.   *Rifle Company, Infantry and Airborne Battle Groups.* 1962.
7-20.   *Infantry, Airborne Infantry and Mechanized Infantry Battalions.* 1962.
7-30.   *Infantry, Airborne and Mechanized Division Brigades.* 1962.
7-40.   *Infantry and Airborne Battle Groups.* 1960.
21-50. *Ranger Training and Ranger Operations.* 1962.
30-5.   *Combat Intelligence.* 1960, 1963.
31-15. *Operations Against Irregular Forces.* 1961.
31-16. *Counterguerrilla Operations.* 1962, 1963.
31-21. *Guerrilla Warfare and Special Forces Operations.* 1955, 1958, 1961.
33-5.   *Psychological Operations.* 1962.
41-10. *Civil Affairs Operations.* 1962.

57-35. *Army Transport Aviation-Combat Operations.* 1957.
    Airmobile Operations. 1963.
61-100. *The Division.* 1961.
100-5. *Field Service Regulations: Operations.* 1939, 1944, 1954, 1962.
Pamph. 20-243. *German Antiguerrilla Operations in the Balkans.* 1954.

Army Schools Curricula

Civil Affairs School. *Syllabus.* Fort Gordon, Ga. 1963.
Infantry School. *Infantry Battalion in Operations Against Irregular Forces.* Fort Benning, Ga. 1962.
————. *Operations Against Irregular Forces.* (ST 31-20-1). Fort Benning, Ga. 1950.
Special Warfare Training Center. "Program of Instruction for Counterinsurgency Operations" (Course 33-6-F6). Fort Bragg, N.C. 1962.

Army Reports

Army Concept Team in Vietnam. *Airmobile Company in Counterinsurgency Operations.* Saigon: ACTV [MAAC]. 1963.
Director of Combat Aviation. *1957 Estimate of the Situation.* Fort Rucker, Ala.: U.S. Army Aviation School. 1958.
JUSMAPG. "Operations Evaluation: Intelligence." Athens, 1949.
Murden, William and Lt. Col. John Yakshe. *Evaluation of Procedures Employed in Tests of the 1956 Field Army (ATFA-1).* Fort Monroe, Va.: U.S. Army Operations Research Office, 1956.
Special Warfare Board (Howze Board). *Final Report.* Fort Monroe, Va.: USCONARC, 1962.
US Army Combat Operations in Vietnam, (ARCOV). 1966.

Office of the Chief of Military History

Fisher, E. F. *Relationship of the ROAD Concept to Morale Considerations.* Mimeo, n.d.
Gardner, Hugh. *Guerrilla and Counterguerrilla Warfare in Greece 1941–1944.* Mimeo, 1962.
Howell, Edgar. *Soviet Partisan Movement 1941–44* (DA-Pam 10-244). 1950.

Lanz, Hubert. *Partisan Warfare in the Balkans.* 1952.
Sawyer, Robert. *Military Advisors in Korea: KMAG in Peace and War.* 1962.

Advanced Research Projects Agency

Counterguerrilla Operations in the Philippines 1946–1950: A Symposium at the Special Warfare School 15 June 1961. Mimeo. 1961.
French High Command, Saigon. Crozier, Brian (trans.) *Lessons from the Indo-China War.* Mimeo, 1955.

Secretary of the Army

Deputy Chief of Staff for Operations and Plans, Office of the Director of Strategic Plans and Policy, Special Warfare Division. *Counterinsurgency Operations: A Handbook for the Suppression of Communist Guerrilla Terrorist Operations.* 1962.

Navy Department

Annual Report 1917–1933. Washington, D.C., 1918–1934.

U.S. Marine Corps Manuals

FMFM 8-2. *Operations Against Guerrilla Forces.* 1962.
Landing Force Bulletin #12. "Concept of Future Amphibious Operations." HQMC: 15 December 1955.
Small Wars Manual (SWM). 1940.

U.S. Marine Corps Reports

Fleet Marine Force Organization and Composition Board (Hogaboom Board). *Report.* HQMC. 7 January 1957.
Smith, Julian et al. *Review of the Organization and Operations of the Guardia Nacional de Nicaragua.* Quantico, Va.: Marine Corps Schools, 1937.

Office of the President

The President's Committee to Study the U.S. Military Assistance Program
(Draper Committee). *Final Composite Report to the President's
Committee.* 1959.

Department of State

*Aggression from the North: The Record of North Vietnam's Campaign to
Conquer South Vietnam* (FE Series 130). 1965.
Aid to Greece and Turkey (Pub 2802). 1947.
Assistance to Greece and Turkey: First Report to Congress. 1947.
Assistance to Greece and Turkey: Second Report to Congress. 1948.
Assistance to Greece and Turkey: Fifth Report to Congress. 1949.
Assistance to Greece and Turkey: Eighth Report to Congress. 1949.
Foreign Relations of the United States. 1928–1933, 1947–1951.
Notes on Strategic Hamlets. USOM. Saigon. 1963.
Report of the Allied Mission to Observe the Greek Elections (Pub 2522).
1947.
A Threat to Peace: North Viet-Nam's Effort to Conquer South Viet-Nam
(FE Series 110). 1961.
The United Nations and the Problem of Greece (Pub 2909). 1947.

Congressional Reports

U.S. House Armed Services Committee. "Department of Defense Appropriations FY 1964." 88th Congress: First Session. 1963.
U.S. Senate Committee on Foreign Relations. "Use of US Navy in Nicaragua." Seventieth Congress: First Session. 1928.
———. "Vietnam and Southeast Asia." Eightieth Congress: First Session.
1963.

III. GOVERNMENT DOCUMENTS, FOREIGN

Great Britain

Lord Mountbatten of Burma. *Southeast Asia.* London: HMSO, 1951.
Central Office of Information. *The Fight Against Communist Terrorism in
Malaya.* London: HMSO, 1953.

Secretary of State for Colonies. "Federation of Malaya Agreement." London: HMSO, 1941.

Greece

Ministry of Public Works. *Sacrifices of Greece in the Second World War.* Athens: Graphic Arts, Aspiotis-Elka, 1946.

Federation of Malaya

Annual Report. Kuala Lumpur: Government Printing Office, 1950–1956.
Legislative Council Minutes and Council Papers. "Report of the Consultive Committee." Kuala Lumpur: Government Printing Office, 1947.
———. *Report of the Committee Appointed to Investigate the Squatter Problem.* Kuala Lumpur: Government Printing Office, 1949.
———. *The Squatter Problem in the Federation of Malaya.* Kuala Lumpur: Government Printing Office, 1950.
———. Council Paper #23. *Resettlement and the Development of New Villages in the Federation of Malaya.* Kuala Lumpur: Government Printing Office, 1952.
———. *High Commissioner's Semi-Annual Report.* Kuala Lumpur: Government Printing Office, 1948–1954.
Legislative Minutes. "High Commissioner's Speech, Meeting of the 6th Session." 18 March 1953.
Office of Information. *Communist Banditry in Malaya.* Kuala Lumpur: Government Printing Office, 1951.

Republic of Korea

Ministry of Education. *Korean War History for Year One.* Seoul: ROK, 1955.

Philippines

Philippine Armed Forces. "Annual Report of the Chief of Staff." Manila, 1946, 1948.

Philippine Armed Forces. "Intelligence Summary." Tarduc: G-2 MPC, 14 Oct. 1946.
Philippine Armed Forces. "Intelligence Summary." Manila: G-2 HQ, 30 June 1949.

Government of Vietnam

Ministry of Information. *Vietnam's Strategic Hamlets*. Saigon, 1963.
RVN Embassy. "Policy on Programs of GVN as Announced by General Nguyen Khanh, Prime Minister GVN on 7 March 1964." Washington, D.C.

United Nations

UNO, Security Council. *Official Reports: First Year, Series Two, Number Four*. N.Y.: UNO, 1946.

IV. BOOKS, MONOGRAPHS, AND COMPENDIA

Abaya, Hernando. *Betrayal in the Philippines*. N.Y.: Scribners, 1946.
Acheson, Dean. *Present at the Creation*. N.Y.: Norton, 1969.
Aguinaldo, Emilio. *A Second Look at America*. N.Y.: Speller, 1957.
Appleman, Roy. *South to the Naktong; North to the Yalu*. Washington, D.C.: USGPO, 1961.
Baclagon, Uldarico. *Lessons From the Huk Campaign in the Philippines*. Manila: M. Colcol, 1956/1960.
Ball, George. *The Past Has Another Pattern: Memoirs*. N.Y.: Norton, 1982.
Barton, Fred. *Salient Operational Aspects of Paramilitary Warfare in Three Asian Areas*, (ORO-T-228). Chevy Chase, Md.: Johns Hopkins University, Operations Research Office, 1963.
Battleground Korea: The Story of the 25th Infantry Division. Atlanta, Ga.: Albert Lone, 1961.
Berstein, David. *The Philippine Story*. N.Y.: Dutton, 1947.
Blaufarb, Douglas. *The Counterinsurgency Era*. N.Y.: The Free Press, 1977.
Buttinger, Joseph. *The Smaller Dragon*. N.Y.: Praeger, 1950.

Callwell, C. E. *Small Wars: Their Principles and Practice*, 3rd Ed. Wakefield, West Yorkshire: E. P. Publishing, 1976.

Carlson, Evans. *The Chinese Army: Its Organization and Military Effectiveness*. N.Y.: Institute of Pacific Relations, 1940.

Chamberlan, W. C. and J. D. Iams. *Rise and Fall of the Greek Communist Party*. Washington, D.C.: Department of State, Foreign Service Institute (mimeo), 1963.

Chapman, R. Spencer. *The Jungle Is Neutral*. London: Chatto and Windus, 1949.

Chin Kee Onn. *Malaya Upside Down*. Singapore: Jitts, 1946.

Condit, D. M. et al. *Challenge and Response in Internal Conflicts*. 3 Vols. Washington, D.C.: Center for Research in Social Systems, 1967.

Condit, Kenneth. *The History of the Joint Chiefs of Staff and National Policy, 1947–1949*. Wilmington, Del.: Glazier, 1979.

Condit, Kenneth and Turnbladh, Edwin. *Hold High the Torch: A History of the 4th Marines*. Washington, D.C.: HQMC, 1960.

Counterguerrilla Operations in the Philippines 1946–1957: A Symposium, 15 June 1961. Fort Bragg, N.C.: Special Warfare Center, 1961.

Davis, Burke. *Marine!: The Life of General Lewis Puller*. Boston: Little, Brown, 1962.

Dyer, Murray et al. *The Developing Role of the Army in Civil Affairs*. Bethesda, Md.: Operations Research Office, 1961.

Firth, Raymond, *Report of Social Science Research in Malaya*. Singapore: Institute for Social Science Research, 1948.

Fishel, Wesley, ed. *Problems of Freedom: Vietnam Since Independence*. N.Y.: Praeger, 1961.

Galula, David. *Counterinsurgency Warfare: Theory and Practice*. N.Y.: Praeger, 1962.

Gavin, James. *War and Peace in the Space Age*. N.Y.: Harper, 1958.

Greene, T. N. *The Guerrilla and How to Fight Him*. N.Y.: Praeger, 1962.

Grunder, Garel and Livezey, William. *The Philippines and the United States*. Norman, Okla.: University of Oklahoma Press, 1951.

Hammer, Ellen. *The Struggle for Indochina*. Stanford, Ca.: Stanford University Press, 1954.

Hanrahan, Gene. *The Communist Struggle in Malaya*. N.Y.: Institute of Pacific Relations, 1954.

Hausrath, Alfred. *Civil Affairs in the Cold War.* Bethesda, Md.: Operations Research Office, 1961.

Heilbrunn, Otto. *Partisan Warfare.* N.Y.: Praeger, 1962.

Heilbrunn, Otto. *Warfare in the Enemy's Rear.* N.Y.: Praeger, 1963.

Heilbrunn, Otto and Dixon, C. D. *Communist Guerrilla Warfare.* N.Y.: Praeger, 1955.

Henniker, M. C. A. *Red Shadow Over Malaya.* London: William Blackwood, 1955.

Hermes, Walter. *Truce Tent and Fighting Front.* Washington, D.C.: USGPO, 1966.

Heymont, Irving. *Combat Intelligence in Modern Warfare.* Harrisburg, Pa.: Stackpole, 1960.

Higgins, Gerald. *Civil Affairs in Future Armed Conflicts.* Bethesda, Md.: Operations Research Office, 1960.

Hilsman, Roger. *To Move a Nation.* N.Y.: Doubleday, 1964.

Ind, Allison. *Allied Intelligence Bureau.* N.Y.: McKay, 1958.

James, Doris Clayton. *The Years of MacArthur.* 2 Vols. Boston: Little, Brown, 1970, 1975.

Jones, Joseph. *Fifteen Weeks.* N.Y.: Viking, 1955.

Jones, S. W. *Public Administration in Malaya.* London: Royal Institute of International Affairs, 1953.

Jureidini, Alfred. *Casebook on Insurgency and Revolutionary Warfare.* Washington, D.C.: Special Operations Research Office, 1963.

Lacouture, Jean. *Vietnam: Between Two Truces.* Translated from the French by Konrad Keller and Joel Carmichael. N.Y.: Vintage, 1966.

Lam Swee. *My Accusation.* Kuala Lumpur: Benar, 1951.

Lansdale, Edward. *In the Midst of Wars.* N.Y.: Harper, 1972.

Lindholm, Richard, ed. *Vietnam, the First Five Years.* Lansing, Mich.: Michigan State University Press, 1959.

Linebarger, Paul. *Psychological Warfare,* 2nd ed. N.Y.: Hawthorne, 1954.

Low, N. I. *This Singapore.* Singapore: City Bookshop, 1946.

Malayan Communist Party. *Strategic Problems of the Malayan Revolutionary War.* Singapore: n.p., 1948.

McCrocklin, James. *Garde d'Haiti 1915–1934.* Annapolis, Md.: U.S. Naval Institute Press, 1956.

McCuen, John. *The Art of Counter-Revolutionary War.* Harrisburg, Pa.: Stackpole, 1966.

McNamara, Robert. *The Essence of Security: Reflections in Office*. N.Y.: Harper, 1968.

McNeil, William. *The Greek Dilemma: War and Aftermath*. Philadelphia: Lippincott, 1947.

Mataxis, Theodore and Goldberg, Seymour. *Nuclear Tactics*. Harrisburg, Pa.: Military Service Publishing Co., 1958.

Miers, Richard. *Shoot to Kill*. London: Faber, 1959.

Miller, Harry. *The Communist Menace in Malaya*. N.Y.: Praeger, 1954.

Molnar, Andrew et al. *Undergrounds, Resistance and Revolutions*. Washington, D.C.: American University, Special Operations Research Office, 1963.

Montross, Lynn et al. *US Marine Operations in Korea 1950–1953: East Central Front*. Washington, D.C.: USGPO, 1962.

Moran, J. W. G. *Spearhead in Malaya*. London: Peter Dansie, 1959.

Munro, Dana. *The United States and the Caribbean Area*. Boston: World Peace Foundation, 1934.

Ney, Virgil. *Notes on Guerrilla War: Principles and Practices*. Washington, D.C.: Command Publications, 1961.

O'Ballance, Edgar. *Malaya: The Communist Insurgent War 1948–1960*. Hamden, Conn.: Archon, 1966.

Oldfield, J. B. *The Green Howards in Malaya (1949–1952)*. Aldershot: Gale and Polder, 1953.

Onraet, Rene. *Singapore—A Police Background*. London: Crisp, 1947.

Osanka, Mark. *Modern Guerrilla War*. N.Y.: The Free Press, 1962.

Osborne, Milton. *Strategic Hamlets in South Vietnam*. Ithaca, N.Y.: Cornell University, Department of Asian Studies (mimeo), 1965.

Pentagon Papers, Senator Mike Gravel Edition, 4 Vols. Boston: Beacon Press, 1971.

Peterson, A. H. et al. *Symposium on the Role of Airpower in Counterinsurgency and Unconventional Warfare*, (Rand 3652-PR). Santa Monica, Calif.: 1963.

Pike, Douglas. *Viet Cong*. Cambridge: MIT Press, 1966.

Porter, Gareth. *Vietnam: The Definitive Documentation of Human Decisions*. Stansfordville, N.Y.: Coleman, 1979.

Possony, Stefan. *A Century of Conflict*. Chicago: Regnery, 1953.

Purcell, Victor. *The Chinese in Malaya*. London: Oxford University Press, 1948.

————. *The Chinese in Southeast Asia.* London: Oxford University Press, 1951.

————. *Malaya: Communist or Free?* Stanford: Stanford University Press, 1954.

Pye, Lucien. *Guerrilla Communism in Malaya.* Princeton: Princeton University Press, 1956.

Rinehardt, G. C. *Atomic Weapons in Land Combat* 3rd ed. Harrisburg, Pa.: Military Service Publishing Co., 1954.

Rostow, W. W. *The Diffusion of Power.* N.Y.: Macmillan, 1972.

Saraf, Stefano. *Greek Resistance Army.* London: Birch, 1947.

Scaff, Alvin. *The Philippine Answer to Communism.* Stanford: Stanford University Press, 1955.

Seaton-Watson, Hugh. *East European Revolution.* London: Metheun, 1950.

The Seizure of Haiti by the United States. Washington, D.C.: Foreign Policy Association, 1922.

Sharp, U. S. G. *Strategy for Defeat: Vietnam in Retrospect.* San Rafael, Calif.: Presidio Press, 1978.

Slover, Robert. *Symposium: The US Army's Limited War Mission and Social Science Research, 26–28 March 1962.* Washington, D.C.: American University, [SORO], 1962.

Smith, Joseph B. *Portrait of a Cold Warrior.* N.Y.: Putnam, 1976.

Smith, Thomas. *Population Growth in Malaya.* London: Royal Institute of International Research, 1952.

SORO. *Case Studies in Insurgency and Revolutionary Warfare.* Washington, D.C.: American University, 1963.

Tanham, George et al. *War Without Guns.* N.Y.: Praeger, 1966.

Taruc, Luis. *He Who Rides the Tiger.* N.Y.: Praeger, 1967.

Taylor, Maxwell D. *The Uncertain Trumpet.* N.Y.: Harper, 1960.

Thompson, Robert. *Defeating Communist Insurgency.* N.Y.: Praeger, 1966.

Thompson, Virginia. *Labor Problems in Southeast Asia.* New Haven: Yale University Press, 1947.

Thompson, Virginia and Adloff, Richard. *The Left Wing in Asia.* N.Y.: Sloane, 1947.

Traeger, Frank, ed. *Marxism in Southeast Asia.* Stanford: Stanford University, 1959.

Von Clausewitz, Karl. *On War.* Translated from the German by J. J. Graham. 3 vols. London: Routledge and Kegan Paul, 1968.

Warner, David. *The Last Confucian.* N.Y.: Praeger, 1963.

Westmoreland, William. *A Soldier Reports.* N.Y.: Doubleday, 1976.

Wise, Frederick. *A Marine Tells It to You.* N.Y.: J. H. Sears, 1929.

Woodhouse, C. M. *Apple of Discord.* London: Hutchinson, 1948.

Worley, Marvin. *A Digest of New Developments in Army Weapons, Tactics, Organization and Equipment.* Harrisburg, Pa.: Military Service Publishing Co., 1958.

Wyatt, Woodrow. *Southwards from China.* London: Hodder and Stoughton, 1952.

V. ARTICLES

The following abbreviations are used:

Air University Quarterly Review, AUQR

Army Information Digest, AID

Infantry School Quarterly, ISQ

Journal of the Royal United Services Institute, JRUSI

Marine Corps Gazette, MCG

Military Review, MR

US Naval Institute Proceedings, USNIP.

Adams, Paul. "Strike Command" *MR* 42 (May 1962): 2–10.

"After Nineteen Years We Leave Haiti" *MCG* 19 (Aug. 1934): 21–29.

"Antiguerrilla Operations" *Officer's Call* 3 (Mar. 1951): 1–15.

"Army Operations in Limited War" *AID* 13 (Jun. 1958): 41–48.

Atkinson, James. "American Military and Communist Unorthodox Warfare" *MCG* 42 (Jan. 1958): 21–25.

Baldwin, Hansen W. "Land Forces as an Element of National Power" *Army Combat Forces Journal* 7 (Jan. 1956): 16–24.

Bashore, Boyd. "Dual Strategy for Limited War" *MR* 40 (May 1960): 46–62.

———. "Vertical Counterattack by Counterinsurgents" *Army* 12 (Apr. 1962): 23–30.

Baughman, G. C. "United States Occupation of the Dominican Republic" *USNIP* 51 (Oct. 1925): 2306–17.

Beebe, John. "Beating the Guerrilla" *MR* 35 (Dec. 1955): 3–18.

Bellinger, John. "Civilian Role in Antiguerrilla Warfare" *MR* 41 (Sep. 1961): 91–94.

Bentz, Harold. "Psychological Warfare and Civic Action" *Army* 13 (Jul. 1963): 62–65.

Bleasdale, Vicator. "La Flor Engagement" *MCG* 16 (Feb. 1932): 29–40.

Carlson, Evans. "The Guardia Nacional de Nicaragua" *MCG* 21 (Jun. 1937): 7–20.

Clarke, Bruce. "The Designing of New Divisions for our Army" *Armor* (May–Jun. 1955): 22–25.

Clutterbuck, F. C. "Bertrand Stewart Prize Essay—1960" *Army Quarterly* 81 (Jan. 1961): 161–81.

Coffey, R. B. "A Brief History of the Intervention in Haiti" *USNIP* 48 (Aug. 1922): 1325–44.

Collier, Thomas. "Partisans—The Forgotten Force" *Infantry* 50 (Aug. 1960): 4–8.

"Considerations in Fighting Irregular Forces" *Infantry* 52 (Jul.–Aug. 1961): 8–9, 39–41.

Coyle, Randolph. "Service in Haiti" *MCG* 1 (Dec. 1916): 343–48.

Crozier, Brian. "The Diem Regime in Southern Vietnam" *Far Eastern Survey* 24 (Apr. 1955): 49–56.

Davis, H. C. "Indoctrination to Latin American Service" *MCG* 5 (Jun. 1920): 157–63.

Dodson, Charles. "Special Forces" *Army* 11 (Jun. 1961): 44–52.

Dohnanyi, Ernst. "Combatting Soviet Guerrillas" *MCG* 39 (Feb. 1955): 50–70.

Easterbrook, Ernest. "Realism in Counterinsurgency Training" *AID* 17 (Oct. 1962): 12–21.

Edson, Merrit. "The Coco River Patrol" *MCG* 20 (Aug. 1936): 18–23, 38–40; (Nov. 1936): 40–41, 60–72; 21 (Feb. 1937): 35–43, 57–63.

Ellis, E. H. "Bush Brigades" *MCG* 6 (Mar. 1921): 1–15.

Esson, D. C. "The Secret Weapon—Terrorism" *Army Quarterly* 78 (Jul. 1959): 167–80.

Fellows, Edwin. "Training Native Troops in Santo Domingo" *MCG* 8 (Dec. 1923): 215–33.

Fisher, Thomas. "Limited War—What Is It?" *AUQR* 9 (Winter 1957–1958): 127–42.

Gavin, James. "Cavalry, and I Don't Mean Horses" *Harpers* (Apr. 1954): 54–60.

––––––. "Why Limited War" *Ordnance* 42 (Mar. 1958): 809–13.

Gray, David. "When We Fight a Small War" *Army* 10 (Jul. 1960): 26–30.

Gray, John. "The Second Nicaraguan Campaign" *MCG* 17 (Feb. 1933): 33–41.

Greathouse, R. H. "King of the Banana Wars" *MCG* 17 (Jun. 1960): 29–33.

"Guerrilla Warfare as the High Command Sees It" *Army* 12 (Mar. 1962): 38–64.

Hadd, Harry. "Orders Firm But Flexible" *USNIP* 88 (Oct. 1962): 81–89.

Haffner, L. E. "Guerrilla War and Common Sense" *MCG* 46 (Jun. 1962): 20–23.

"Haitian Gendarmarie" *MCG* 11 (Jun. 1926): 73–81.

Hall, Donald. "Organization for Combat Propaganda" *Soldiers* 6 (May 1951): 11–16.

Hamlett, G. "Special Forces: Training for Peace and War" *AID* 16 (Jun. 1962): 2–9.

Hampton, Ephram. "Unlimited Confusion Over Limited War" *AUQR* 9 (Spring 1957): 28–47.

Hanneken, H. H. "A Discussion of the Voluntario Troops in Nicaragua" *MCG* 26 (Nov. 1942): 118–20, 247–66.

Harrington, Samuel. "The Strategy and Tactics of Small Wars" *MCG* 6 (Dec. 1921): 474–91.

Hilsman, Roger. "Internal War: The New Communist Tactic" *MR* 42 (Apr. 1962): 11–22.

Howze, Hamilton. "Helicopters in the Army" *Ordnance* 43 (Jan. 1958): 634–38.

HQMC Division of Operations and Training. "Combat Operations in Nicaragua" *MCG* 13 (Mar. 1929): 3–16; 14 (Jun. 1929): 81–94; 14 (Sep. 1929): 170–79.

"The Individual Side" *Army* 12 (Aug. 1962): 26–32.

Jacobs, Walter. "Wars of National Liberation" *MR* 42 (Jul. 1962): 45–52.

Johnson, Chalmers. "Civilian Loyalties and Guerrilla Conflict" *World Politics* 14 (Jul. 1962): 646–61.

Johnson, Harold. "Subversion and Insurgency: Search for a Doctrine" *Army* 15 (Nov. 1965): 40–42.

Johnson, J. R. "Antiguerrilla Exercise" *MCG* 39 (Dec. 1955): 20–22.

Johnson, S. A. "Junior Marines in Minor Irregular Warfare" *MCG* 6 (Jun. 1921): 152–63.

Kelly, George. "Revolutionary Warfare and Psychological Action" *MR* 40 (Oct. 1960): 4–13.

Kilmartin, R. C. "Indoctrination in Santo Domingo" *MCG* 7 (Dec. 1922): 377–86.

King, James. "Determinate and Limited War" *Army* 8 (Aug. 1957): 21–26.

Kleinman, Forrest. "Report From Vietnam" *Army* 12 (Sep. 1962): 21–36, 90, 92.

Kock, Harlan. "Terrain Tailors Tactics in Indo-China" *Army* 4 (Apr. 1954): 22–50.

Lane, Rufus. "Civil Government in Santo Domingo in the Early Days of the Occupation" *MCG* 7 (Jun. 1922): 127–46.

Lansdale, Edward. "Civic Action Helps Counter Guerrilla Threat" *AID* 12 (Jun. 1962): 50–53.

Leach, D. R. and O'Shea, C. J. "Artillery vs Guerrillas" *MCG* 46 (Sep. 1962): 48–51.

LeMay, Curtis. "Counterinsurgency and the Challenge Imposed" *Airman* 6 (Jul. 1962): 2–9.

Lesh, Burton. "Antiguerrilla SOP" *Infantry* 52 (Jul.–Aug. 1962): 30–31.

"Limited War: The Prospects and Possibilities" *AID* 13 (Jun. 1958): 6–20.

Little, John. "Counterinsurgency Campaign" *AID* 17 (Jun. 1962): 52–55.

McClellen, D. N. "Supervising Nicaraguan Elections" *USNIP* 59 (Jan. 1933): 33–38.

McClintock, Robert. "The American Landing in Lebanon" *USNIP* 88 (Oct. 1962): 65–72, 74–77, 79.

McClure, Robert. "Trends in Army Psychological Warfare" *AID* 7 (Jun. 1952): 8–14.

McConaughy, John. "Communist Strategy in Southeast Asia" *MR* 42 (May 1962): 39–53.

Mangold, Harold. "Defense of Rear Areas (2)" *ISQ* 41 (Jul. 1952): 55–67.

"Military Operations Against Irregular Forces" *Infantry* 52 (Jul.–Aug. 1962): 12–13, 44–46.

Murray, J. C. "The Anti-Bandit War" *MCG* 38 (Jan. 1954): 14–23; (Feb. 1954): 50–59; (Mar. 1954): 40–47; (Apr. 1954): 52–60; (May 1954): 52–58.

"The Nature of the Beast" *Infantry* 52 (Mar. 1962): 7–8, 60–61.

"Noll" (pseud). "The Emergency in Malaya" Army Quarterly 68 (Apr. 1954): 46–65.

Norman, Lloyd and Spore, John. "Big Push in Guerrilla War" Army 12 (Mar. 1962): 28–37.

Palmer, Bruce and Flint, Roy. "Counterinsurgency Training" Army 12 (Jun. 1962): 32–39.

Papathanasiades, Theodossios. "The Bandits' Last Stand in Greece" MR 46 (Jan. 1962): 22–31.

Paret, Peter and Shy, John. "Guerrilla War and US Military Policy: A Study" MCG 46 (Jan. 1962): 24–32.

Peard, Roger. "The Tactics of Bush Warfare" Infantry 38 (Sep.–Oct. 1952): 409–16.

Pelzer, Kenneth. "Resettlement in Malaya" Yale Review 41 (Mar. 1952): 391–404.

Pezzelle, Roger. "Special Forces" Infantry 45 (Jun. 1959): 13–19.

Railsback, E. H. "Let's Face It" MCG 42 (Nov. 1958): 52–60.

"Readiness for the Little War: Optimum Integrated Strategy" MR 37 (Apr. 1957): 14–26.

"Readiness for the Little War: A Strategic Security Force" MR 37 (May 1957): 14–21.

Reid, William. "Tactical Air in Limited War" AUQR 8 (Spring 1956): 40–48.

Rigg, Robert. "Twilight War" MR 40 (Nov. 1960): 29–32.

Rostow, W. W. "Guerrilla War in Underdeveloped Areas" Department of State Bulletin 45 (Aug. 1961): 233–38.

Scigliann, Robert. "Vietnam, a Country at War" Asian Survey 3 (Jan. 1963): 48–54.

Slover, Robert. "Action Through Civic Action" AID 17 (Oct. 1962): 7–11.

———. "This is Military Civic Action" Army 13 (Jul. 1963): 48–52.

Sollom, A. H. "Nowhere But Everywhere" MCG 42 (Jun. 1958): 38–44.

Sparks, Michael. "Guerrillas, Small Wars and Marines" MCG 46 (Jan. 1962): 50–53.

"Special Forces: Europe" Army 12 (Jan. 1962): 56–61.

Stewart, H. D. "How to Fight Guerrillas" USNIP 88 (Jul. 1962): 23–37.

Taylor, Maxwell. "Safety Lies Forward—Technologically and Tactically" Army 7 (Dec. 1956): 19–24.

———. "Our Changing Military Policy" Army 12 (Mar. 1962): 54–56.

Thorpe, C. G. "Dominican Service" *MCG* 4 (Dec. 1919): 315–26.

Thrasher, Thomas. "The Taking of Fort Riviere" *MCG* 15 (Feb. 1931): 31–33.

Tirona, Tomas. "The Philippine Anti-Communist Campaign" *AUQR* 7 (Summer 1954): 42–55.

"Two More Pentomic Divisions" *Army* 7 (May 1957): 10–15.

Utley, Harold. "The Tactics and Techniques of Small Wars" *MCG* 18 (Aug. 1933): 44–48.

Vicellio, Henry. "Composite Air Strike Force" *AUQR* 9 (Winter 1956–1957): 22–38.

Villa-Real, Luis. "Huk Hunting" *Army* 5 (Nov. 1954): 32–36.

Wade, Sidney. "Operation Bluebat" *MCG* 43 (Jul. 1959): 10–23.

Wainhouse, Edward. "Guerrilla War in Greece" *MR* 36 (Jun. 1957): 17–25.

Walraven, J. G. "Typical Combat Patrols in Nicaragua" *MCG* 14 (Dec. 1929): 243–53.

Walterhouse, Harry. "Civic Action: A Counter and Cure for Insurgency" *MR* 42 (Aug. 1962): 47–54.

Warmbrod, Karlton. "Defense of Rear Areas (1)" *ISQ* 40 (Apr. 1952): 5–16.

Weyland, Otto. "Airpower in Limited War" *Ordnance* 44 (Jul.–Aug. 1959): 40–43.

White, Thomas B. "USAF Doctrine and Limited War" *Air Force* 41 (Jan. 1958): 47–51.

Widder, David. "Ambush—The Commander's Hidden Attrition Punch" *Army* 12 (Nov. 1961): 38–42.

Wilkinson, J. B. "The Company Fights Guerrillas" *MCG* 46 (Jan. 1962): 54–57.

Yarborough, William. "Troubleshooters on the Spot" *AID* 17 (Sep. 1962): 52–55.

Zasloff, J. J. "Rural Resettlement in South Vietnam: The Agroville Program" *Pacific Affairs* 35 (Winter 1963): 327–40.

INDEX

Agency for International Development [AID], 151, 198
Albania, 17, 26
ARC LIGHT, 269
Army of the Republic of Vietnam [ARVN], 186, 193, 209, 213, 244, 248–249, 252

Ball, George, 269–270
BARREL ROLL, 250, 258
Bien Hoa airfield attack, 230, 237–238; reaction by LBJ administration, 242
Biggs, Harold, 79, 83
Bundy, McGeorge, 211; recommendation of 25 May 1964, 217; report to LBJ, February 1965, 251–254; on Soviet or Chinese intervention, 265–266
Bundy, William, 207; draft memos of September 1964, 227–229

Central Intelligence Agency [CIA], 52, 191, 217, 221; assessment of South Vietnamese stability, September 1964, 227, 238–239; comprehensive infiltration study, December 1964, 245; Twelve-Point Covert Action Plan, 262, 267
Chen Peng, 72
Clausewitz, Karl and U.S. military doctrine, 113–115, 177, 283, 285
Cline, Ray, 259
Commander-in-Chief, Pacific [CINCPAC], 193, 241, 251, 257, 265
Commander, U.S. Military Assistance Group, Vietnam [COMUSMACV] and ARCOV, 2–3; assessment of infiltration, 223; reaction to Bien Hoa attack, 237;

concurs in the need for ground troops, 241; proposal for the use of additional ground troops, 268
Cooper, Chester, 260, 269

Democratic Republic of Vietnam [DRV], 186
DESOTO patrols, 221, 225, 229; resumed, 247
Draper Committee, 153–154

Economic Development Corps [EDCOR], 58–60, 66
Edson, Merrit, 102–103

FARMGATE, 219, 229, 246
Ferret Force, 77
FISHNET reporting system, 254
Forrestal, Michael, 211
Forty-one Point Program, 260–261

Gavin, James, 117, 126
Gilpatrick, Roswell, 188, 193
Graduated military pressure proposal, 209, 217, 247, 252, 254
Greece, guerrilla strength, 12; battle of Konitza, 16–17; Operation DAWN, 19; Operation CROWN, 19–20; closure of border with Yugoslavia, 23–25, 28
Greek National Army, 12, 18
Griswold, Dwight, 13
Gulf of Tonkin Resolution, 226–227

HARDNOSE, 244
Henderson, Loy, 15–16

Hilsman, Roger, 196–197, 211
Ho Chi Minh, 186
Hogaboom Board, 159–160
Howze Board, 126
Hukbalahap, 44; outbreak of insurgency, 49–50; program of, 51; initial American appreciation of, 52–53, 60–61
Hukbasahap, 45

Johnson, Harold, 257–258
Johnson, Lyndon Baines, 1961 trip to South Vietnam, 189; authorizes interdiction, 246
Joint Chiefs of Staff, 160, 188, 190; 1962 recommendations to JFK, 195; operations plans, 218–220; reaction to Bien Hoa, 241–242; recommends deployment of marine brigade, 256; on use of marines, 265
Joint United States Military Assistance Group [JUSMAG], 53, 65
Joint United States Military Assistance Planning Group [JUSMAPG] formation of, 14; General James Van Fleet becomes commander of, 15; and reconstruction of Greek National Army, 18, 21

Kennedy, John, 188; and commitment of American troops to South Vietnam, 189
Korean War and American counterguerrilla operations, 38; Operation RATKILLER, 39–40
Krulak, Victor, 160

Lansdale, Edward, 58–60, 185, 187–188
Laos, 213–214, 244, 246, 250
Lau Yen, 73
Lemnitzer, Lyman, 191
Linebarger, Paul, 56
Lodge, Henry Cabot, 212, 214–215

MacArthur, Douglas, and Luis Taruc, 46; and Manuel Roxas, 47
Magsaysay, Ramon, appointed as secretary of defense, 52; and JUSMAG, 54; and civil affairs, 55–56; and Edward Lansdale, 58; elected president, 61; search for Vietnamese analogue, 281

Malayan Emergency, 71; declared, 73; nature, 80–81; casualties, 92
Malayan Peoples' Liberation Army, 72, 87; changes name to Malayan Races' Liberation Army, 77
Markos, Vaphiadis, appointment as commander of Greek Communist guerrillas, 9–10; conduct of combat operations, 16, 20–21; and the "town campaign," 24–25; replacement of, 25
MAROPS 34A, 220, 225–226
Marshall, George, 21
McCone, John, 207, 221, 262–263
McNamara, Robert, 151, 193, 199–200; December 1963 visit to South Vietnam, 205; report of 17 March 1964, 207–210, 247, 252; plan of June 1965, 270–271
McNaughton, John, 207, 243
Military Assistance Advisory Group [MAAG], 186; function of, 187, 190

National Liberation Front [NLF], 186
National Security Action Memorandum [NSAM] 65, 190–191; NSAM 288, 218–219
National Security Council, 15, 207
Ngo Dinh Diem, 185, 200–201
Nguyen Khanh, 206, 210, 214–215
Nha Trang, 143, 146
Nicaraguan National Guard [GNN], 103, 105; created, 98; effectiveness, 101; and Anastacio Somoza, 107
Nuclear war and the "New Look" Army, 116

Operation Plan 32-59, 193
Operation Plans 37-64, 98-64, 98A-64, 218–220

Pacification program, 196, 205, 213, 249, 257, 261
Papagos, Alexander, 13, 23; and final offensive, 26
Pentomic division, 117
Peoples' Army of Vietnam [PAVN], 186, 223; first introduction of units into the South, 268

Philippine Armed Forces, formation, 49; American appreciation of, 53; reorganization of, 54; 1951 offensive operations, 57
Philippine Islands elections of 1946, 48; elections of 1949, 50
Pohang Guerrilla Hunt, 39
Porter, Paul, 11
Puller, Louis [Chesty], 105–106; and Lewis Walt, 106, 162

Quang Ngai Special Platoons, 261
Qui Nhon attack, 254

Reorganization Objective Army Division [ROAD], 118
Rogers Board, 126
ROLLING THUNDER, 258, 267
Rusk, Dean, 26, 190, 211, 213

Sandino, Augosto, 98, 107
Sharp, Ulysses, 250, 264–265
Shepherd, Lemuel, 158–159
Shoup, David, 160
South Korean Labor Party, 33–34; and the outbreak of the Korean War, 35, 37
Southeast Asian Coordinating Committee [SEACORD], 244, 250, 257, 266
Special Branch, 83, 88, 91
Squatters, 74–77; regulations concerning, 78; resettlement efforts, 79
State War Executive Committee, 83; and "morning prayers," 84–85, 86
Strategic Hamlet Program, 190–191, 196–199
Sullivan, William, 207

Taruc, Luis, 44–45, 60–61; and General Douglas MacArthur, 46; surrender of, 62
Taylor, Maxwell, 118, 191; reports to JFK, 192–193; visits South Vietnam with McNamara in September 1963, 199–200, 206, 210; reaction to Bien Hoa attack, 239–240; concurs in Bundy recommendations, February 1965, 252; comments on graduated response proposal, 254; on deployment of marines, 256, 258, 262–264; assessment of air war, 266

Templar, Sir Gerald, 85; and food control, 86
Thompson, Sir Robert, 197
Tit-for-tat response proposal, 209, 211–212, 227, 239–240
Twenty-one Point Military Program, 262

U.S. Air Force doctrine, 174; the Tactical Air Command, 175–176; close air support, 194
U.S. Army doctrine, 113–115; unconventional war, 119; irregular forces, 120; intelligence and guerrilla war, 121–122, 123, 131–132; airmobility, 125–126; firepower, 127–129; command and control, 129–130; ideological sponsorship of guerrillas, 133–135; psychological warfare, 149–151; civic action, 152–154; and the creation of the South Vietnamese Army, 179–180
U.S. Army Special Forces, 141; formation of, 142; mission of, 143–145; counterguerrilla function, 146; impact upon the American view of guerrilla war, 147–149
U.S. Marine Corps doctrine, 159; nature of guerrilla war, 162–163; psychological warfare, 164; civic action, 165; patrolling, 168; refugees, 169, 170–171
U.S. Marine Corps operations, in Korea, 39, 96; land in Nicaragua, 97–98; El Chipote attack, 99–100; Neuva Segovia campaign, 101, 158; Lebanon, 160
U.S. Operations Mission [USOM], 205, 261

Viet Cong, 195; infiltration, 213, 222–225, 245; assessment of strength, March 1965, 259–260
Voluntarios, 104

Walt, Lewis, 161
Westmoreland, William, 237, 241–242, 251–252, 254–255, 259, 264; on tiedown ratios, 268
WHITE STAR, 229
Whitney, Courtney, 46

YANKEE TEAM, 229, 246